Venetia Redeemed

Venetia Redeemed

FRANCO-ITALIAN RELATIONS

1864–1866

JOHN W. BUSH

SYRACUSE UNIVERSITY PRESS

To William and Mildred,
My Brother and Sister

L'Italie . . . [c'est] . . . une maison que le
voisin laisse brûler pour faire la part de feu.

PRINCE RICHARD METTERNICH
September 27, 1866

Preface

THIS STUDY grew out of my interest in Franco-Italian relations during the decade preceding the War of 1870–71. One of the main concerns of students of this period is to know why Napoleon III failed to make an ally of the Kingdom of Italy, whose cause he had championed in 1859–60. The reason for the failure of their relations in the 1860's has been sought hitherto in the difficulties over the city of Rome. The Italians considered Rome their natural capital, but the French insisted on preserving it under the sovereignty of the Pope: this conflict of interests was the essence of the so-called Roman question. However, between two important dates in the history of the Roman question, 1864, when a convention over Rome was signed by France and Italy, and 1867, when Rome was attacked by Italian troops under Garibaldi, Franco-Italian relations revolved almost entirely about another item in the still incomplete program of Italian unification—Venetia.

I was attracted to this short but active period (1864–66) because the threads of Franco-Italian relations needed to be put together amid the complications of the Austro-Prussian War. It seemed necessary to know as accurately as possible how Venetia was won for Italy, from Austria, by France, and weigh the effects of this transaction upon the relationships involved. Such an investigation promised not only some solution to the problem posed above but also an understanding of the Roman question and indeed of the whole puzzling subject of the Bonapartes in Italy.

For the period just prior to the outbreak of the Austro-Prussian War there are a number of excellent studies such as Chester W. Clark, *Franz-Joseph and Bismarck: The Diplomacy of Austria Before the War of 1866,* Charles W. Hallberg, *Franz-Josef and Napoleon III, 1852–1864,* and Adolf Kulessa, *Die Kongress-idee Napoleons III im mai 1866;* and articles such as Heinrich von Srbik, "Der Geheimvertrag Oesterreichs und Frankreichs vom 12 juni 1866," César Vidal, "La question vénitienne et la diplomatie française en 1866," and Nancy Nichols Barker, "Austria, France, and the Venetian Question, 1861–1866." Of special importance is E. Ann Pottinger's *Napoleon III and the German Crisis, 1865–1866.* But the concern of these authors is mainly Franco-Austrian or Franco-Prussian relations, and none continues through the Austro-Prussian War. Lynn M. Case, *Franco-Italian Relations, 1860–1865,* still the standard work for that period, treats the Venetian question only in passing. No completed studies to my knowledge take Franco-Italian relations through the final annexation of Venetia or dwell at any length on the diplomatic and military aspects of the Venetian question during the Austro-Prussian War.

This subject led me to the diplomatic, military, and domestic archives of France, Austria, Italy, and Great Britain, where I studied the pertinent material for the period from 1864 to 1866 as well as for other relevant years. Also helpful was the collection of documents edited under the direction of the French Foreign Ministry, *Les origines diplomatiques de la guerre, 1870–1871,* which contains extensive selections of correspondence between the Quai d'Orsay and the French diplomatic posts in Europe during the period 1864 to 1871. On the Italian side valuable sources were Baron Bettino Ricasoli's *Lettere e documenti* and General La Marmora's correspondence, which is available in his own publications and in Italian books and periodicals published after his death.

I am deeply grateful to the many who assisted me directly and indirectly in the course of this investigation. Professor Ross S. J. Hoffman's wisdom and guidance were indispensable, as were the friendship and encouragement of my colleagues in the history profession, especially Professor John C. Olin of Fordham University, Professor G. Charles Paikert of Le Moyne College, and Professor James M. Powell of Syracuse University. I wish also to take the opportunity to thank those who assisted me in my researches in Europe. Professor Louis Girard of the Sorbonne and Professor René Rémond of L'Institut d'Etudes politiques de

Paris were generously available for frequent interviews. Invaluable assistance was afforded by archivists, among whom Madame Osanam at the Quai d'Orsay in Paris, and Dr. Gebhard Raath and Dr. Anna Benna in Vienna, deserve special mention. I am grateful for pleasant and helpful conversations with Professor Lynn M. Case, Professor E. Ann Pottinger, Professor Norbert Miko, and Professor Pierre Renouvin, who share my interest in this subject. Father William T. Noon, S.J., and Professor Anthony J. Vetrano gave generously of their talents when I was preparing the manuscript. I received the skilful assistance of Mrs. Judith Powell in making the index. Last but not least, tribute is due to my students at Le Moyne College. The translations that appear throughout the work are my own.

JOHN W. BUSH, S.J.

October 3, 1967
Syracuse, New York

Abbreviations

APP   Germany, Historische Reichskommission, *Die Auswär-tige Politik Preussens, 1858–1871* (Berlin: Staling, 1939).

Archivio   Italia, Ministero degli affari esteri, Archivio Storico,
Storico   Rome.

Evénements   Alfonso La Marmora, *Un peu plus de lumière sur les événements politiques et militaires de 1866* (Paris: J. Dumaine, 1874).

FAE   France, Archives du ministère des affairs étrangères, Quai d'Orsay, Paris.

GBFO   Great Britain, Public Record Office, Foreign Office, London.

HHS   Haus, Hof und Staatsarchiv, Vienna, Austria.

OD   France, Ministère des affaires étrangères, *Les origines diplomatiques de la guerre, 1870–1871.* 20 vols. (Paris: Imprimerie Nationale, 1910–32).

Oncken   Hermann Oncken, *Die Rheinpolitik Kaiser Napoleons III von 1863 bis 1870 und der Ursprung des Krieges von 1870–71.* 3 vols. (Stuttgart: Deutsche Verlagsanhelt, 1926).

Contents

Venetia Redeemed

INTRODUCTION

The Venetian Question, 1859-64

THROUGHOUT the 1860's Venetia continually required the attention of European chancelleries. On the agenda of several proposed Congresses, included in many projects and secret negotiations, the question of Venetia's disposition was seldom absent from discussions of major issues. In the early part of the decade, it was considered along with such questions as those of the Danubian Principalities, Poland, and Schleswig-Holstein; it even lurked in the background of the French expedition in Mexico.[1] But as the two great unification movements on either side of the Alps gained momentum, Venetia, as link and common ground between them, took on a defined and truly universal importance.

As a political and geographic unit, Venetia of the 1860's was an Austrian crownland embracing a cluster of Italian provinces between the Adriatic Sea and the Mincio River, extending northward to the Carnic Alps and the Austrian border and southward to the Po River. Ancient home of the Veneti, this area was for centuries a major portion of the stately Republic of Venice but passed under foreign control with the Napoleonic Wars. During these wars the Republic met its end by partition between France and Austria. The Venetian provinces first became part of the various French satellites in Italy and then, as a result of the Congress of Vienna, formed with the Milanese (an Austrian possession since 1713) the Lombardo-Venetian Kingdom. This combination was disrupted by the Austro-Sardinian war of 1859, and subsequently Lombardy, together with the Hapsburg possessions in central Italy, went to Victor Emmanuel II, leaving Venetia the only Austrian possession on the peninsula. As such, Venetia awaited "redemption" by the newly proclaimed Kingdom of Italy.

[1] See Nancy Nichols Barker, "France, Austria, and the Mexican Venture, 1861–1864," *French Historical Studies,* Vol. III, No. 2 (Fall, 1963), 224–45.

The Boundaries of Venetia, 1740–1947

Soon after its acquisition under the Treaty of Vienna this territory had become the Austrian "jewel of empire" prized in the Hapsburg house not only for the prestige adhering to the glorious city of Venice but for the access it gave to the sea and to Italy and for the solidarity it afforded with the western reaches of the Empire in Germany. The loss of Lombardy accentuated these virtues of Venetia, and then in the mid-1860's as the Austrians re-evaluated their policy of economic isolation they saw Venice as a commercial outlet of incalculable importance.

Still within the confines of Austrian Venetia after 1859 was the famous Quadrilateral, which Prince Clemens Metternich had built up into one of Europe's most formidable military frontiers. The Quadrilateral was a series of forts constructed in the vicinities of four sizeable towns, Peschiera, Verona, Legnano, and Mantua. Together they formed roughly a parallelogram on the southwestern corner of Venetia and were surrounded by a natural moat formed by Lake Garda and the Po, Mincio, and Adige rivers. The effectiveness of this fortress lay in the fact that it stood across the only naturally accessible ground on the Venetian border. High mountains running from Lake Garda to Stelvio Pass at the tip of Switzerland protected the western approaches; the Po River running along the southern border extended the defenses of Venetia to the Adriatic. Railroads and highways connected the two principal forts, Mantua and Verona, then led northward to Trent, Bolzano, and Brenner Pass and eastward to Venice and thence to the Austrian border. The Quadrilateral had stopped a Piedmontese force during the revolutions of 1848 and had caused Napoleon III to think better of his march to the Adriatic in 1859. Thus Austria still had in Venetia a position of command looking both northward and southward, and the Quadrilateral was a symbol as well as a physical sanction of Austria's undying opposition to Italian, and in a more remote sense, German unification. General Joseph Radowitz, Prussian military expert and early champion of German unification, presaged in 1848 the full role of the Venetian fortresses when he remarked, "Germany must be defended on the Mincio." [2]

For the Kingdom of Italy to have Venetia was as important for a new order of things as it was indispensable to Austria for the old. It meant the promise of liberation from Austria, a guarantee of security and economic solvency, and, above all, vindication of the principle of nationalities to which Italy appealed for her right to exist.

[2] Luigi Chiala, Le général La Marmora et l'alliance prussienne, 28.

Hardly less important were the concerns of the other European powers. For Prussia, to disengage Venetia from Austria meant not only to weaken her Germanic rival in the south but also to draw the attention of France to the Mediterranean and away from the Rhine. Venetia was for Prussia, as a German observer once said, "a fortress on the Rhine."[3] Great Britain kept an active if remote vigilance over this "apple of discord" which might drive central Europe to a general quarrel and destroy the coveted equilibrium. And to Roman Catholics in every European state, an Austrian Venetia was a last outpost of protection for the temporal power of the Pope.

Finally, for Louis Napoleon, the emotional, ideological, and political heir of his Corsican uncle, Venetia held manifold attractions. To obtain Venetia for Italy would be the completion of the program begun at Plombières. More concretely, Venetia, since Villafranca, had succeeded Lombardy as the symbol of the old dynastic struggle between the rulers of France and the house of Hapsburg. In the 1860's Louis Napoleon wished to realize the French ambition (once so important in the plans of the first Bonaparte) to possess that historic window on the east through an Italian protégé. Venetia would also be a gift that might quiet the clamor of Italians for Rome, which for partly domestic reasons he could not bestow upon them. The Emperor was by background and by certain overtones in his character devoted to a principle that later would be called "self-determination of nations." As a principle in his diplomacy it never quite stood by itself independent of balance-of-power and dynastic considerations. Yet in Venetia, unlike Germany,[4] Louis Napoleon could reconcile his idealism with the exigencies of dynastic and international politics, giving him, if not available means, at least a clear objective. Above all, there was a certain urgency attached to the Venetian question since he considered the prestige of Bonaparte to ride on its solution. If he died before detaching Venetia from Austria, he would leave his son, as he himself expressed it, "seated on a barrel of gunpowder."[5]

After 1859 attention to Venetia became acute because its separation from Lombardy made it vulnerable. The French armies, after two victories at Magenta and Solferino, stopped at the Quadrilateral in June, 1859, and the armistice of Villafranca was confirmed by the Treaty of

---

[3] Meroux de Valois to Drouyn de Lhuys, Oct. 19, 1864, *OD*, IV, 274–76.

[4] E. Ann Pottinger, *Napoleon III and the German Crisis, 1865–1866*, 207–10.

[5] Cowley to Clarendon, May 6, 1866, in R. C. Wellesley (Lord Cowley), *The Paris Embassy During the Second Empire*, 302.

Zurich on November 10, 1859. By this treaty the Lombardo-Venetian Kingdom was carved up; Lombardy minus the province of Mantua went to the Kingdom of Sardinia, the eight Venetian provinces plus Mantua remaining with Austria.[6]

Zurich also provided that the Hapsburg princelings of central Italy be reinstated and that the Pope be made president of an Italian federation. Italian patriots, however, nullified these provisions by holding plebiscites in Tuscany, Parma, Modena, and the Papal province of Romagna and voting to join the Kingdom of Sardinia. Napoleon accepted this *fait accompli* and exacted benefit for himself in the cession of Nice and Savoy, a transaction that was sealed in the Treaty of Turin on March 24, 1860. However, Napoleon III was prevented from merely gathering up his prize and departing by the precipitous action of Garibaldi in Sicily and Naples and the subsequent march of Victor Emmanuel II from the north during which he took two Papal provinces. Although Victor Emmanuel II and Garibaldi rode through the streets of Naples together in triumph on November 9, 1860, Italy was not yet unified because French troops encamped around Rome prevented an attack on the Holy City and the Austrian army held the Quadrilateral and Venetia.

The refusal of Napoleon III to let Italy have Rome and the unfinished liberation of northern Italy were the two outstanding and correlative problems in the Emperor's Italian program after 1860. Of more immediate importance was the Roman question because it threatened the very security of his position in France. French Catholics objected to their government as accessory to the loss of Romagna by the Pope and insisted that at least Rome and the surrounding province be preserved by the maintenance of a French garrison around the city. Louis Napoleon was willing, nevertheless, under the influence of Count Cavour, to extricate himself from his position as guardian of

[6] At present writing the Italians speak of "Tre Venezie" as a result of the boundary changes that took place after World War I and World War II. Venetia proper, comprising eight provinces of Belluno, Padova, Rovigo, Treviso, Udine, Venice, Verona and Vicenza, is known as "Venezia Euganea" and corresponds to the territory with which we are dealing. When the "Italian Tyrol" or the Trentino and the Upper Adige regions were given to Italy in 1919 they were called "Venezia Tridentina," and the region comprising Trieste and Istria to the east was given the name "Venezia Giulia." After World War II Istria was given to Yugoslavia and Trieste was made a free city, but a narrow strip along the Isonzo River was left to Italy and this, added to Friuli, was named "Friuli-Venezia Giulia." See maps on p. 2. See also the article "Tre Venezie," *Enciclopedia italiana*, XXXV, 78–112.

Rome and in April, 1861, was on the point of agreeing to exchange the withdrawal of his troops for a moral guarantee by the new Kingdom of Italy. But Cavour's untimely death on June 6, 1861, ended negotiations. The failure of these negotiations left a deadlock on the Roman question which was to last until the fall of 1864—a deadlock interrupted only by the unsuccessful attempt of Garibaldi to take Rome in August, 1862. In the meantime, the French Emperor kept his troops at Civita Vecchia to block further attack and turned his attention to Venetia.

The period of the early 1860's was witness to a great and sudden expansion of the French Empire. The expedition to China in 1860 to gain economic and religious concessions in the Orient was followed by the incredible venture in Mexico. Eager for Russian friendship, Napoleon III did not immediately concern himself with the Polish revolt that broke out on January 27, 1863, but in the context of this revolt he later would propose a radical scheme for revision of the treaties of 1815. These were all evidently meant to exploit to the full the prestige won at Magenta and Solferino and to make the Empire worthy of its name on a world-wide scale, but never did Louis Napoleon lose sight of his unfinished business in northern Italy. In his offering of the Mexican throne to the brother of Francis Joseph [7] and in his attempt to carry off an Austrian alliance during the Polish crisis, his concern with Venetia is discernible.

In Italy, after Cavour's death a ministry under Baron Bettino Ricasoli continued to emphasize the Roman question, but there was great popular sentiment for an expedition to Venetia after Garibaldi's failure at Aspromonte on August 29, 1862. Such sentiment was both stimulated and expressed by a loosely organized extremist party known popularly as the Party of Action (Partito d'Azione). This group had a small but increasing representation in the Camera (the Italian Chamber of Deputies) and claimed the followers of Mazzini and Garibaldi and indeed all who now dared to advocate a dramatic seizure of Venetia by internal revolution assisted by the Italian government's armed intervention. Successive ministries had to pay more and more attention to this radical party as the Venetian question came more prominently into view.

[7] See Sartiges to Drouyn de Lhuys, Aug. 14, 1863, FAE, Italie, Vol. 8, pp. 76–79. See also Barker, "France, Austria, and the Mexican Venture, 1861–1864."

Ricasoli was outwardly faithful to Cavour's program. He tried to get France to agree to withdraw her troops from Rome in exchange for a guarantee against further aggression upon Papal territory. But his basically hostile attitude toward France and careless diplomacy caused him to fail in his effort, and he resigned in March, 1862.[8] The ministry of Urbano Rattazzi, which followed, also failed to make any progress on the Roman question; then came a period of deathly silence on that question under the ministry of Marco Minghetti, who assumed office in December, 1862.

While the Minghetti ministry seemed less interested than its predecessors in Rome, it gave greater attention to the Venetian question. It began paying more heed to the popular agitation for Venetia, set off especially by the Polish revolt, and Rome seemed to be receding more and more into the background. The French Foreign Office noted in the Minghetti ministry a new realism on the question of Rome and a willingness to wait for internal developments or the illness of Pius IX to provide a solution. The French hoped that Minghetti could achieve some sort of control of the popular movement which was placing Venetia in first place in the unification program.[9]

The Mazzinian faction among the radicals had been proclaiming ever since Villafranca that the sequence should be Venetia first, then Rome, and blamed the disaster of Aspromonte upon the mistake of wrong emphasis. But it was the revolt of the Poles in January, 1863, that turned the full force of the radical movement toward Venetia. Garibaldian committees began to organize immediately in order to discuss means of helping the Poles,[10] and in April small attacks began on the Tyrol with the hope of pushing the Italian government to action in Venetia.[11] In the plans of the international Mazzinians, Venetia was linked with Poland for a general liberation movement of central European peoples. "The salvation of Poland is at Venice, at Belgrade, at Pesth," they proclaimed from London.[12] The enthusiasm

[8] Lynn M. Case, *Franco-Italian Relations 1860–1865*, 113–63.
[9] See Malaret to Drouyn de Lhuys, Feb. 24, 1863, FAE, Italie, Vol. 6, pp. 153–55; Drouyn de Lhuys to Malaret, Feb. 26, 1863, *ibid.*, 160–61; Malaret to Moustier, Oct. 24, 1866, *OD*, XIII, 10–16.
[10] Malaret to Drouyn de Lhuys, Feb. 9, 1863, FAE, Italie, Vol. 6, p. 110.
[11] Sartiges to Drouyn de Lhuys, Apr. 6, 1863, FAE, Italie, Vol. 6, pp. 343–47; and Apr. 21, 1863, *ibid.*, 361–67.
[12] Mazzinian proclamation annexed to Sartiges to Drouyn de Lhuys, Apr. 5, 1863, *ibid.*, 320–28.

caught on in Venice, too, as the Venetians began to feel that the moment of liberation was at hand.[13]

The Polish question offered the opportunity of bringing the Venetian question—and, for the first time since the Treaty of Paris of 1856, the whole Italian question—into the field of European diplomacy. Napoleon III and the Minghetti ministry both were interested in this, but it was the French Emperor who took the initiative. When, for the purpose of preventing the spread of the Polish revolution into her territory, Prussia joined Russia in a pact called the Alvensleben Convention, the French Emperor, who at first had hesitated to declare himself in favor of the Poles, finally decided to unite with London and Vienna to block the convention.[14] Although the proposition met no favor with either chancellery, he decided not to pass up this opportunity.

An approach was made directly to Austria through the Empress Eugénie. On February 21, 1863, she had a three-hour conversation with Prince Richard Metternich, the Austrian ambassador, in which she outlined a fantastic plan to reorganize the western political map from Poland to Mexico. The plan bears the characteristic mark of the grandiose schemes that came out of the Imperial court, but in it can also be read the main objective of French policy: to induce Austria to release Venetia. In return for Venetia and Galicia, a Hapsburg archduke could be king of a reconstructed Poland; Silesia would go to Austria outright; a free hand would be given Austria south of the Main, and her Adriatic coastline would be extended.[15] Metternich merely smiled at the idea, and Napoleon III made haste to disavow it. Later, in March, Napoleon offered his own proposals to Austria, substituting general promises of Austrian hegemony in the Middle East and support for her attempts to gain control in Germany. The Austrian Ambassador at least relayed this request to the Hapsburg court, but there it met the rigid resistance of Francis Joseph.[16]

As early as the summer of 1861 and continuing through 1863, Napoleon attempted another scheme—equally ineffective—to entice Austria to yield up Venetia. He said he was willing to sacrifice Italian

[13] Malaret to Drouyn de Lhuys, Dec. 22, 1863, FAE, Italie, Vol. 8, pp. 486–95.

[14] W. E. Mosse, *The European Powers and the German Question, 1848–1871*, 110–17.

[15] Henry Solomon, "Le Prince Richard Metternich et sa correspondance pendant son ambassade à Paris 1859–1871," *Revue de Paris*, Vol. I (1924), 515–17.

[16] Charles W. Hallberg, *Franz-Josef and Napoleon III, 1852–1864*, 317–27.

unity for the idea of federation in Italy, giving Venetia to a truncated northern Kingdom, resurrecting the Kingdom of the Two Sicilies, and allowing the Papal States (with a lay government) to be a third member.[17] He renewed these overtures after the Battle of Aspromonte in 1862 and again in the wake of the Polish crisis, but to the Austrian court and government destruction of Italian unity—desirable as it might be—was insufficient compensation for the loss of Venetia.

The attitude of the Austrian Empire toward its dynastic prize on the Adriatic is revealed in the draft of a secret memorandum prepared for Prince Metternich in March, 1863. The memo was destined to be communicated to Napoleon III and contained the only positive assurances Austria could give him at that time. The general principle enunciated was that Austria could not engage in an active diplomatic effort with France, though it was possible that future events might make Napoleon's proposals more attractive. Such events would have to yield great compensation for Austria in terms of the equilibrium of Europe and in concrete territorial gains in the Middle East or Germany. The memorandum went on to estimate the pitfalls for Austria in any policy that implied the sacrifice of Venetia. It would have meant pursuing a policy of adventure, renouncing the conservative traditions of the house of Hapsburg, and most certainly reviving "dangerous tendencies amid the nationalities at home," thus risking disintegration of the Empire. Furthermore, voluntary cession of Venetia would have meant a collision with Prussia since the *sine qua non* of such a cession would have to be compensation in Germany, which was not possible without "the annihilation of Prussia" and the subsequent assumption of greater responsibilities in Germany by the already overextended house of Hapsburg. This was not meant to discourage all hope in the French court but only to state that a high price must be offered: aggrandizement of territory—meaning certainly Silesia—and extension of influence in Germany and the Middle East.[18] The proposals of Eugénie and her husband made in the context of the Polish crisis had offered this compensation, but it was obvious that

[17] Nancy Nichols Barker, "Austria, France, and the Venetian Question, 1861–1866," *Journal of Modern History*, Vol. XXXVI, No. 2 (June, 1964), 146–48.

[18] Memorandum from Rechberg to Metternich, Mar. 21, 1863, found in HHS, published in English translation in Chester W. Clark, *Franz-Joseph and Bismarck: The Diplomacy of Austria Before the War of 1866*, Appendix A, No. 1, 527–29. Clark, p. 310, states that the memorandum probably was never actually shown to Napoleon III. I have used it only as an index of the attitude of the Austrian cabinet toward a policy involving Venetia.

at the Hofburg there was a more realistic evaluation of what was possible. Also, the reconstituting of the Kingdom of Poland would have meant giving up Galicia.

When negotiations with Austria failed, Napoleon III appealed to England and Russia, this time for a restoration of the constitution granted Poland by Alexander I. When Russia showed herself willing at least to discuss this and other proposals, Napoleon in late April of 1863 presented a favorite solution of his: a general European congress. This attempt again foundered because of Austrian resistance, and the Polish question dragged on without solution through the summer of 1863.[19]

During that summer the Minghetti administration, with full approval of Victor Emmanuel II, began to fish in the troubled waters. In June, Constantino Nigra, the Italian ambassador to Paris, while on vacation with the Imperial couple at Fontainebleau, attempted to encourage Eugénie to continue her intercession for Venetia. The astute Nigra adapted his approach to the audience and the occasion; he sang his appeal as a barcarole while "en promenade" with the Empress and her chaperon in a Venetian gondola.[20] But the Empress, no doubt remembering her experience of the previous February, told him he was wasting his time.

In Turin more realistic plans were afoot. The Italian government in July initiated secret talks in London and Paris on an idea that had been conceived shortly after the Treaty of Zurich as a solution to the problem of Venetia.[21] The Minghetti Cabinet now thought that Russia's antagonism toward the western powers could be used to good advantage by suggesting to Austria a trade of the principalities of Moldavia and Wallachia for Venetia. Austria would take over the coveted principalities and in turn yield Venetia to Italy. Essential to

---

[19] Hallberg, *Franz-Joseph,* 324–35.

[20] The barcarole translated from the Italian is roughly as follows: "Lady, if some time on your tranquil lake the silent Emperor rocks with you, tell him that on the Adriatic, poor, nude and cadaverous, groans and languishes Venice, but she exists . . . and waits . . ." See Solomon, "Le Prince Richard Metternich et sa correspondance pendant son ambassade à Paris 1859–1871," 517; Emile Ollivier, "L'entrevue de Biarritz, 1856," *Revue des deux mondes,* Period 5, Vol. 9 (June, 1902), 512. Nigra was a poet and littérateur in his own right; see Lanfranco Vecchiato, *Constantino Nigra, diplomatico, erudito, poeta.*

[21] During the Crimean War Napoleon III had proposed trade of Venetia and Lombardy for the Danubian Principalities, and Cavour brought it up at the Congress of Paris in 1856. Thaddeus W. Riker, *The Making of Roumania: A Study of an International Problem, 1856–1866,* 39–40.

the plan, however, was a preliminary agreement between France and England to approach Austria. When in July the Italian representative visited the chancelleries at London and Paris, he found them, though agreeing in principle, unwilling to take the initiative. They both felt Austria would simply refuse, and even if she accepted, the exchange would be likely to bring on war with Russia. Besides, Lord Palmerston, the British prime minister, did not want to be first to propose the dismemberment of the Ottoman Empire, and the French Emperor, to fortify his objections to the plan, raised another, perhaps irrelevant, issue—the necessity of consulting the people of the principalities.[22]

The efforts of Napoleon III both on his own and in responding to the initiative of Italy were, to say the least, ineffectual. They did not even seem serious. Either the Emperor and his foreign minister sensed Austria's intransigence or felt that to challenge Russia would be too great a strain on the peace of Europe. It is also important to note that in his conversations with the Italian representative, Count Guiseppi Pasolini, Napoleon III repeatedly switched the subject to Rome.[23]

What the Emperor did do, however, was to resume the idea of the congress first suggested in April. On November 4, 1863, he sent invitations to all European powers to convene for discussions on the peaceful settlement of such questions as Poland, Denmark, the Danubian Principalities, Rome, and Venetia. To make it as acceptable as possible to Austria, the Venetian question was phrased in an extremely vague and guarded way. The invitation merely suggested as a question to be discussed, "Should Italy and Austria remain eternally enemies face to face in a hostile attitude?" [24] The Italians and the Pope accepted, but England and Austria declined, the latter because she sensed the danger for Venetia.

Italian attempts to raise the Venetian question in the general diplomatic field then languished. Action was lacking in the winter and spring of 1864, so much so that the government was under attack for its inertia.[25] Napoleon III, too, seemed to slacken in his cultivation of Austria after the latter excluded the question of Venetia from the Polish and Danish crises and turned down the congress because Venetia was to be discussed. As an escape from his responsibilities to the Ital-

[22] Nigra to La Marmora, Feb. 24, 1866, Archivio Storico, Vol. 838; Sartiges to Drouyn de Lhuys, Aug. 14, 1863, FAE, Italie, Vol. 8, pp. 76–79.

[23] Case, *Franco-Italian Relations*, 257.

[24] Visconti-Venosta to Nigra, Dec. 24, 1863, FAE, Italie, Vol. 8, No. 504.

[25] Malaret to Drouyn de Lhuys, May 24, 1864, FAE, Italie, Vol. 9, pp. 321–46.

ian cause he began to explore the possibilities of Prussia, now coming into conflict with Austria, as an ally of Italy. Otto von Bismarck, Prussian minister-president, however, in November, 1863, and January, 1864, brushed off attempts made in this direction.[26]

By the spring of 1864, both Italy and France were feeling the full effects of Austria's immovability and of their own isolation from the other European powers. Evidently the resolution of the question lay between France and Italy, but France was growing less and less enthusiastic about seeking an answer. Things were at such a standstill that on May 12 the Italian foreign minister, Visconti-Venosta, had to appear before the Camera to answer in open debate the accusation of the opposition that the government had abandoned the cause of both Rome and Venetia.[27]

Then suddenly, in late May, diplomatic activity began again, and the interest of the Emperor was revived. But the action did not involve Venetia. On the very day that Visconti-Venosta was feebly trying to justify the cabinet's inertia, Gioacchino Pepoli, the ambassador to St. Petersburg and a relative and friend of Napoleon III, sent a memorandum to the French Emperor about a plan for the evacuation of Rome and the guarantee of Papal territory. Pepoli had first gone to the Tuileries on his own initiative and had had a confidential visit with the Emperor to see what could be done about reopening the Roman question. In official circles, too, there was a revived interest. The Italian cabinet had taken up the matter in the summer of 1863, and then after the illness of Pius IX in January, 1864, members of the cabinet privately discussed the possibility of going to Emperor Napoleon on the Roman question. As a result of such discussions among his ministers, cabinet chief Minghetti was about to send General Alfonso La Marmora, another personal friend of Napoleon III, to Paris to open the question of evacuating Rome. Minghetti decided however, when he heard of Pepoli's attempts, to let him try first.[28]

Why did the Italian cabinet suddenly come alive again to the Roman question? Indeed there was the scare caused by Pius IX's attacks of erysipelas in January and May, 1864. La Marmora had suggested to Minghetti that it was imperative to settle the Roman ques-

[26] Clark, *Franz-Joseph and Bismarck*, 40–54.
[27] Speech of Visconti-Venosta annexed to Malaret to Drouyn de Lhuys, May 24, 1864, FAE, Italie, Vol. 9, pp. 321–46.
[28] Case, *Franco-Italian Relations*, 267–72.

tion with France before Pius IX died.[29] Yet the new ministry in the
summer of 1863 had already changed its position on Rome, to the
point of promising to take the initiative at the opportune time.[30] The
reason for the move would seem to lie in the new realism that the
Minghetti ministry brought to the question of Rome and in the ministry's willingness to seek compromise with the French. Nor is it unrea-
sonable to suspect that the action on Rome was related to the failure
of both France and Italy to attract international attention to the Venetian question.

At any rate, the overtures begun by Pepoli led unexpectedly to serious negotiations for a definitive treaty on Rome. Pepoli was allowed
to follow his first successful attempts at personal dealing with the
French Emperor. He arrived in Paris June 11 upon the invitation of
the Emperor, stayed at Fontainebleau a while, and by the end of June
was able to send to Turin a project he and Napoleon III had agreed
upon.[31]

The plan, based on the project proposed by Cavour in 1861, required that Italy herself respect the Pope's remaining territory and
that she protect the Papal territory from any irregular attacks; in return France would evacuate Rome. But there was one important addition to the Cavourian project. Napoleon III was indeed eager to withdraw his troops from the Eternal City, but he did not want the op-
probrium of seeming to abandon the Roman pontiff. Catholics needed
more assurance than a mere agreement between France and Italy.
Therefore, Napoleon III in his talks with Pepoli had agreed upon a
practical guarantee that would dispel from the minds of Catholics the
notion that the Italian government was keeping its capital at Turin
only until the seat of government could be transferred to Rome. In
order to have the French withdraw from Rome, therefore, Italy, according to the proposed convention, would have to change its capital
to another city.[32]

Although Turin was not an entirely satisfactory capital and though
the clause was to remain secret, changing the capital under these circumstances gave the Italian cabinet pause. They discussed the project

[29] *Ibid.*
[30] See the discourse of Minghetti in the Chamber of Deputies on June 18, 1863,
quoted in *ibid.,* 267.
[31] *Ibid.,* 272–73.
[32] See Nigra Report to Minghetti, June 14, 1864, quoted in *ibid.,* 272–73.

through the month of July, all the while seeking from Napoleon III a relaxation of terms. The capital transfer would indeed be a difficult move to explain to the Italian people at large, and naturally the Piedmontese faction opposed it. Yet by August, 1864, the Italian Council of Ministers, reflecting their anxiety to resolve the Roman question, agreed upon the capital transfer as proposed; they decided to represent it to the public as a strategic move designed to protect the capital from Austrian attack.[33]

Before the King could be persuaded to accept the transfer of the capital from his native Piedmont, La Marmora and Luigi Menabrea had to attempt last-minute bargaining. They were unsuccessful, however, and the King, confronted with Minghetti's threat of resignation, was all but forced to accept the capital transfer.[34]

Thus a document of major importance in Franco-Italian relations was signed on September 15, 1864. According to its provisions Italy was restrained from attacking the city of Rome, and she agreed to prevent any external attack. She also was to allow the formation of a corps of Catholic volunteers recruited from all over Europe for the purpose of helping to protect the frontier of the Papal territory and of keeping peace within. In addition, Italy agreed to assume "a proportional part of the debt of the former States of the Church," i.e., those territories now incorporated in the Kingdom of Italy. In return for such concessions, France was to withdraw her troops from the Papal territory "gradually and as fast as the army of the Holy Father shall be organized." But in any case the evacuation was to be completed not later than two years from the signing of the treaty. The transfer of the capital was consigned to a protocol separate from the convention and made a necessary condition of its validity.[35]

The course of these negotiations forms a kind of parenthesis between two periods of concern over Venetia, one leading up to the stalemate in the autumn of 1863 and the other to be resumed immediately after the convention was signed. This study properly begins when the Venetian question is taken up again after the signing of the September Convention.

[33] Case, *Franco-Italian Relations*, 282.
[34] *Ibid.*, 293.
[35] See text of convention in *ibid.*, 299–300. Although not designated in the treaty, Florence was later chosen as the new capital.

CHAPTER I

Venetia and the September Convention

ALLEGED SECRET CLAUSES

THE NEWS of the September Convention between France and Italy had scarcely reached the courts of Europe when there arose an almost universal suspicion that Napoleon III had given his word to another pact of Plombières. In France, Italy, Austria, the Papal Court, and Venice itself, in official as well as unofficial circles, there ran the interpretation, based in some cases on alleged secret clauses, that the French Emperor in temporarily closing the road to Rome had opened one to Venice.

While no official word had come from the Tuileries speculation was rife in Paris. Ambassadors spread the alarm to their home offices that the real thrust of the convention was against Austria. Lord John Russell, British foreign secretary, received a report that this feeling was nearly universal.[1] Count Rudolf Mülinen, the Austrian chargé d'affaires in Paris, reported secret clauses in the convention providing for war against his country.[2] Newspapers carried a similar interpretation. One commentator singled out the transfer of the Italian capital as a measure to make the seat of government more defensible in the event of a war against Austria.[3] Others noted that recent Austrian moves, such as the sudden return of Metternich to his post in Paris and the movement of troops to the Quadrilateral could only mean that panic had broken out in Vienna at news of the convention.[4]

Count Bernard von Rechberg, the Austrian foreign minister,

[1] Grey to Russell, Sept. 29, 1864, GBFO 27, Vol. 1534, No. 114.
[2] Mülinen to Rechberg, Sept. 26, 1864, HHS, Karton 78, No. 36C.
[3] *Le Constitutionnel,* Oct. 12, 1864.
[4] Mülinen to Rechberg, Oct. 3, 1864, HHS, Karton 78, No. 37; and Sept. 26, 1864, *ibid.*, No. 37F. In Rome Baron von Hübner, the Austrian ambassador to the Vatican, had the story that Victor Emmanuel II boasted of a secret article in the September Convention guaranteeing him possession of Lombardy should any conflict with Austria arise. Hübner to Mensdorff, Apr. 3, 1866, HHS, Karton 208, No. 13B.

though he received assurances to the contrary from the Quai d'Orsay,[5] could not help but put credence in the report of the two secret articles reported by Mülinen.[6] It seemed logical to him that Victor Emmanuel II would have consented to the transfer of the Italian capital only if some important concessions on Venetia were made.[7] These fears were shared by the Viennese public, which demanded a guarantee for Venetia against the menace implied in the September Convention.[8] More alarming to the Austrian government were the demonstrations and proclamations being made in the city of Venice. The Central Venetian Committee (said to be supported by the Italian government) in early October issued a proclamation announcing the conclusion of an alleged Franco-Italian alliance, defensive and offensive, in which Napoleon III was to give armed assistance for the conquest of Venetia in the spring of 1865.[9] Articulate public opinion made some of the same assumptions as did Count Rechberg. Hopeful Venetians argued that some recompense besides the evacuation of Rome must have been offered to Italy and that this recompense could only have been a guarantee of Italy's present territory and a promise of help for the day when it would be thought possible to redeem Venetia.[10]

Diplomats at other centers of activity expected action upon Venetia. Bismarck was not slow in taking advantage of Austria's threatened position by refusing concessions in Schleswig and offering only benevolent neutrality in the event of a Venetian war. He reacted similarly in his relations with France, for whose nonintervention he no longer felt he had to promise compensation on the Rhine. A Kiel newspaper summed up rumors of such calculations pithily in mid-October, 1864: "For Prussia Venice has become a fortress on the Rhine." [11] The same article made the further point that the convention, as a concession to the extremists in Italy, would precipitate an internal revolution in Rome overwhelming the unprotected Pope and

[5] Bloomfield to Russell, Oct. 1, 1864, Bloomfield Papers, GBFO 356, Vol. 20, No. 518.

[6] Bloomfield to Russell, Sept. 29, 1864, *ibid.*

[7] Bloomfield to Russell, Oct. 1, 1864, *ibid.*, No. 524.

[8] Gramont to Drouyn de Lhuys, Sept. 30, 1864, *OD*, IV, 205–208.

[9] Rechberg to Mülinen, Oct. 12, 1864, HHS, Karton 80, No. 4; Gramont to Drouyn de Lhuys, Oct. 2, 1864, FAE, Autriche, Vol. 487, No. 74.

[10] Pilet, Consul General at Venice, to Drouyn de Lhuys, Sept. 25, 1864, FAE, Venise, Vol. 25, No. 44.

[11] Annexed to Meroux de Valois to Drouyn de Lhuys, Oct. 19, 1864, *OD*, IV, 274–76.

lead readily to the next step, an attack on Venetia. In last analysis it spelled grave danger for Austria.[12] Other areas of the German Confederation were alerted to this possibility by news from Milan (published in an Augsburg newspaper) that a revolutionary committee in that city had declared the annexation of Venetia to be an objective of the September treaty, that an offensive and defensive alliance had been signed, and that action was expected in 1865.[13] The anti-Austrian interpretation of the September Convention was so strong in Rome that it gave temporary comfort to the Ultramontane party. Hearing that it was a thrust against the northern powers, they were less inclined to fear it as a prelude to the fall of Rome.[14]

In the Kingdom of Italy revolutionary circles made much of the connection between Venetia and the September Convention. They were spreading more than rumors; the Mazzinians published texts of the alleged secret articles.[15] They also had gained possession of two letters which they claimed documented the negotiation of an agreement on Venetia, and in an effort to embarrass the government, they circulated copies. The letters (allegedly an exchange of notes between Visconti-Venosta and Pepoli) presumed to record certain confidential talks with the French Emperor. According to the letters, dated September 9 and September 14, 1864, Napoleon III was to "give guarantee to Italy for the solution of the Venetian question" and to receive in return rectification of the Franco-Italian frontier at Nice.[16]

In face of such widespread suspicion, the principal concern of the French Foreign Office was to continue assurances to Austria. Baron Joseph von Hübner, Austrian ambassador to the Papal Court, on a visit to Paris, his former post, was assured that the Emperor's health was too poor for him to be thinking of starting a war.[17] In Vienna Antoine duc de Gramont, the French minister to Austria, read to

---

[12] *Ibid.*

[13] Bloomfield to Russell, Oct. 1, 1864, Bloomfield Papers, GBFO 356, Vol. 20, No. 526. Cardinal Antonelli, however, did not commit himself on an interpretation. He said the correct meaning of the Convention existed "only in the Emperor's mind." Bloomfield to Russell, Nov. 22, 1864, *ibid.*, No. 76.

[14] Odo Russell to Earl Russell, Nov. 8, 1864, GBFO 43, Vol. 91B.

[15] Drouyn de Lhuys to Malaret, Nov. 28, 1865, FAE, Italie, Vol. 13, No. 44. The letters were picked up by the Consul at Milan and are annexed to his dispatch to Drouyn de Lhuys, Nov. 8, 1865, FAE, Milan, Vol. 4, pp. 150–51.

[16] *Ibid.*

[17] Hübner to Rechberg, Oct. 2, 1864, annexed to Mülinen to Mensdorff, Oct. 3, 1864, HHS, Karton 78, No. 37F.

Count Rechberg a statement denying any hostile intent in the September Convention.[18] And Edouard Drouyn de Lhuys, the French minister of foreign affairs, told Mülinen that all the talk about secret articles plotting a war was absurd.[19]

Instead of openly repudiating the rumors in Paris, Drouyn de Lhuys chose to speak to the French people in a series of articles in *Le Constitutionnel* written under the name of M. Paulin Limayrac. Nine articles in successive issues presented the official interpretation of the September Convention as a treaty that safeguarded the Pope, placated Italy, and showed the continuity of Napoleon III's policies. In the October 12 issue, he assured Austria that she had no reason to fear the September Convention, that it related only to Rome and not to Venetia, and that rumors about "war in the spring" were perennial.[20]

The letters of Pepoli and Visconti-Venosta present a special problem. The French Foreign Office never dealt with them in public statements. Possibly Drouyn de Lhuys was unaware of their circulation until the Consul at Milan sent him copies of both letters one year later, at which time he merely scribbled on them the words "false and absurd." [21] He then sent copies to Baron Joseph Malaret, the French ambassador to Turin, who was to bring them to the attention of La Marmora with the request that he do something about such "false propaganda." [22] The accusation in the letters was to haunt Marquis Pepoli some years later because they implied his having offered more Italian territory on the border of Nice and Savoy to the French. Pepoli denied having written the letters, and since investigation could not authenticate the documents his denials were accepted.[23]

[18] Bloomfield to Russell, Oct. 1, 1864, Bloomfield Papers, GBFO 356, Vol. 20, No. 526.

[19] Mülinen to Rechberg, Oct. 12, 1864 (tel) HHS, Karton 78, No. 42B.

[20] *Le Constitutionnel*, Oct. 12, 1864. Mülinen's dispatch of Oct. 12 states that the articles were written by a M. Limayrac under Drouyn de Lhuys's direction. Professor Case, *Franco-Italian Relations*, states that Limayrac was a nom de plume of Drouyn de Lhuys.

[21] Consul at Milan to Drouyn de Lhuys, Nov. 8, 1865, FAE, Milan, Vol. 4, pp. 150–51. Copies were annexed to this dispatch.

[22] Drouyn de Lhuys to Malaret, Nov. 28, 1866, FAE, Italie, Vol. 13, No. 44.

[23] In 1880 the famous letters turned up in the hands of an Italian historian, Professor Maineri, of Turin, who challenged Pepoli with them. Pepoli invited Maineri to look through all his correspondence with Napoleon III to see if any trace of such talks existed. Maineri did so and declared after the investigation that he accepted Pepoli's denial and judged the letters apocryphal. See letters between Pepoli and Maineri and Pepoli and Carpi in Luigi Carpi, "Biografia di M. Pepoli," *Risorgimento italiano, Biografie*, III (1885), 370–426. Also, in 1880 a publication entitled *Politica segreta italiana* (Turin: Roux e Fanale, 1880) con-

As a result of the Quai d'Orsay's denials and the fact that there was no overt action on Venetia, the tension created by the September Convention slowly subsided. The Austrians accepted the explanations offered for the time being, though Prince Metternich's careful reports show that the Viennese cabinet did not for a moment relax its vigilance over the French Emperor's every move. The air of expectancy died out in Venice, and the Italian government soon appeared preoccupied with domestic problems, especially economic reconstruction and the transfer of the capital from Turin to Florence.

THE LOGIC OF CIRCUMSTANCE

Despite the widespread suspicion and accusation, the lack of documentary evidence prevents us from contesting the statements of the French that they promised no military assistance to Italy for the winning of Venetia.[24] However, the French foreign minister confined himself to disavowing any hostile intent concerning Austria. Moreover, it is difficult to dismiss as pure speculation the instinctive reaction of journalists and diplomats all over Europe in associating the September Convention with Venetia. Even assuming that the reports and the documentary evidence circulated were spurious, the reasoning contained in the reports demands attention even though it might challenge widely accepted views of the September Convention.[25] Arguing either that Venetia was promised or that Lombardy was guaranteed in case of a conflict with Austria, the speculations invariably rested on the assumption that such agreements must have been made because the evacuation of Rome by French troops was inadequate compensation for the sacrifices made by the Italian government.[26]

---

tained an article by Aurelio Saffi treating the Venetian article in the September Convention circulated by Mazzini as authentic. See Carpi, pp. 413–16.

[24] None of the three principal studies of the September Convention—Case, *Franco-Italian Relations;* Norbert Miko, "Zur Geschichte der Konvention vom 15 September 1864 Zwischen Frankreich und Italien," *Römische Historische Mitteilungen,* Vol. II (1957–58); and Renato Mori, *La questione romana, 1861–1865*—contains any hint of secret clauses or negotiations.

[25] A. J. P. Taylor in his *Struggle for Mastery in Europe, 1848–1918,* 155, suggests that the Convention was a clear victory for Italian diplomacy in that it was merely a postponement of Rome's acquisition.

[26] Pilet to Drouyn de Lhuys, Sept. 25, 1864, FAE, Venise, Vol. 25, No. 44; Hübner to Mensdorff, Apr. 3, 1866, HHS, Karton 208 (Vatikan), No. 13B; Bloomfield to Russell, Oct. 1, 1864, Bloomfield Papers, GBFO, No. 524.

The sacrifices referred to were the renunciation of Rome and the transfer of the capital from Turin,[27] but if we also consider Italy's assumption of an enormous Papal debt and Italy's agreement to allow an army of Papal volunteers to be formed to replace the French forces —all provisions of the September Convention—the ubiquitous suspicion of secret compensations is even more understandable. Moreover, for the moment it was only Italian honor that was saved by the withdrawal of French troops—an honor being engaged anew to keep the Eternal City inviolate.

That Venetia should be supplied as the missing item in the seemingly incomplete convention is also understandable. There seems little question that within the Italian government at the time just previous to the signing of the September Convention the Venetian question was primary. It has already been noted that the Minghetti ministry inaugurated a shift of emphasis from Rome to Venice in 1863 which it maintained throughout the following year. The ministers ignored Rome during most of their term of office until the sudden burst of activity in May, 1864.[28] Both the sudden revival of negotiations on Rome and the emphasis on Venetia reflected the realistic attitudes acquired by Minghetti as well as the skill he had gained in directing and moderating the activists. Not only the activists but also the liberal wing of Minghetti's party definitely preferred to concentrate on Venetia, for they considered it a more immediately realizable objective than Rome.[29] Thus the Venetian question was less complicated and was one upon which the Government could achieve wider agreement. It was to Minghetti, Visconti-Venosta, and others like them that Baron Malaret alluded when he reported that at the time of the September Convention Venetia had eclipsed Rome as the immediate and principal object:

> At the time of the September Convention, for the population as well as for the political leaders, the independence of Venice was not only the first but the principal end to achieve; the Roman question came only in second place.[30]

[27] *Ibid.*
[28] See *supra,* pp. 12–13.
[29] See address of Bettino Ricasoli to the Liberal Association of Florence, July 11, 1864; Bettino Ricasoli, *Lettere e documenti,* VII, 314–20; Ricasoli to Celestino Bianchi, Sept. 23, 1864, *ibid.,* VII, 249–52.
[30] Malaret to Moustier, Oct. 24, 1866, *OD,* XIII, 10–16.

Malaret further explained that on all levels there was hope of a direct transaction with the Holy See for a definitive solution of the Roman question, but for the winning of Venetia they felt the absolute need of France.[31]

Rome and Venetia were also linked together in a broader, international context. Since its inception the French occupation of Rome had caused a diplomatic isolation to fall around the new Italian Kingdom.[32] The Italians had felt the full effect of that isolation when they attempted unsuccessfully to negotiate for Venetia during the Polish revolution of 1863. The first requisite for any resumption of the unification program was breaking out of this isolation, bringing Italian problems back into the mainstream of European diplomacy as was done after the Crimean War, and especially winning the cooperation of France and England.[33] This was the very line of thinking Visconti-Venosta presented to the Camera in May, 1864, when he had to answer the charge that the government was lagging in its efforts to push on to Rome and Venetia. He explained that the whole European picture must change for the better before action could be taken, and one of the hopes he held out was based upon a recent speech of Napoleon III in which a requiem was spoken on the treaties of 1815 insofar as they "weighed upon the legitimate aspirations of peoples." [34]

The general advantage of gaining a better image in European diplomatic circles by settling the Roman question with France was itself sufficient motivation for the September Convention. Even more advantageous and more concrete would have been some commitment, somewhere in the context of the September Convention, of French assistance for the acquisition of Venetia. Such commitment could have been in the form of an understanding or pledge of diplomatic support for negotiations with Austria or at the very minimum the Emperor's blessings upon a military alliance with another power.

The events following the September Convention strengthen these latter possibilities and tend to confirm the hypothesis that Venetia was the missing item in the September Convention.

---

[31] *Ibid.*

[32] Francesco Cataluccio, *La politica estera di E. Visconti-Venosta,* 27.

[33] Ricasoli to Celestino Bianchi, Sept. 23, 1864, Ricasoli, *Lettere,* VII, 249–52.

[34] Speech of Visconti-Venosta, May 12, 1864, *Gazzetta ufficiale,* Turin, May 24, 1864; Malaret to Drouyn de Lhuys, May 12, 1864, FAE, Italie, Vol. 9, n.n., pp. 93–100; see also Report to the King by outgoing ministry, Sept. 19, 1864, annexed to Malaret to Drouyn de Lhuys, Oct. 5, 1864, FAE, Italie, Vol. 10, No. 90.

GENERAL LA MARMORA AND THE CAPITAL TRANSFER

It was to implement the program of seeking closer French ties that General La Marmora, a friend of Louis Napoleon ever since the battle-fields of the Crimea and Solferino, was chosen to be Minghetti's successor. To follow the General's career is to be led from the September Convention directly to the heart of the Venetian question.

La Marmora had first been chosen to start the negotiations for the convention, but he stepped aside for Pepoli, who had unexpectedly opened an avenue for dealing with the Emperor of the French on Rome. The General carried out certain ad hoc assignments during the negotiations, but Pepoli and Nigra accomplished the main task. Just before the convention was signed, Minghetti, perhaps to have the influential La Marmora talk Napoleon III out of posing the transfer of the capital as a *sine qua non* of the treaty, asked La Marmora to go to St. Cloud and confer with the Emperor and his foreign minister. The transfer of the capital had actually turned him against the whole project because, being from Piedmont, he recognized that such a measure might alienate this important region. La Marmora did not effect any changes in the project, but he nevertheless came away from his talks at St. Cloud disposed to accept the convention. This was because, in his words, he was able to convince himself *"how favorably disposed was the French government in our regard relative to the question of Venetia."* [35]

Within a fortnight after his talks with the Emperor and Drouyn de Lhuys, La Marmora was asked to interrupt a short vacation to come to Turin to accept the presidency of the Italian Council and the portfolio of foreign affairs. He had been sought after as a possible cabinet chief during the earlier stages of the negotiations for the September Convention because he alone, as a soldier and a Piedmontese, was thought capable of convincing the people of Piedmont that they should accept the removal of the capital from Turin. At that time he refused.[36] Now, after his conversations with the Emperor and Drouyn de Lhuys on the eve of the Roman settlement, he accepted and soon took up with conviction his assignments as cabinet chief and foreign minister.

[35] *Evénements,* 47.
[36] Case, *Franco-Italian Relations,* 278f.

La Marmora immediately set to work cementing relations with France and selling the September Convention to the Italian people.

His first task was to win approval of the convention in the Camera and Senato at the session that began on October 24, 1864. Legally the convention did not need formal approval of the legislative bodies, but movement of the capital required financial appropriations as well as understanding and support on the part of the deputies.[37] If the government had not been fairly sure that it could carry the motion easily, it would not have brought the issue up for debate. The results justified the government's confidence, for the motion carried by a greater majority than any vote taken in the same chambers since 1859.[38]

The important factor in these debates is not the government victory but the manner in which discussion turned so naturally from the transfer of the capital to the Venetian question. The deputies were encouraged by one of the government's spokesmen, Deputy Ferrari, not to regret so much the renunciation of Rome since a capital, after all, is not a "question of architecture." [39] As to the transfer of the capital from Turin, Deputies Pepoli and Rattazzi, speaking in defense of the government's policy, admitted that the seat of government was to be changed as pledge of Italy's serious purpose not to attack Rome or allow it to be attacked.[40] But government spokesmen hastened to explain that a move from Turin was necessary in any case since the Piedmontese capital was too vulnerable to Austrian attack and that Florence had more advantages strategically.[41] Pepoli and others then pointed out how the September Convention, the accomplishment of diplomacy, prepared the way for the acquisition of Venetia, a question that might have to be resolved by military action. They made the point that the Italian government had to establish its prestige before the world by eliminating the French occupation of Rome.[42] Carlo Buoncampagni explained how both questions of Rome and Venetia could now be solved: Italy might make some private settlement with the Pontifical government or perhaps an internal revolution in Rome might even take place, leaving Italy free to resume the quest of Vene-

[37] *Ibid.*, 300n85.

[38] Malaret to Drouyn de Lhuys, Nov. 20, 1864, FAE, Italie, Vol. 11, pp. 202–21.

[39] Session of Nov. 10, 1864, *Gazzetta ufficiale*, Turin, Nov. 11, 1864.

[40] Session of Nov. 14, 1864, *ibid.*, Nov. 19, 1864.

[41] See Report of the Senato's Commission, annexed to Malaret to Drouyn de Lhuys, Nov. 28, 1864, FAE, Italie, Vol. 11, pp. 238–43.

[42] Session of Nov. 14, 1864, *Gazzetta ufficiale*, Turin, Nov. 19, 1864.

tia. He suggested that neither term of the program—"Roma e Venezia"—need be abandoned. They need now only to be inverted.[43]

Opposition to the convention came largely from disgruntled Piedmontese and from the radicals who in principle objected to this kind of settlement of the Roman question and fretted over Napoleon III's intentions to insist upon a federation for Italy. Yet they picked up with great enthusiasm—more than the government desired—the suggestion concerning Venetia. Venetia, yes, but diplomacy was not the solution to questions of Italian unity. Alfredo Carlo called for proceeding directly to the liberation of Venetia.[44] Deputy Pinelli, of the loyal opposition, advocated accepting the convention (because it was a *fait accompli*) and reaping some advantage from it by turning directly to Venice. He would also invert the terms of the formula as Buoncampagni had suggested and would implement it by an offensive and defensive alliance with France. He declared that there was no security while Austria was encamped behind the Quadrilateral.[45] The ministry, however, rejected Pinelli's resolution because of its open expression of hostile intentions.[46]

Thus, the government and the opposition were of one mind on the immediate program. The Roman question would be better solved by proceeding immediately to the Venetian question. The former question hopefully would take care of itself either by an understanding with the Vatican, an internal revolution, or a chance no one dared express—the death of Pius IX. As Baron Bettino Ricasoli put it earlier in addressing the Liberal Association of Florence, "after the September Convention Italy ought not go to Rome but Rome ought to go to Italy." [47]

The most significant remarks on the Venetian question, however, were to be made by General La Marmora. In his main speech of November 12, 1864, he began by telling of his former objection to the September Convention—that it would be an "apple of discord" thrown among the Italians. He declared however that he had now overcome his apprehensions and was resolved to accept the treaty. His address was a plea for confidence in Napoleon III, which he justified by a long review of the history of Louis Napoleon's disinterested

[43] Session of Nov. 9, 1864, *ibid.*, Nov. 11, 1864.
[44] Session of Nov. 18, 1864, *ibid.*, Nov. 20, 1864.
[45] *Ibid.*
[46] *Ibid.*
[47] Manifesto to the Liberal Association of Florence, Sept. 27, 1865, Ricasoli, *Lettere*, VII, 333.

efforts for a united Italy. As for the two tasks that lay ahead, he shared Buoncampagni's thoughts. The question of Rome might best be put aside for the moment:

> For this question [of Rome] I have confidence in time and the Emperor of the French. If there is a man who by his position and capacity can aid us, it is the Emperor of the French and we owe gratitude to him.

As for the question of Venice, he conveyed the subtle but assuring hope of help from the Emperor to the accompaniment of the knowing aha's of the deputies. He continued:

> But I go further, sirs; I hope also for his support in the question of Venetia. I strip myself of my position as minister of foreign affairs, ignoring the fact that it is impossible to do it (laughter).

Emphasizing the fact that, although the statement was unofficial, he was quite serious about it, he continued: "Notice, sirs, that what I say to you is neither official nor unofficial; it is an idea that is personal to me." Furthermore, he read in the recent behavior of England as well as France an attitude favorable to Italy's rights on the upper Adriatic. As for France, concern over the Venetian question could be seen in the Mexican adventure since an Austrian archduke was chosen for the Mexican throne. La Marmora noted significantly that England, which always manifested a lively interest in Italy, had ceded the Ionian Islands to Greece—"these Ionian Islands situated in the same Adriatic which washes the steps of the Ducal Palace of Venice."

The General went so far as to indicate the means by which Venice would come into Italian hands:

> All this has inspired me with a hope, knowing the excellent intentions of the Emperor in all that concerns our interests, that a day can come when it will be possible to put together some arrangement for our benefit. And if ever that day comes, not entering ourselves into any direct relation with the Austrian government, it would be natural that we have an intermediary and it is certain that no one could serve us better than the Emperor of the French.[48]

[48] All above quotations are taken from the recorded speech of General La Marmora sent in French translation by Malaret to Drouyn de Lhuys and found in Malaret to Drouyn de Lhuys (circa) Nov. 12, 1864, FAE, Italie, Vol. 11, dispatch No. 115, pp. 103–15.

Were these words inspired by his talk with Napoleon III and Drouyn de Lhuys during the negotiation of the September Convention? Not only is this obvious from the circumstances, but one can read a clear affirmation in La Marmora's recollections published later in his life.[49]

The subsequent course of parliamentary debate further elucidates La Marmora's meaning. The understanding implied in the speeches from both sides of the hall was that the winning of Venetia with French help was a program already decided. It was only a question of how it might be accomplished. Pepoli tried to re-echo the confidence of La Marmora in the diplomatic intervention of Napoleon III. After the September Convention, he declared, there remained only the "Austrian question" which he was willing to commend to the skills of General La Marmora.[50] Members of the opposition, while applauding the direction that policy was taking, wanted to discuss more specific steps to implement it.[51] Some openly called for a war against Austria.[52] Pinelli finally introduced a resolution that the ministry take "practical steps" with France to make Austria withdraw from Venetia, but La Marmora, noting the thinly veiled bid for a war, asked that the motion be thrown out.[53]

FIRST DIPLOMATIC MOVES

The significance of La Marmora's speech was not missed by European diplomats. Drouyn de Lhuys read the discourse carefully and with much pleasure and accepted it as the official thought of the Italian government.[54] On the other hand, Austrian fears were aroused anew. Count Alexander von Mensdorff, the foreign minister, was astonished to hear that the president of the Italian council had announced publicly that he counted on the aid of Napoleon III in what he called "the Venetian question." The Austrian minister wondered if this meant a change in Napoleon's avowal that he would not go to war for Venetia or even make it an object of diplomatic pressure.[55]

Indeed, the debates in the Italian parliament and especially La

[49] *Evénements*, 47. See *supra*, p. 22.
[50] French translation of the recorded speech found annexed to Malaret to Drouyn de Lhuys, Nov. 19, 1864, FAE, Italie, Vol. 11, pp. 119–36.
[51] Annexed to Malaret to Drouyn de Lhuys, Nov. 16, 1864, *ibid.*, 138–71.
[52] Session of Nov. 18, 1866, *Gazzetta ufficiale*, Florence, Nov. 19, 1864.
[53] *Ibid.*
[54] Drouyn de Lhuys to Malaret, Nov. 15, 1864, FAE, Italie, Vol. 11, pp. 116–18.
[55] Mensdorff to Metternich, Nov. 19, 1864, HHS, Karton, 79, pp. 380–85.

Marmora's speech were sufficient to set off important diplomatic moves and to accelerate the trend of certain alignments in Europe. Rumblings of trouble between Austria and Prussia over Schleswig-Holstein had already come to the ears of the Italian Chief Minister along with feelers from Prussia. Count Karl von Usedom, the Prussian ambassador in Turin, had been making frequent long visits to La Marmora, speaking of the possibility of a diplomatic rupture with Austria and asking what Italy would do in the event of such a rift.[56] La Marmora was not then ready to consider the action suggested by these questions, as he demonstrated to Drouyn de Lhuys, assuring the latter that he would abide only by a peaceful solution to the Venetian question in cooperation with France.[57] Assured or not, France had to present some plan to counteract in the Italian cabinet the enticing picture of cooperation with Prussia. But there was as yet no avenue open to Venice. The Austrian cabinet had already made it clear that though it wanted agreement—even an entente—with France on the Roman question, the question of Venetia must remain out of the discussion.[58] Nigra and Drouyn de Lhuys discussed the purchase of Venetia, but the French Minister knew Austria would decline and substituted rather hopelessly the "dream of Lord Russell," namely, the previously proposed combination whereby Austria would acquire the sovereignty now held by the Ottoman Empire over the Danubian Principalities and in exchange give Venetia to Italy.[59] As before, it was to go unrealized for want of initiative on the part of either France or England, the only ones who could bring up the subject in Vienna.

Meanwhile, the Party of Action in Italy was trying to draw attention to Venetia by two attempted revolts in Udine and Friuli. One was a commotion caused on October 16 by a group of forty men in Garibaldian costumes in the town of Spelimbergo; they disarmed the police and looted communal banks in the town.[60] The second was an attempt of Garibaldian volunteers from Brescia to invade Friuli and excite the population to insurrection.[61] The Party of Action continued to collect arms, money, and ammunition and to train young volunteers

[56] Evénements, 52.
[57] Drouyn de Lhuys to Gramont, Oct. 29, 1864, FAE, Autriche, Vol. 487, pp. 217–22.
[58] Mensdorff to Metternich, Nov. 11, 1864, HHS, Karton 79, No. 2.
[59] Diplomatic Circular, Drouyn de Lhuys to Gramont, Oct. 29, 1864, FAE, Autriche, Vol. 487, pp. 217–22; Nigra to La Marmora, Nov. 22, 1864, Evénements, 50.
[60] Mensdorff to Mülinen, Oct. 21, 1864, HHS, Karton 79, n.n.
[61] Nigra to La Marmora, Nov. 3, 1864, Archivio Storico, Vol. 836.

with a view to setting off an insurrection in Venetia. The Venetians, who had believed since the September Convention that they were on the eve of deliverance, by November began to lose hope and look to France.[62]

By the end of November both Italy and Austria were ready for some definite word from the French Emperor. Both Nigra and Metternich followed the Imperial family to the chateau at Compiègne where they were able to have long conversations with the Emperor and his foreign minister. Metternich, as it were, spoke in one ear and Nigra in the other.

It was the obvious intention of the Austrians to stave off any combination on Venetia and to facilitate an agreement on Rome. Metternich received instructions from his chief early in the month to seek an entente with France on the question of preserving the temporal power of the Pope under the new situation.[63] And there also lingered the unanswered question of whether the September Convention actually meant hostile intent toward Austria. Finally, Metternich wanted to know Napoleon's aspirations concerning Venetia. On November 29 Metternich finally had an interview alone with the Emperor in which he got an answer on the intentions of the September Convention vis-à-vis Austria. The answer was that no hostility was meant. Napoleon elaborated by describing the negotiations of the convention to show that they came about on the initiative of the Italian government and that the reason for moving the capital was to offer a practical guarantee that Italy had fixed a capital other than Rome. This, the French Emperor stated, was the only condition upon which he would evacuate the city of the Popes.[64]

As to Napoleon III's intentions in Venetia, several points were made clear for Metternich. First of all, the French Empire had not pledged itself to support the Italians in a war for the coveted provinces. The Emperor reminded the Austrian that he had not made war for Poland and that he would not make war for Venetia.[65] Yet, if Italy were to attempt peaceful negotiations with Austria for recognition and for the exchange of Venetia, Napoleon III would support

---

[62] Pilet to Drouyn de Lhuys, Nov. 1, 1864, FAE, Venise, Vol. 25, No. 50.

[63] Mensdorff to Metternich, Nov. 1, 1864, HHS, Karton 80, No. 1.

[64] Metternich to Mensdorff, Dec. 5, 1864, HHS, Karton 79, No. 65B. He got substantially the same answer from Drouyn de Lhuys, Drouyn de Lhuys to Gramont, Dec. 6, 1864, FAE, Autriche, Vol. 847, No. 85.

[65] Metternich to Mensdorff, Dec. 5, 1864, HHS, Karton 79, No. 65B

his Italian protégé. Only if Austria attempted to take away territory that Victor Emmanuel II already possessed might France assist Italy materially. Metternich reported in full on the conversation, quoting the Emperor's words:

> This is the complete truth on my intentions. I want Italy to conserve what she has—*no more no less*—I will support, I caution you in all loyalty, every peaceful attempt between Rome and Italy to arrive at a relationship of neighborly coexistence as well as every chance of an entente between you and us, or between you and Italy, for a peaceful solution of the difficulties which the Venetian question can again create—either by way of friendly arrangements with Italy or by way of political combinations or finally by a system of compensations.[66]

In conclusion, and in order further to assure Austria, both the Emperor and his foreign minister used a phrase they would repeat often in dealing with Austria: If Italy attacked Austria, she would do so "at her own risk and peril." [67]

Metternich returned from his visit to Compiègne convinced that Napoleon III had not promised material support to the Italians on the Venetian question. Yet he still held to his opinion that the September Convention was a capitulation to the revolutionary party, and he wondered about Napoleon's declaration of support of peaceful attempts to get Venetia. Perhaps the Frenchman might eventually try to force Austria out of her reserve on this question.[68]

Nigra used his opportunity at Compiègne to reopen the one avenue to the Venetian question possible at the time—the "dream of Lord Russell." This idea of exchanging the Danubian Principalities for Venetia was first suggested by the English shortly after the Treaty of Zurich; it was attempted in 1863 during the Polish crisis and brought up by Drouyn de Lhuys again a month after the signing of the September Convention. The Emperor now raised two questions concerning the exchange, probably to disguise his real conviction that Austria simply would not hear of it. He was favorable provided account could be taken of the will of the people of Moldavia and Walla-

[66] *Ibid.*

[67] *Ibid.*; Drouyn de Lhuys to Gramont, Dec. 6, 1864, FAE, Autriche, Vol. 847, No. 85.

[68] Metternich to Mensdorff, Dec. 5, 1864, HHS, Karton 79, No. 65C; and Dec. 15, 1864, HHS, Karton 80, No. 2.

chia. He also felt that it was Great Britain's place to take the initiative at the Viennese court since Britain was not in such a delicate position as France after Magenta and Solferino.[69]

Nigra's attempt to carry the suggestion to London got no further than the British ambassador in Paris, Lord Cowley, who said the present time was inopportune. Thus for the moment Austria obtained assurances and Italy a slight deferment, but in either case it was shown that the September Convention had brought Italy to the threshold of action on Venetia.

[69] Nigra to La Marmora, Dec. 13, 1864, Archivio Storico, Vol. 836.

CHAPTER II

Napoleon III and the Prussian-Italian Alliance

VENETIA AND THE GERMAN CRISIS IN 1865

THE TRANSFER of the capital from Turin to Florence was the only provision of the September Convention put into effect immediately. On October 13, 1864, a declaration annexed to this document provided for the complete evacuation of Roman territory by French troops not earlier than two years after the decree from the Italian King transferring the capital from Turin,[1] which was issued on December 11, 1864. The other major concern of the convention, that is the assumption by Italy of the public debt adhering to the confiscated Papal States, was not taken up actively until the summer of 1866.[2] The so-called Antibes Legion,[3] which was to replace the French garrison as security for the Pope, was not organized until January, 1866;[4] nor was the project of seeking a modus vivendi between the Roman and Italian governments undertaken by the French Emperor until more than two years after the signing of the convention itself.

There are several possible explanations for the delayed action. One was the demoralizing effect of Pius IX's *Syllabus Errorum* upon French-Papal relations. Oddly, however, within a year of the issuing of the Papal document these relations took a decidedly favorable turn.[5] Another was the sad state of internal affairs, especially financial,[6] which troubled the Italian government. Yet during the year 1865 the Italians were considering a far riskier and more expensive undertaking than the assumption of the Papal debt, namely, a war against

[1] *OD*, XII, 384n1.

[2] Malaret to Drouyn de Lhuys, Aug. 24, 1866, FAE, Italie, Vol. 15, p. 386. See also *OD*, XII, 384n1 for short summary of negotiations.

[3] The Antibes Legion was a corps of supposedly volunteer Catholics which was in reality under supervision of the French government. Jean Maurain, *La politique ecclésiastique du second empire de 1852–1869*, 738.

[4] *Ibid.*

[5] Maurain, *La politique ecclésiastique,* 736.

[6] André Cochut, "La situation financière en Italie," *Revue des deux mondes,* Period 2, Vol. 63 (May, 1866), 221–51.

Austria.[7] A third explanation is that the governments of France and Italy wanted to become occupied promptly with their program for Venetia, exploiting the effect of the recently signed September Convention. Doubtless they already foresaw opportunities to their profit arising from the Danish War and from subsequent complications in Schleswig-Holstein. It might reasonably be supposed that part of the underlying *quid pro quo* in the settlement for Rome was that some efficacious action against Venetia should precede complete execution of the September Convention.

Opportunity certainly appeared in 1865. From the time of the Danish War it had become evident that neither Austria nor Prussia would be able to act efficaciously without the help or at least approval of the French Emperor. Bismarck was extremely wary of the intentions of both Italy and France all during the crisis over the Elbe Duchies; in fact he settled for such a compromise as the Gastein Convention because he feared French intervention.[8] On the other hand, the Austrians blamed their own lack of resolution in dealing with Prussia on built-in fears of French ulterior motives with regard to Venetia.[9] Some eight months before the September Convention, when difficulties were foreseen between Prussia and Austria, Napoleon III observed to Pasolini that opportunity to acquire Venetia might lie in an alliance between Italy and Prussia.[10] Such a possibility became likelier in April, 1865, when the Austrians rejected Bismarck's first compromise proposals on Schleswig-Holstein.[11]

What the intentions of the Emperor might be in the period leading up to the Gastein Convention—February to August, 1865—was of grave importance to all parties concerned, including, to be sure, the Italians. Yet all this concern met with a continued air of reticence in the French court and its Ministry of Foreign Affairs. The Emperor was as yet unable to make a clear decision on which course to take in seizing the opportunities before him. Should he support a possible Prussian-Italian alliance, or should he cultivate Austria for a peaceful

---

[7] Malaret to Drouyn de Lhuys, Apr. 20, 1865, FAE, Italie, Vol. 12, No. 32.

[8] Pottinger, *Napoleon III*, 9–10. This volume contains a superb treatment of the Prussian phase of Napoleon III's policy up to the opening of hostilities between Prussia and Austria.

[9] Metternich to Mensdorff, Mar. 19, 1865, HHS, Karton 81, No. 16C; see also a publication attributed to Benedetti, *La Convention de Gastein* (Paris: E. Dentu, 1865), 23.

[10] Emile Ollivier, "L'entrevue de Biarritz, 1865," *Revue des deux mondes*, Period 3, Vol. 9 (June, 1902), 481–518.

[11] Benedetti to Drouyn de Lhuys, Apr. 9, 1866, *OD*, VI, 131–34.

solution of the Venetian question? Indications throughout the spring and summer of 1865 were that he was leaning toward the second alternative. As early as February he declared before the Sénat and Corps législatif that he had no intentions of intervening militarily in Germany.[12] Both he and Drouyn de Lhuys backed this up with continued assurances to Metternich that Italy would take advantage of Austria at Italy's own "risk and peril."[13]

In late May an incident occurred that tended to prove French assurances to Austria to be more than mere diplomatic stereotype. The event is worth recording here because it shows continuity with serious efforts exerted since 1861 to cultivate Austria's good will.[14] The notoriously pro-Italian "Plon-Plon," Prince Jerome Napoleon, had just been appointed vice president of the Conseil privé. He was subsequently commissioned to deliver an address on the occasion of the unveiling of a monument to Napoleon I at Ajaccio, Corsica. Deciding to exploit his new ascendancy by turning his eulogy into an attack on Austria, Prince Jerome compared the "true liberty" engendered by the Bonapartist concept with the "false liberty" fostered by the Austrian Empire, and he warned of the fatal influence inherent in any Austro-French alliance. His speech so much upset Prince Metternich that the latter sent a copy to his home office, underlining in red the many passages that he found offensive.[15] Napoleon III's reaction to the speech was as unexpected as it was satisfactory to the Austrian cause. In less than a fortnight the Emperor published in the *Moniteur* a personal letter to Prince Jerome repudiating the sentiments expressed in the Prince's Ajaccio speech and chiding him for a breach of unity and discipline within the Imperial family.[16] As a consequence the Prince promptly offered his resignation as vice president of the Conseil privé; it was accepted by the Emperor.[17] Metternich was understandably elated over this victory of the Austrian cause at the Imperial court. He applauded this act of the Emperor as a veritable coup d'état within

[12] See reprint of speech appended to Metternich to Mensdorff, Feb. 15, 1865, HHS, Karton 81, No. 10.

[13] Metternich to Mensdorff (tel), Aug. 12, 1865, HHS, Karton 81, No. 48; Nigra to La Marmora, Aug. 13, 1865, *Evénements*, 57.

[14] See Barker, "France, Austria, and the Mexican Venture, 1861–1864," *French Historical Studies*, Vol. III, No. 2 (Fall, 1963), 224–45.

[15] Metternich to Mensdorff, May 27, 1865, HHS, Karton 81, No. 26A and B, with annexed copy of *La Presse*, May 19, 1865, containing the address.

[16] *Moniteur*, May 27, 1865.

[17] Metternich to Mensdorff, June 1, 1865, HHS, Karton 81, No. 29B.

the Imperial household and noted that such energetic action coming from the Tuileries was a most welcome change.[18] In the following July Metternich went on holiday with the Imperial couple. During the holiday Napoleon III fell back into his former reticence, merely brushing off Metternich's inquiries: Austria, Napoleon noted laconically, need have no fear about Venetia.[19] When Austria finally accepted the Gastein Convention as a compromise on Schleswig-Holstein, Napoleon III was in Algeria, where apparently he had gone so as to be unavailable for comment. Meanwhile Drouyn de Lhuys was repeating the warning to Italy that she would become belligerent in the situation "at her own risk and peril."[20]

Napoleon's apparent leanings toward a peaceful or negotiated settlement with Austria goaded the activists in Italy in their typical impatience to push for a more direct assault on the Venetian question. Encouraged by vague feelers from Count Usedom, Bismarck's ambassador in Florence, Nigra now began his campaign, one that he now would pursue relentlessly, in order to convince General La Marmora that Italy should ally herself with Prussia in the coming crisis, even without the help of France.[21] La Marmora, though he felt the pressures of Nigra and was sensitive to anti-French public opinion throughout Italy, insisted upon having Napoleon III's advice and cooperation.[22] "You understand," he had already told Usedom, "how important it is for us, and for you likewise, to know if France will be favorable or opposed to this war."[23]

It was just this puzzled concern that induced Count Otto von Bismarck to seek out the Emperor at the latter's retreat at Biarritz in October, 1865. The conversations between the French Emperor and the Prussian Minister-President as they sat at luncheon or paced the sands of Biarritz cannot be documented, but enough is known about them to manifest Bismarck's intentions and to indicate the nature of the topics the two men discussed.[24] Bismarck had come to Biarritz to dis-

---

[18] *Ibid.*

[19] Metternich to Mensdorff, July, 1865, HHS, Karton 81, No. 34.

[20] Nigra to La Marmora, Aug. 13, 1865, *Evénements*, 57.

[21] Nigra to La Marmora, Aug. 8, 1865, *ibid.*, 55–56.

[22] Drouyn de Lhuys to Viscomte Treilhard, Aug. 17, 1865, FAE, Italie, Vol. 12, No. 32; La Marmora to Nigra, Aug. 4, 1865, *Evénements*, 53–54.

[23] La Marmora to Nigra, Aug. 4, 1865, *Evénements*, 53–54.

[24] Certainly the most satisfying account of the Biarritz interviews as far as French and German sources are concerned is Pottinger, *Napoleon III.* She has gleaned a remarkable amount of information from conversations held by Bismarck and Napoleon III with confidants, ministers, ambassadors, and other officials be-

pel French misgivings about the Gastein Convention and to explain Prussia's need for French neutrality and support. Therefore, Bismarck talked with Napoleon III about such relevant subjects as the Gastein Convention, the German constitution, Moldavia and Wallachia, and a possible alliance between Prussia and Italy.[25] Admittedly Bismarck had great ambitions in Germany. As for what compensation he proposed to Napoleon III, it is quite clear that either before or during the talks at Biarritz the area offered was Belgium.[26]

What was said specifically of Venetia at Biarritz? Emile Ollivier in his account of the meeting gives an imaginative clue. He describes the two statesmen bent over a European atlas while Bismarck traced with a pencil the frontiers with which Prussia would be content around Schleswig. From German-speaking lands he then turned to the atlas for Italy; finding the Isonzo River with his pencil, he remarked that this would be a good frontier for Italy when "Venice" (sic) was returned to her.[27] Ollivier was doubtless using one of his "literary forms" in depicting this scene, but it is certain all the same that Bismarck's desires to know Napoleon III's mind on a possible Prussian-Italian alliance found ample expression at the Biarritz meeting. This expression comes out clearly in two long interviews that Bismarck held with Nigra after the Minister-President's return from Biarritz.

Bismarck first sought out Nigra in Paris on November 3, seemingly in order to gather from him some clearer insights into the Emperor's intentions than those he was able to gain at Biarritz. In his responses to Bismarck's questions, Nigra tried his best to convey that Napoleon III would not insist on German territory as compensation. He also assured Bismarck that the Emperor would allow Italy to join Prussia in any combination calculated either to force Austria to war or to compel her to accede to Prussian demands in Germany. This was a most remarkable interview, for Nigra soon took the lead, telling Bismarck that Prussia must lose no time in starting hostilities with Austria; the situation was already ripe. Austria was in poor condition financially

---

fore and after the interview. See also Willard Allen Fletcher, *The Mission of Vincent Benedetti to Berlin, 1864–1866;* R. Fester, "Biarritz, eine Bismarck-Studie," *Deutsche Rundschau,* Vol. CXIII (November, 1902), 212–36; Ollivier, "L'entrevue de Biarritz, 1865"; Friedrich Frahm, "Biarritz," *Historische Vierteljahrschrift,* Vol. XV (1912), 337–61.

[25] Pottinger, *Napoleon III,* 25–33.
[26] *Ibid.,* 30.
[27] Ollivier, "L'Entrevue de Biarritz, 1865," 502–503.

and militarily inferior to Prussia. France was favorable, as was Russia; and England was neutral or impotent.[28]

After such unexpected success with Nigra, Bismarck decided to return to the Tuileries for another interview with the Emperor to see if he could verify some of Nigra's judgments. The Minister-President could not get any assurances over and beyond those he had obtained at Biarritz. He found the Emperor "in good dispositions" but still noncommittal. Bismarck then returned to Nigra, and they resumed their enthusiastic talk about the cooperation of Italy and Prussia. Bismarck astounded the Italian Ambassador with the confidences he offered, explaining how he hoped to precipitate hostilities with Austria in the Frankfort Diet and even discussing with him some steps in the military strategy that would follow. Nigra was deeply impressed by the revealed might of the Prussian military machine and reported back to La Marmora that he thought that even by itself the Prussian army could defeat Austria.[29] And what was more, Italy, reported Nigra, had an essential role in the Prussian plans. He passed on to his chief Bismarck's dull witticism, "If Italy did not exist, it would be necessary to invent her." [30]

The dialogue between Bismarck and Nigra in Paris had much greater issue than that which took place at Biarritz. Napoleon III's reticence was largely necessitated by the fact that his attitude towards the problems in Germany had not yet clarified. For one thing he could not at the time of the Biarritz meeting respond effectively to an offer of Belgium. Despite the obvious advantages of gaining Belgium, historically viewed as a logical area for French expansion, such an adventure was for the moment too risky. Great Britain's well-known opposition to French interest here had been reaffirmed vigorously when the German crisis loomed in the spring of 1865. Furthermore, the internal situation in France in the fall of that year, including an agricultural depression, the beginnings of a wave of antimilitarism, and the growing influence of Adolphe Thiers' party in the Corps législatif precluded an understanding with Bismarck on military terms, howsoever seriously Bismarck might present them.[31] Poor health, too, forced

[28] Nigra to La Marmora, Nov. 3, 1866, Sandro Bortolotti, *La guerra del 1866,* 75–78.

[29] Nigra to La Marmora, Nov. 4, 1866 (a postscript to the communication of Nov. 3, 1866), *ibid.,* 80.

[30] *Evénements,* 71.

[31] Pottinger, *Napoleon III,* 30–40. This section of Pottinger's book also contains

the Emperor to delay taking an active part in the German crisis and caused frequent absences from Paris. Metternich attributed Napoleon's subdued demeanor to illness,[32] symptoms of which had appeared as early as 1863 and were discovered around this time to be caused by a debilitating bladder stone.[33] The "Sphinx of the Tuileries," as Metternich had once dubbed him, was a human Sphinx, flesh and blood.

The Gastein Convention and the unsatisfactory nature of the Biarritz talks turned Napoleon III's attention once again in the direction of Austria, and thus he renewed his search for a peaceful arrangement on Venetia. For the moment the ailing Emperor had no choice but to give the pro-Austrian Drouyn de Lhuys his head. In November, at the request of his minister of foreign affairs, Napoleon III gave permission for an Austrian loan of ninety million gulden to be listed on the Paris Bourse.[34] By December, Drouyn de Lhuys and Metternich were speaking of an alliance in view of the way Prussian overtures had agitated Italy. Drouyn de Lhuys spoke what was probably his own mind on further consequences of action against Venetia. Austria, he observed, could crush Italy with one blow, and once Italy were reduced to a "geographic expression" Austria could then grant autonomy to Venetia.[35] The talks of Metternich and Drouyn de Lhuys were so enthusiastic that Mensdorff had to caution his minister in Paris not to exceed the limits to which the Austrian cabinet would go in achieving an entente with France: there would be no entente unless the Italians actually attempted to seize Venetia by an outright attack.[36]

Aside from conspicuous evasion of any discussion of Venetia, Vienna showed a genuine desire to receive and respond to French attentions. On December 7 Francis Joseph and the Austrian Empress gave a ceremonial dinner at Schönbrunn in honor of Gramont as an expression of gratitude for his efforts in securing the loan.[37] Throughout the winter the Austrian court extended other courtesies, such as bestowing

---

an excellent evaluation of the effect of the subsequent army reductions upon possible military backing for a strong policy in Germany. She finds these of less consequence than the lack of support in French public opinion.

[32] Metternich to Mensdorff, June 26, 1865, HHS, Karton 81, No. 32B.
[33] Ollivier, "L'Entrevue de Biarritz, 1865," 518.
[34] Pottinger, Napoleon III, 43–44.
[35] Metternich to Mensdorff, Dec. 2, 1865, HHS, Karton 81, No. 49.
[36] Mensdorff to Metternich, Dec. 12, 1865, ibid., n.n.
[37] Gramont to Drouyn de Lhuys, Dec. 9, 1865, OD, VII, 216–17.

the Grand Order of St. Stephen upon the French Prince Imperial.[38] While the conversations were going on between Drouyn de Lhuys and Metternich in Paris, negotiations for a commercial treaty were resumed on Austria's initiative. These negotiations did not come to fruition until December 11, 1866,[39] but the preliminary talks were part of an attempt to establish amicable relations in the winter of 1865–66. Even these attempts left unclear an issue that should have been their focus—Venetia.

THE ISOLATION OF LA MARMORA

Considerably before the Gastein Convention but certainly in anticipation of an eventual rupture, both Austria and Prussia made initial approaches to Italy via commercial negotiations. Austria chose an opportunity presented by long-standing customs difficulties between the Venetian provinces and the bordering territories of the Kingdom of Italy. In August, 1865, Metternich asked if the French government would undertake to facilitate better relations in this special area.[40] Although Metternich explicitly stated that taking up trade negotiations did not imply Austrian recognition of the Kingdom of Italy,[41] such a move on Austria's part was encouragement enough for General La Marmora. Amid clamor in Italy for action on Venetia, La Marmora launched the first of two attempts to negotiate the Venetian question directly with Austria. In September, 1865, he dispatched Count Malaguzzi, a private citizen of Modena, to Francis Joseph to offer one billion lire for the cession of Venetia; this offer also included both a political alliance and a commercial treaty. In addition, the dynastic friction between the house of Hapsburg and the house of Savoy was to be ended by the marriage of Prince Humbert to the daughter of Archduke Albert. This offer, to be sure, ran into the rigid opposition of the Hapsburg court toward political recognition of Italy and cession of Venetia to Italy by any means. In fact, they considered the

[38] Drouyn de Lhuys to Gramont, Jan. 5, 1866, *OD*, VII, 247.

[39] Dwight C. Long, "The Austro-French Commercial Treaty of 1866," *American Historical Review*, Vol. XLI (April, 1936), 474–91. Negotiations for a commercial treaty were begun in the fall of 1864 but were interrupted by the Schleswig-Holstein problem. They were one aspect of Austria's final decision to terminate her commercial isolation in view of the coming conflict in Germany.

[40] Drouyn de Lhuys to Gramont, Aug. 1, 1865, *OD*, VI, 366–67.

[41] *Ibid.*

offer presumptuous.[42] After this General La Marmora refused to talk
of commercial relations unless political negotiations were also clearly
intended and Venetia itself discussed.[43]

In the meantime Bismarck was developing a plan to bring Italy
into the new Zollverein. (The old Zollverein agreement was due to
expire December 31, 1865.) The commercial negotiations with Prussia
not only offered Italy economic benefits. They also implied political
recognition by the lesser German states, which announced around
November 20 that they would ratify the agreement between the Zollverein and Italy.[44] The treaty was ready for formal signatures by December 7, 1865.[45] The Prussian Order of the Black Eagle was
awarded to Victor Emmanuel II,[46] a bounty thrown in for good measure.

La Marmora continued to keep the door open to Austria on commercial relations, and Austria continued to respond in quite concrete
terms, offering an application of the commercial treaty signed between Sardinia and Austria in 1851.[47] Throughout the winter of
1865–66 the Austrian Minister of Commerce spoke frequently with
Gramont, stressing the mutual advantages of such an agreement yet
offering no hope on the Venetian question.[48] Finally, on February 23,
1866, the Italian cabinet declared it would postpone further discussion
until after a parliamentary crisis had been solved.[49] Thus this success
of Prussian efforts over those of Austria provided some forecast of the
outcome of the contest for Italy's allegiance.

It is clear that General La Marmora did all in his power to effect a
situation whereby with the help of the French he could reach an
agreement with Austria and stave off pressure to turn to Prussia. It is
also clear that his position was becoming more and more difficult as
the months of the crisis wore on. Since early April, 1865, he was being
plied with Usedom's questions about an alliance.[50] As early as Au-

[42] Clark, *Franz-Joseph and Bismarck,* 307–308.
[43] La Marmora to Nigra, Jan. 11, 1866, *Evénements,* 78–81; see circular of
General La Marmora, London *Times,* Dec. 13, 1865.
[44] Usedom to Bismarck, Nov. 27, 1865, *APP,* VI, 479–80; see also London
Times, Dec. 12, 1865.
[45] London *Times,* Dec. 12, 1865.
[46] *Evénements,* 87.
[47] Nigra to La Marmora, Jan. 19, 1865, *Evénements,* 81–85.
[48] Gramont to Drouyn de Lhuys, Feb. 8, 1866, *OD,* VII, 285–86; see also dispatches of Gramont, Feb. 13 and 18.
[49] Drouyn de Lhuys to Gramont, Feb. 23, 1866, *OD,* VII, 314.
[50] Drouyn de Lhuys to Malaret, Apr. 13, 1866, FAE, Italie, Vol. 12, 172–73.

gust, 1865, Nigra was urging him to help form an Italian-Prussian alliance.[51] But more important was the spirit that seized the Italian populace as soon as word of the developments in Germany began to be bruited about. Stimulated not only by rumors from Germany but also by increased agitation in Venice [52] which had been fiercely burning underground since the attempted uprising of Garibaldi and Mazzini in 1864,[53] Italians in the spring of 1866 were in a state of anxious expectation. Malaret reported from Turin that the right of the Venetians to be part of Italy was being proclaimed as a kind of political dogma in the press and on the streets throughout Italy. He predicted that the conservatives, who differed from the actionists only on the means of acquiring Venetia, would be carried along on a tidal wave of public opinion as soon as it were known that Prussia had offered a definite alliance to Italy.[54] Mazzini's voice resounded in an inflammatory challenge to the Venetian people: "Rise up against your oppressors!"[55] The Party of Action secretly began to organize another revolution in Venice now involving collaboration with Louis Kossuth and György Klapka, the Hungarian patriots, and their Polish counterparts in Galicia.[56] Garibaldi's comings and goings from Caprera and the departure of his recruits for the Trentino were by no means entirely a secret.[57]

It is difficult to assess the impact of first stirrings of public opinion upon the parliamentary elections held throughout Italy in October, 1865. Issues seething in the wake of the September Convention were still a major preoccupation.[58] Thus the Party of Action, probably for tactical reasons, did not push its program on Venetia very vigorously during the campaign,[59] and the Moderate Liberal party, because La Marmora, its titular chief, was trying to stem the tide of feeling for

[51] Nigra to La Marmora, Aug. 8, 1865, *Evénements*, 55–56.

[52] Malaret to Drouyn de Lhuys, Mar. 24, 1865, FAE, Italie, Vol. 12, pp. 137–43; Pilet to Drouyn de Lhuys, May 13, 1865, FAE, Venise, Vol. 25, pp. 88–90.

[53] Anselmo Osti, *Rapporti fra Vittorio Emmanuele II e Giuseppe Mazzini, passim*.

[54] Malaret to Drouyn de Lhuys, Apr. 20, 1865, FAE, Italie, Vol. 12, pp. 182–90.

[55] Circular of Mazzini, FAE, Italie, Mémoires et documents, 354–55; see also Dieudé Defly to Drouyn de Lhuys, Nov. 8, 1865, FAE, Italie, Milan, Vol. 4, n.n.

[56] Dieudé Defly to Drouyn de Lhuys, Nov. 8, 1865, FAE, Italie, Milan, Vol. 4, pp. 146–49.

[57] *Ibid.*

[58] Mori, *La questione romana*, 446–47.

[59] Treilhard to Drouyn de Lhuys, Oct. 1, 1865, FAE, Italie, Vol. 13, pp. 166–71.

Venetia, soft-pedaled the issue.[60] Nevertheless, while the Moderates won a numerical victory, the Party of Action increased its seats to 83 (out of 380),[61] and what was more important the liberal wing of the Moderate party gained considerable strength,[62] causing it to seek independence from La Marmora and the other conservative leaders. No great influence could be expected from the clericals since only a handful had been seated during the elections.[63] Whether because of the Roman issue or the Venetian issue, the elections had so weakened the government that La Marmora was in serious trouble by the beginning of December.[64] Metternich singled out Mazzini's activity as the cause,[65] but also involved was pressure from La Marmora's own party to include more liberal ministers, such as the anti-French Ricasoli.[66] The cabinet was dissolved on December 21, and La Marmora, though he retained his own seat, had a difficult time finding suitable men to fill his cabinet.[67] He formed a government within ten days, but since Ricasoli was not included he continued to lose support. A new crisis was in the offing by early February,[68] and now the issue was more clearly the alliance with Prussia.[69] The General continued to maintain his dignified expectation of a peaceful solution of the Venetian question without rushing into Prussia's arms; he spoke of "waiting a few more years." [70] Finally La Marmora's isolation became complete when King Victor Emmanuel II, betraying his secret collaboration with Mazzini on the Venetian program,[71] told the Prussian ambassador that he favored a war for Venetia.[72]

[60] Treilhard to Drouyn de Lhuys, Sept. 19, 1865, FAE, Italie, Vol. 13, pp. 141–46; and Oct. 10, 1865, *ibid.*, 166–71.

[61] Malaret to Drouyn de Lhuys, Nov. 1, 1865, *ibid.*, 197–200.

[62] Mori, *La questione romana*, see also Luigi Chiala, *Le général La Marmora*, 6–7. Many were newcomers seeking recognition by a policy of opposition.

[63] Malaret to Drouyn de Lhuys, Nov. 1, 1865, FAE, Italie, Vol. 31, pp. 197–200.

[64] Minghetti to Pasolini, Dec. 8, 1865, Marco Minghetti, *Carteggio tra Marco Minghetti e Giuseppe Pasolini*, IV, 127.

[65] Metternich to Mendsdorff, Dec. 2, 1865, HHS, Karton 81, No. 49C.

[66] Minghetti to Pasolini, Dec. 8, 1865, Minghetti, *Carteggio*, IV, 127.

[67] Malaret to Drouyn de Lhuys, Dec. 3, 1865, FAE, Italie, Vol. 13, No. 103. See London *Times*, Dec. 29, 1865, reporting the rumor that La Marmora stayed in office because the French government wanted him there.

[68] Usedom to Bismarck, Feb. 16, 1866, APP, VI, 586.

[69] *Ibid.*

[70] Usedom to Bismarck, Feb. 7, 1866, *APP*, VI, 571; Usedom to King William I, Feb. 3, 1866, *APP*, VI, 563.

[71] Osti, *Rapporti, passim.*

[72] Usedom to Bismarck, Feb. 16, 1866, *APP*, VI, 586.

On January 10, shortly after the formation of the new cabinet, La Marmora sent off an urgent dispatch to Nigra asking him to assess possible forms of aid from Napoleon III for solution of the Venetian question. Since Rome and Venice were competing for the attention of the Italian government, La Marmora wondered if both could not be solved together: could Venetia be given Italy in exchange for her renunciation of Rome? Nigra reported home that this exchange was out of the question because the Emperor did not wish to jeopardize the September Convention and did not want to evacuate Rome until the time fixed in the agreement. Nigra also discussed the only other two possibilities according to which Italy could expect French cooperation, namely, armed intervention and the oft-mentioned exchange for the Danubian Principalities. While France now chose not to make war for Venetia, neither would she hinder Italy in profiting from the imminent rupture between Prussia and Austria. As for the exchange, Nigra reported, Metternich had said that it was not beyond the realm of possibility but would actually take place only if affairs in Euorpe finally rendered necessary a territorial modification.[73] Thus La Marmora's only hope of saving his government and still remaining loyal to Napoleon III lay in the flimsy chance of exchanging Venetia for some territory now in possession of the embarrassed Sultan of Turkey.

So it came about in early February, 1866, that General La Marmora and the Austrian government, in some unofficial way, established contact and discussed the exchange of Venetia for Turkish territory. Usedom on February 7 sounded the alarm that there was some danger of the Venetian question being settled peacefully in the context of Austria's commercial approaches to Italy.[74] Shortly after this Count Robert von Goltz, the Prussian ambassador in Paris, picked up threads of a story that a French secret agent in Vienna had discovered Austria to be ready to offer Venetia for the Danubian Principalities together with Bosnia or Serbia.[75] When told of it by his friend Goltz, Nigra apparently believed this story and expressed his dismay at the

---

[73] Nigra to La Marmora, Jan. 19, 1866. E. Passamonti, "Constantino Nigra ed Alfonso La Marmora dal 1862–1866," *Risorgimento italiano*, Vol. XXII (1929), 436–43. Both La Marmora's instructions and Nigra's dispatch are in Nigra's letter; La Marmora's letter is not available.

[74] Usedom to Bismarck, Feb. 7, 1866, *APP*, VI, 571, together with Metternich to Mensdorff, Mar. 22, 1866 (secret), Oncken I, 115–17. We have concluded that the report mentioned by Eugénie to Metternich on March 12 was the source of Nigra's information here given to Goltz.

[75] Goltz to Bismarck, Feb. 16, 1866, *APP*, VI, 586–88.

possibility of Austria's gaining such preponderance in eastern Europe.[76] In its full-blown form this rumor had Hübner communicating unofficially with La Marmora, private citizen, proposing the cession of Venetia for the Danubian Principalities, "Northern Serbia," and Bosnia plus an unspecified sum of money.[77] But more believably the compensations to Austria were simply Bosnia-Herzegovina and an indemnity.[78]

It is true that Francis Joseph denied any such thought was ever in his mind when confronted with the accusation in mid-March.[79] The idea nevertheless was entertained favorably within the Austrian government,[80] and one imagines there must have been talks between lesser officials in both governments such as were held between Gramont and the Austrian minister of commerce on trade negotiations. General La Marmora has omitted from his own writings all evidence that might betray his secret and unofficial negotiations because attacks upon him after the war centered precisely on these alleged negotiations as betrayals of the true interests of his country.[81] But he did admit that he expected overtures from Austria through January after he decided to hold out against any commercial negotiations that did not include Venetia.[82] In view of the prevalence of unofficial negotiations during this period,[83] it would be unrealistic to dismiss the evidence that a fresh attempt to bargain privately for Venetia was made in February and perhaps continued through March, 1866. Their importance lies not only in the controversy that ensued in Italy and Germany after the war but also in establishing the fact that for La

[76] Ibid.

[77] Oubril to Gorchakov, Feb. 25, 1866, APP, VI, 605. It was in this form that Bismarck passed on the rumor to the Russian Chancellor, Gorchakov. It doubtless contained Bismarck's embellishments, the more to turn Russia against the plan. See also Oubril to Gorchakov, Mar. 13, 1866, APP, VI, 663–65; and Mar. 6, 1866, APP, VI, 699–701.

[78] See Drouyn de Lhuys to Gramont, Mar. 13, 1866, OD, VII, 420.

[79] Gramont to Drouyn de Lhuys, Mar. 17, 1866, OD, VII, 11–12; Mensdorff to Metternich (tel), Mar. 16, 1866, Oncken I, 110–11.

[80] Gramont to Drouyn de Lhuys, Mar. 17, 1866, OD, VIII, 11–12; Chiala, Le général La Marmora, 59–60, says the one obstacle to the peaceful exchange for Venetia was Francis Joseph, to whom it was a point of "military honor."

[81] Carlo Castellani, La Marmora e Ricasoli nel 1866 con documenti, 9–11; Luigi Chiala, Ancora, un po' più di luce sugli eventi politici e militari dell'anno 1866, p. iii.

[82] La Marmora to Nigra, Jan. 11, 1866, Evénements, 78–81.

[83] See Demetrio E. Diamilla-Müller (ed.), Politica segreta italiana, 1863–1870. See supra, p. 38, for the Malaguzzi mission and infra, 54–55, for the Landauer mission. Malaguzzi was still trying, but La Marmora had already despaired of this mission.

Marmora a peaceful solution of the Venetian question was primary. On the unofficial level he was indeed now working quite independently of Napoleon III, though on the official level the opposite was true.

Rumors continued to circulate through March, but hope for an arrangement with Austria died in mid-February.[84] Talks between Gramont and the Austrian minister of commerce about commercial relations between Italy and Austria ground to a halt.[85] Victor Emmanuel II was nodding encouragement to Usedom, and the latter had all but decided to circumvent La Marmora [86] when the breakthrough came. La Marmora, during a reception in Florence, February 21, took Usedom aside from the festivities and told him quietly that as long as Bismarck was set on war the two of them should "make some serious proposals." [87] It is possible that La Marmora was able to obtain the consent of Napoleon III before thus opening the door to Bismarck.[88] At any rate La Marmora had finally abandoned his earlier position and had saved his cabinet. Statesmen generally believe they cannot serve their country from the sidelines.

NAPOLEON III's "ADVICE AND CONSENT"

While he had opened the door to Bismarck, La Marmora did not cease hoping that somehow Venetia might still drop, as he had once said, "like a ripe fruit into Italy's lap." [89] Scarcely two days after his talk with Usedom something happened that nearly shook the fruit from its branch. On February 23 a conspiracy in Bucharest forced Prince Cusa to abdicate and signaled what could have become a general revolution throughout Moldavia and Wallachia—a possibility with wide implications to the Turkish Empire and consequently of much concern to all European powers. To Nigra, who had begun to despair of a war in Germany, this seemed to be the opportunity to renew efforts on the exchange project. The day after the coup d'état

[84] Usedom to Bismarck, Feb. 16, 1866, APP, VI, 586.
[85] See dispatches of Gramont to Drouyn de Lhuys, Feb. 13, 18, and 23, 1866, OD, VII, 296–314.
[86] Usedom to Bismarck, Feb. 16, 1866, APP, VI, 586.
[87] Usedom to Bismarck, Feb. 22, 1866, APP, VI, 596.
[88] Usedom asked permission to get in touch with Prince Jerome Napoleon on February 17, obviously as a way of facilitating La Marmora's change of position. Bismarck to Usedom, Feb. 22, 1866 (tel), ibid.
[89] Usedom to King William I, Feb. 3, 1866, APP, VI, 563–64.

in Bucharest, the Italian minister in Paris sent a seventeen-page dispatch to La Marmora describing the situation in remarkable detail and explaining its uniqueness. On former occasions when talk about the trade was attempted, for instance during the Conference of Paris in 1856 and during the Polish crisis in 1863, fear of reviving hostilities with Russia prevented the successful execution of the plan. Now Russia was sufficiently isolated to allay Austria's fears. And Napoleon III was at the moment the logical person to broach the question in Vienna.[90] La Marmora leaped at this opportunity. He immediately telegraphed Nigra to "set your sights without delay and move as energetically as you can towards the exchange between Venetia and the Principalities." He added that "at Berlin they are becoming very bellicose and even are making us new offers." [91]

On February 28, immediately upon receipt of the telegram from his chief, Nigra gained audience with Napoleon III [92] and laid before him the two salient facts of the situation: the revolution in Bucharest and Prussian overtures to Italy.[93] Doubtless the Emperor already knew of these two facts, but Nigra was presenting them in an arresting juxtaposition. The sovereignty of the Porte over Moldavia and Wallachia might be ceded to Austria in exchange for the latter's cession of Venetia to Italy, who would offer financial indemnification to the Sultan. To France this would not only carry the advantage of acquitting herself of obligations to Italy but would offer a welcome chance to checkmate Russia in the Balkans and even to have revenge for her diplomatic defeat during the Polish crisis of 1863. Such a prospect was indeed attractive to the Emperor, and he thought it would be so to all the Western powers. But there was one serious obstacle: Austria almost certainly would refuse. In response to this difficulty the Italian Minister confided to the Emperor the information he had on a change of mood in unofficial circles in Austria; he suggested that here lay the significance of Prussia's offers. The Austrian cabinet could not long hold out if they knew they would have to face "an armed and

[90] Nigra to La Marmora, Feb. 24, 1866, Archivio Storico, Vol. 282.

[91] Nigra to Prince Eugène de Savoie–Carignano, June 23, 1866, Ricasoli, *Lettere*, VIII, 8–18. These quotations represent Nigra's reconstruction of the telegram as recorded in this long letter to Prince Eugène.

[92] Nigra to La Marmora, Mar. 1, 1866, Passamonti, "Constantino Nigra ed Alfonso La Marmora dal 1862–1866," 446–50. Nigra states that he was bringing this question up "for the second time," suggesting the possibility that at some previous time he had occasion to consult the Emperor on the trade idea.

[93] *Ibid.*

hostile Italy" in the event of their refusal.[94] Nigra wanted Napoleon III to speak confidentially with English officials and then try, with or without England's cooperation, to entice Austria to attend a general congress. The Emperor did not show much enthusiasm for approaching Austria, but he did respond to Nigra's bait: the threat of a two-front war might soften the resistance of the Viennese cabinet, making "the danger of a rupture with Prussia . . . truly serious." [95] Here Nigra and Napoleon III found common ground: they were both anxious for Prussia to overcome her hesitations and back Bismarck's challenge to Austria. On that common ground they formulated a proposal to present to La Marmora: the Emperor would confer with England and then broach the matter with the Viennese cabinet; meanwhile Italy would "ardently push Prussia to war" while making warlike preparations herself. Thus the Emperor might be able to tell Austria that if she did not accept, she could be at war with Italy and with Prussia without the benefit of assistance from France.[96]

Although in a later letter (June 23 to Prince Eugène de Savoie-Carignano) narrating the course of the negotiations on the Venetian question Nigra said that Napoleon III advised La Marmora "to push her [Prussia] to conclude a defensive and offensive alliance with you," nowhere can such advice be found in his letter to La Marmora of March 1, 1866.[97] The advice given in the earlier letter to La Marmora urging him to conclude an alliance with Prussia is clearly Nigra's own, formed as a result of his discussion with the Emperor. It was not the first occasion on which La Marmora was confused concerning whose advice Nigra was reporting, the Minister's own or that of Napoleon III.[98] In fact, in this letter of March 1 Nigra attributed an expression

[94] *Ibid.*
[95] *Ibid.*
[96] *Ibid.*
[97] In discussing this interview *post factum* with others, once in the letter to Prince Eugène de Savoie–Carignano on June 23, 1866 (Ricasoli, *Lettere*, VIII, 8–18) and again in an interview with the Austrian historian, Heinrich Friedjung (reported in the latter's volume, *The Struggle for Supremacy in Germany, 1859–1866*, trans. A. J. P. Taylor and W. L. McElwee, Appendix III, p. 321) Nigra said Napoleon III counseled the defensive and offensive treaty with Prussia, though all is subordinated to making Prussia bold enough to attack Austria. Nigra told Friedjung that Napoleon advised Italy to make the treaty "for only then will Prussia dare to attack Austria." We find it not difficult to see how Nigra, in writing to Prince Eugène or talking to Friedjung, would make seem explicit in the Emperor's advice what was at best implicit. In the controversy that followed the battle of Custozza, no Italian wanted to take responsibility for the treaty with Prussia.
[98] *Evénements*, 136.

("Se l'Austria avesse alla testa del suo governo uomini sensati...")
to the Emperor that is precisely identical with one he had used earlier
in giving his own opinion while relaying information to his chief
about the Biarritz meeting.[99] After a long and somewhat rhetorical
build-up of the case for a Prussian alliance, Nigra ended with a vision
of the promised land: "Have courage then, dear General, and inspire
the Prussian and in three months, if God wills it and if fortune is with
us, we can be in Saint Mark's." [100] By the end of the March 1 letter,
Nigra was so carried away by his plea for the Prussian alliance that
the project of the trade for Moldavia-Wallachia had been relegated to
dim and distant possibility: "Let us make no exchange. If the powers
want to do it, we will accept." [101] The Italian Ambassador's previous
efforts for an alliance with Prussia and his earlier tutelage under
Cavour [102] invite conjecture that the Machiavellian plan proposed to
La Marmora came from none other than Nigra. As for the role of Napoleon III, it was at best one of "advice and consent."

At this juncture (early March, 1866) Napoleon III wanted Italy to
make whatever motions would be necessary to help Bismarck overcome the hesitations in the Prussian court and military staff. This
would either bring on a prolonged contest in which he would intervene as arbiter or at least drive Prussia and Austria to the conference
table. But it is highly questionable whether he would have actually
advised an offensive and defensive treaty until he might have assured
himself of participation by way of a triple alliance. He had lacked
that assurance ever since the Biarritz meeting, nor had it been forthcoming in the talks with Goltz in early March.[103] These talks with
Goltz once again brought the offer of Belgium, but the Emperor was
in March, 1866, even more fearful of such a risk, and all he could now
do was hint that "anyone could easily see the difference in the map
between the present boundaries of France and those of 1814." [104]
Nigra, knowing of Napoleon's earlier talks with Goltz, was annoyed at

[99] "If Austria had men of sense at the head of her government," Nigra to La
Marmora, Oct. 25, 1865, Bortolotti, La guerra, 75–78, esp. 77.

[100] Nigra to La Marmora, Mar. 1, 1866, Passamonti, "Constantino Nigra ed
Alfonso La Marmora dal 1862–1866," 446–50.

[101] Ibid.

[102] See Riccardo Zagaria, "Constantino Nigra," Aevum, Anno V. (1931) 61–90;
and Delfino Orsi, "Il mistero dei 'ricordi diplomatici' di Constantino Nigra," La
Nuova Antologia (November, 1928), 10–154.

[103] Pottinger, Napoleon III, 68–71.

[104] Nigra to La Marmora, Mar. 17, 1866, Passamonti, "Constantino Nigra ed
Alfonso La Marmora dal 1862–1866," 451–53.

the Emperor's pusillanimous behavior and reminded him that "if he believed it in his interest to have the two Germanic powers draw the sword it would be necessary to give a little spirit to Prussia." [105] The Emperor would indeed have liked to be more explicit in his demands and more cooperative with Prussia. Yet already there were ominous rumblings of discontent with his German policy from the Parisian populace. And, more important, in the Corps législatif, Adolphe Thiers had rallied much support for the ideas he elaborated during the legislative debate of early March when he called for renunciation of any cooperation with Prussia.[106]

The way Nigra relayed the Emperor's advice to La Marmora was crucial. He obviously wanted to cover up Napoleon III's hesitancy and wanted La Marmora to believe that the Emperor offered cooperation for an effective alliance with Prussia. There is reason to believe that the trustful La Marmora while feeling the hairy hand of Esau heard the voice of Jacob.[107] Yet his isolated position forced La Marmora to interpret the Emperor's attitude as the beginning of a French program of assistance that would eventually bring about Italy's winning of Venetia.

THE ADVICE OF A FRIEND

Coincidental with the revolt in Bucharest and the subsequent meeting between Nigra and Napoleon III at the Tuileries came an invitation from Bismarck to La Marmora to send a military expert to Berlin in order to observe improvements in the Prussian army and explore the possibilities of military cooperation between the two countries.[108] By March 8 La Marmora had responded to the invitation and had given his instructions to the agent who was to fulfil the mission, General William Govone, a military expert and part-time diplomat. La Marmora in instructing Govone included a definite assignment to explore the terrain for a possible political alliance between Italy and Prussia. Eventually, with the help of Count Camillo Barral, Florence's minister in Berlin, La Marmora hoped to work toward an

---

[105] *Ibid.*
[106] Pottinger, *Napoleon III,* 64–68.
[107] *Evénements,* 131–33.
[108] *Ibid.,* 88–89; Benedetti to Drouyn de Lhuys, Mar. 16, 1866, FAE, Prusse, Vol. 355, pp. 47–51; Chiala, *Le général La Marmora,* 75–76.

effective pact with Prussia.[109] Govone and Barral, at least by mid-March, had clear instructions to seek an offensive and defensive treaty for a fixed period of time.[110] By means of the steady flow of dispatches from Vincent Benedetti, the French ambassador in Berlin, the Tuileries kept in touch with the progress of these negotiations. Since Napoleon made no attempt to interfere, it may be assumed that he gave tacit approval.

Meanwhile, the other phase of Nigra's scheme was being carried out simultaneously at Downing Street, the Tuileries, and the Ballplatz. In contrast to the negotiations in Berlin these attempts were mere façade. Lord Clarendon, the British foreign secretary, told the French Ministry of Foreign Affairs that he did not want to risk making a proposal that would be turned down.[111] In Paris the task of talking to Count Metternich was assigned to the Empress Eugénie, who apparently was given a prepared script. She presented Metternich with a dispatch from Baron Charles de Talleyrand, the French ambassador at St. Petersburg, which reported that the exchange of Venetia for the Danubian Principalities was easily possible at this moment because Russia was not in a position to stop it. Even in this guise Metternich considered the suggestion offensive; he complained that it was scarcely a return of the loyalty shown by Austria to France. Reflecting the current thinking of the Austrian government, he gave as a reason that for Austria such a trade would mean "to mutilate ourselves and disarm ourselves on the Adriatic in order to still more enforce Italy." [112] Still the rumor persisted in all the capitals of Europe that Austria would be interested in trading off Venetia if compensations such as Bosnia and Herzegovina were offered [113] to balance the loss of Austrian power on the Adriatic. At any rate, Eugénie, when she saw Count Metternich's reaction, retreated behind her feminine defenses

[109] Evénements, 88–89; La Marmora to Govone, Mar. 29, 1866, Evénements, 90–91; La Marmora to Barral, Mar. 9, 1866, Chiala, Le général La Marmora, 76–78. The letter to Barral shows that La Marmora withheld the full import of his instructions from Govone.

[110] Govone to La Marmora, Mar. 14, 1866, Umberto Govone, Il Generale Giuseppe Govone, frammenti di memorie, 423–27; Benedetti to Drouyn de Lhuys, Mar. 18, 1866, FAE, Prusse, Vol. 355, pp. 47–51.

[111] Nigra to La Marmora, Mar. 17, 1866, Passamonti, "Constantino Nigra ed Alfonso La Marmora dal 1862–1866," 451–53.

[112] Metternich to Mensdorff, Mar. 22, 1866, Oncken I, 115–17.

[113] See Nigra to La Marmora, Mar. 17, 1866, Passamonti, "Constantino Nigra ed Alfonso La Marmora dal 1862–1866," 451–53; see also Oubril to Gorchakov, Feb. 25, 1866, APP, VI, 605.

and said she did not know anything about diplomacy anyway. And then the Emperor had to smooth over the situation by assuring Metternich that refusal of Eugénie's proposal would not mean any cooling in France's cordial relations with Austria.[114]

Other realistic motives for Austria's refusal came to light when Gramont brought up the subject in Vienna. There it was learned that Russia had gotten wind of the Venetian project and had declared that she would oppose it with all her power.[115] Perhaps fear of Russian opposition more than anything else was the reason for Austria's hesitancy over any trade for Balkan territories. And here one observes a most ingenious turn of Bismarckian diplomacy. Bismarck had picked up a rumor from Goltz that Austria had made unofficial approaches to Italy involving compensations on the Adriatic, specifically Bosnia and Herzegovina. Then Bismarck began conversations with the Russian ambassador, Count Paul d'Oubril, feeding him the most outlandish versions of the rumor that he could pick up or invent—that La Marmora and Hübner were communicating unofficially, that the Danubian Principalities and a sum of money were included—and even offering Russia an entente to prevent any such development. Taking it all quite seriously, Oubril relayed to Prince Gorchakov all of this information as given him by Bismarck between February 25 and March 18.[116] The information elicited the proper reaction from St. Petersburg: the Tsar declared that Russia would oppose the exchange idea to the point of war.[117] It is not difficult to detect Bismarck's motive for blocking the trade. It offered an escape hatch for his prospective ally whom he counted on to help him both militarily and strategically and who would hopefully furnish the much desired *casus belli*.

When General Govone arrived in Berlin on March 14, Bismarck was fully aware of the likelihood of an Austrian-Italian agreement, though he certainly did not believe all the details he related to the Russian ambassador. When Govone announced to him that his was

[114] Metternich to Mensdorff, Mar. 22, 1866, Oncken I, 115–17.

[115] Nigra to Prince Eugène de Savoie–Carignano, Ricasoli, *Lettere*, VIII, 8–18. The correspondence in the Viennese archives around mid-March is full of references to the problem of the Danubian Principalities showing the deep concern of the Austrian government for this problem (see Karton 82).

[116] Oubril to Gorchakov, Feb. 25, 1866, *APP*, VI, letter, 606–607; secret telegraph, 605; Mar. 13, 1866, *APP*, VI, 663–65; and Mar. 18, 1866, *APP*, VI, 697–99. These conversations have reference to secret, unofficial negotiations, not the formal ones being held through the channels of French mediation, but the effect was the same—to incite Russia's opposition to any such idea.

[117] Talleyrand to Drouyn de Lhuys, Mar. 14, 1866, *OD*, VII, 433–34.

part of a mission to continue serious talks between Usedom and La Marmora, Bismarck welcomed him though he thought it best to be frank. He admitted that at the moment he was not sure that there would ever be a war between Prussia and Austria, given the character of King William and the prevailing climate of opinion in Europe. He stated that his scheme for provoking Austria by means of a proposal for an all-German parliament would take time and that its realization rested upon many contingencies. He certainly had included Italy in his plans, so he said, but what he wanted was a treaty that would take effect only when the proper occasion arose, i.e., if and when Austria should respond in a hostile manner to proposed changes in the German constitution. This came as a disappointment to the Italian delegation. Govone's instructions were to work toward an effective pact providing for immediate action against Austria. Bismarck, not willing to let Italy out of his grasp, made Govone realize that he needed some sort of pact with Italy in order to help him prevail upon King William. On March 14 he offered the alternative of a "general pact of friendship and perpetual alliance" which when the time came might be confirmed with the kind of treaty the Italian government desired. Govone dutifully reported this conversation in a long letter to La Marmora.[118] After another interview, on March 16, Govone reported a sketch of an "eventual treaty" as something a little more specific:

> Prussia will promote the reform of the Germanic Constitution, bringing it in tune with modern times. If this reform is able to disturb the harmony of the confederation and put Austria and Prussia in conflict, Italy, having received word of same, will declare war on Austria and her allies.[119]

At the moment, therefore, Italy had the choice between this proposal and the more vague and "general treaty of friendship." [120] On March 17 Govone and Barral entertained Bismarck at dinner at the Italian legation, but no progress was made except to bring Barral more decisively into the talks.[121]

Meanwhile La Marmora, in trying to overcome his mistrust of Bismarck and his "eventual" or "general" treaty, decided to consult Na-

---

[118] Govone to La Marmora, Mar. 14, 1866, Govone, *Il Generale Govone*, 423–27.
[119] Govone to La Marmora, Mar. 17, 1866, *ibid.*, 428–32.
[120] *Ibid.*
[121] Govone to La Marmora, Mar. 18, 1866, *ibid.*, 432–43.

poleon III once more. Nigra was commissioned to sound the Emperor out on this type of treaty and find out what assurances were forthcoming from France in case Italy were left alone to face Austria. Napoleon III on March 21 told Nigra that Italy had nothing to fear from Bismarck's type of treaty. He overcame all of Nigra's objections. The treaty could not compromise Italy with Austria; it left her free to turn to Vienna if she failed in Berlin. On the other hand, if Austria attacked Italy first, France would defend her. Most important of all, it would help Bismarck push the Prussian King into war:

> Sign a treaty with Prussia, however vague and noncommittal it may be, for it is very desirable to furnish M. de Bismarck with the necessary means to push the King to war.[122]

Before La Marmora had a chance to consider the Emperor's detailed advice as reported by Nigra, he received a telegram from Barral, who had taken over the discussions with Bismarck. Barral asked for instructions on accepting a compromise offered by the Prussian minister.[123] The compromise was to fix a limit of three or six months as the time within which a conflict with Austria had to be produced.[124] La Marmora wired back that Barral should get it in writing "neat and precise." [125] Turning to Nigra's letter, La Marmora was not sure if it contained Nigra's advice or the Emperor's. Perhaps it even came from Goltz. Did the advice concern the compromise version Barral was reporting, or was it the "general treaty of friendship"? [126] La Marmora was so confused at this point and so fearful that he might be abandoned by France to face Austria alone, that he sent a personal friend of the Emperor, Count Arese, to Paris in an effort to make sure of the Emperor's attitudes and intentions.

In talking to Barral, Bismarck was delaying putting his compromise proposals in writing, but finally, after a long conversation with him on March 27, Barral emerged with five points agreed upon for a projected alliance: (1) an alliance would be formed; (2) if negotia-

---

[122] As related and recorded by Heinrich Friedjung, *Struggle for Supremacy*, 114 note 2. Nigra's letter to La Marmora reporting the same conversation may be found in Chiala, *Ancora*, 80–84, and in Bortolotti, *La guerra*, 116–20. Nigra is quite consistent in both reports of the conversation with Napoleon III.

[123] *Evénements*, 113–14.

[124] *Ibid.;* see also Govone to La Marmora, Mar. 22, 1866, Govone, *Il Generale Govone*, 434–37.

[125] *Evénements*, 113–14.

[126] *Ibid.*, 135–39.

tions by Prussia for federal reform failed and if Prussia were obliged to go to war, Italy would declare war against Austria; (3) both Prussia and Italy would pursue war, but once war had begun neither would make peace or sign an armistice without common consent; (4) this consent would not be refused once Austria ceded Lombardy-Venetia to Italy and a territory of equivalent population; (5) the operative term of the treaty would be three months. Before sending this proposed treaty to La Marmora, Barral familiarized Benedetti with its contents and Benedetti sent a copy to Drouyn de Lhuys.[127]

To add to their confusion the Italian government received different reactions from different French officials. Benedetti gave the impression that he personally favored this treaty.[128] Drouyn de Lhuys, however, following a policy of strict neutrality consistent with his talks to Metternich and never privy to the Emperor's advice to La Marmora,[129] wrote Benedetti that he saw no reason to depart from the previously adopted neutrality.[130] To Malaret, Drouyn de Lhuys' directions were more to the point: ". . . we cannot without contradiction advise Italy to take on an enterprise from which we have always kept aloof [;] we must abstain today from every counsel, every encouragement, every influence." [131]

The greatest shock to the sensitive La Marmora was the news that came back almost simultaneously from Nigra and Arese: the Emperor had withdrawn all official support for this treaty. La Marmora's reply to Arese on March 30 was so memorable that it became a refrain in the retelling of this story: The Emperor "finds the signature of this treaty with Prussia useful, but he declares he is giving advice as a friend and without any responsibility." [132] There is no reasonable doubt that the treaty here referred to is the one drawn up by Barral and Bismarck on March 27. Therein lies the explanation of the Emperor's change of advice. Whereas the general treaty was quite innoc-

---

[127] Benedetti to Drouyn de Lhuys, Mar. 27, 1866, OD, VIII, 75–76.
[128] Govone to La Marmora, Mar. 28, 1866, Govone, Il Generale Govone, 439.
[129] Drouyn de Lhuys to Ollivier, Mar. 6, 1870, Emile Ollivier, L'empire libéral, VIII, 56.
[130] Drouyn de Lhuys to Benedetti, Mar. 31, 1866, OD, VIII, 120–21.
[131] Drouyn de Lhuys to Malaret, Apr. 3, 1866, FAE, Italie, Vol. 14, pp. 277–78.
[132] Arese to La Marmora, Mar. 30, 1866, Joseph Grabinski, Un ami de Napoléon III, le comte Arese et la politique italienne sous le Second Empire, 225–26; see also Nigra to Prince Eugène de Savoie–Carignano, June 23, 1866, Ricasoli, Lettere, VIII, 8–18; Nigra to La Marmora, Mar. 29, 1866, and Mar. 31, 1866, Chiala, Ancora, 93–94, 95–96. In Nigra's latter dispatch he said the Emperor advised Italy to "make, or better, accept the alliance with Prussia."

uous and carried hope of assisting Bismarck in his struggle with King William, the newly proposed treaty in view of the situation was fraught with danger: Italy might find herself facing Austria alone. The outlined draft of the treaty left open the possibility that Italy might need to begin the war, and Nigra's letter of March 23 implying the same [133] brought an immediate warning by telegram from Napoleon III: "If Italy takes the initiative in the war, France cannot aid her." [134] Moreover, every indication at that moment was that hope for hostilities between Prussia and Austria had died.[135] Thus, Bismarck could drag out the quarrel with Austria indefinitely or settle with her privately, leaving him in complete control of the situation. Had Napoleon III been able to join the alliance himself, or back up Italy in case she were attacked by Austria—neither of which he could now do—he might have approved the new treaty.

La Marmora, pressed from all sides to go ahead with some form of alliance, felt let down by the Emperor. Yet, too much beset with his own suspicions of Bismarck to give the immediate word to Barral, he fell back on a customary device for delay of negotiations: he needed, so he said, to submit the text of the treaty to King Victor Emmanuel II.[136]

Somewhere during this lull in negotiations with Prussia La Marmora again resorted to secret diplomacy with Austria. He summoned a M. Landauer of the Viennese house of Rothschild to whom he confided his predicament: in the event of his having to go to war with Austria, he would have to launch an attack on Venetia, which he doubted his army could do effectively. But he had the unhappy choice between this and being overcome by the Party of Action in Italy. Would Landauer establish contact for him with the Austrian government and ask for a peaceable cession of Venetia either for a large indemnity to be paid over a period of time, or for sizable territorial compensations such as the Danubian Principalities or territories in Serbia, or Bosnia-Herzegovina? Landauer accepted the mission and confided the task to Baron Anselm Rothschild in Vienna. Rothschild reported on or before April 1, 1866, after an interview with Mensdorff and Count Moritz von Esterhazy, Austrian minister without portfolio, that he could say that such a cession by Austria was not now possible,

---

[133] Nigra to La Marmora, Mar. 23, 1866, Chiala, *Ancora*, 80–84; see also Chiala, *Le général La Marmora*, 90–91.

[134] Nigra to La Marmora, Mar. 24, 1866, *Evénements*, 137.

[135] Nigra to La Marmora, Mar. 23, 1866, Chiala, *Ancora*, 80–84.

[136] Benedetti to Drouyn de Lhuys, Apr. 3, 1866, *OD*, VIII, 135–36.

though Austria was in no way hostile.[137] The Landauer mission, besides revealing La Marmora's anxiety at this point, also indicated that the Austrian government saw less of a threat in a Prussian-Italian alliance than either La Marmora or Napoleon III supposed.

Having failed in a last effort for peace, La Marmora instructed Barral on April 5 to sign the treaty with Prussia as drawn up on March 27, except for one item. He wanted to limit Italy's commitment to a declaration of war on Austria alone, whereas the original project had stipulated that she declare war on all other states in the Germanic Confederation upon which Prussia would serve notice.[138] The General had now to contend with French warnings not to continue on a collision course. Benedetti, probably on instruction from Napoleon III, advised the Italian delegation on April 6 not to sign Bismarck's project but to have another one worked out to present after Prussian mobilization should become an accomplished fact. Benedetti was now gravely cautioning the Italians against the intentions of Bismarck, whom he characterized as "un diplomate maniaque." He urged the Italians to keep the door open to Austria.[139] Prince Jerome was at the court of Victor Emmanuel II in early April on a vacation trip that turned into a mission connected with the Florence-Berlin negotiations.[140] Prince Jerome was known to be opposed to the projected treaty,[141] and the more reliable sources indicate he was carrying much the same advice to King Victor Emmanuel as Benedetti had already given to Barral and Govone.[142] Finally, on April 7, 1866, Barral reported to La Marmora that "in Berlin all indications were that Na-

[137] The report of these negotiations is found in the private papers of the duc de Gramont, but not in the official correspondence preserved at the Quai d'Orsay; Gramont to Drouyn de Lhuys, Apr. 1, 1866, particulière et confidentielle, preserved on microfilm at Archives Nationales, Paris, Correspondance privée, Bobine No. 61. *Note:* The only date assigned to the calling in of Landauer by La Marmora is "towards the end of March." It is barely possible that it occurred before March 29, when La Marmora first heard of Napoleon III's withdrawal of support. Yet we have concluded from the tenor of the communication that it was after that date.

[138] Benedetti to Drouyn de Lhuys, Apr. 9, 1866, *OD*, VIII, 200.

[139] Govone to La Marmora, Apr. 6, 1866, *Evénements*, 152–53.

[140] Ollivier, *L'empire libéral*, VIII, 54; Pottinger, *Napoleon III*, 79–80; La Marmora denied he had any political mission, but so did he deny, at least implicitly, the Landauer mission when he heard that Usedom had picked up rumors of secret overtures being made to Austria. *Evénements*, 154–55.

[141] Pottinger, *Napoleon III*, 79.

[142] Barral to La Marmora, Apr. 7, 1866, Chiala, *Ancora*, 113; Benedetti to Drouyn de Lhuys, Apr. 3, 1866, *OD*, VIII, 152–59. The source of both Barral's and Benedetti's information was probably Usedom, who was the closest witness to this event. Ollivier, *L'empire libéral*, VIII, 57–58, says Jerome was commissioned to advise signing the treaty. La Marmora, *Evénements*, 156, denied any mission was given Jerome. We take neither Ollivier nor La Marmora to be reliable here.

poleon III had withdrawn all support from the treaty." [143] Neverthe-less, the next day Barral and Govone initialed the Prussian-Italian alli-ance. The Emperor may well have given it his final blessing, as Nigra always insisted he did.[144] The realization that he could not prevent the alliance may have impelled him to make a gesture of consolation to his friend La Marmora. Also for La Marmora's consolation was the stipulation in the final text of the treaty that Prussia should take the initiative in the war.[145]

Some final attempt to reconstruct the Emperor's attitude toward the alliance can be made here. The clue is in the risk-and-peril refrain repeated to both Austrians and Italians ever since the beginning of the German crisis. Italy might be entering into a partnership in which she would be used by Bismarck to do what he could not do himself —precipitate a war. Italy might then find herself overcome with a quick Austrian invasion, or even find herself facing Austria alone.[146] If so this would necessitate a premature intervention by the French in order to save their work of 1859. At any rate, it would leave Bismarck completely free to seek a quarrel with Austria or settle with her pri-vately; the treaty would give him a veritable "blank check." Another aspect of the Emperor's attitude toward the alliance was his inability, already realized in mid-March, actively to participate in it himself, thus prohibiting a clear commitment on the Prussian-Italian side. He could not join the alliance for two reasons: he could not obtain such compensations from Bismarck as would justify this policy before French public opinion, and he did not want to tip the scales so deci-sively as to cause Austria to seek peaceful settlement. With France unable to join a Prussian-Italian alliance, the scales were too finely balanced for comfort. Austria might well defeat both her antagonists.

Although it is possible to discern the Emperor's intentions, it is not easy to know what advice he gave to La Marmora and King Victor Emmanuel II. During that important interview with Nigra on Febru-ary 28, the Emperor had advised only that the Italians help push Prussia to war. Speaking of an alliance to Bismarck, if Nigra insisted, might help. And so Napoleon consented to Italy's taking up negotia-

---

[143] Barral to La Marmora, Apr. 7, 1866, Chiala, *Ancora*, 113.
[144] Interview with Friedjung in his *Struggle for Supremacy*, Appendix III, 321.
[145] Text of treaty, *OD*, VIII, 462–63.
[146] Even after Provision No. 2 was rephrased to make it clearer that Prussia should begin the war, Bismarck did not consider himself bound to go to war if Austria attacked Italy first. Chiala, *Le général La Marmora*, 108–109.

tions in Berlin while he himself made the seemingly empty gesture of approaching Metternich on the subject of the Danubian Principalities exchange. He saw no difficulty in proceeding this way as long as it went no further than a harmless general pact of peace and friendship. But when La Marmora rejected such an arrangement out of hand and when Barral and Govone subsequently came up with an immediate defensive and aggressive alliance, the Emperor backed off for reasons given above. While still giving assurance that he would support Italy if she suffered an unprovoked attack from Austria, he made his support as weak as possible—the "counsel of a friend." There will always remain the difference between the way Nigra interpreted the Emperor's words and how they came from Arese. One took them to mean dissuasions; the other, advice without formal commitment. At any rate, La Marmora felt sufficiently reassured to go ahead with the treaty with Prussia. The Emperor's withdrawal of support did not at all signify that he was abandoning La Marmora. There was yet time, he thought, to redeem his pledge to the General. Bismarck had certainly not made his last offer. Then there were congresses and the other subtle potions that might boil up from the witches' cauldron now brewing in Germany.

CHAPTER III

Venetia: The Price of French Neutrality

FIRST AUSTRIAN OFFERS

WITHIN twenty-four hours of the signing of the Prussian-Italian Treaty, the Prussian representative at Frankfort unfurled the red flag for the Austrian bull—the proposal of a new Germanic parliament based on universal suffrage.[1] Austria, however, did not respond to this provocation as readily as expected. Unfortunately for Bismarck's plans, the secret of the treaty with Italy was not well kept. The Viennese cabinet learned the gist of the pact and had its fears increased by the sudden excited language of Italian newspapers and the public air of expectancy in Venice.[2] Instead of breaking with Prussia, Austria chose to keep Bismarck at bay by continuing with him the disarmament negotiations which had begun March 28, meanwhile giving attention to the possibility of an attack on the Venetian border. The Austrians, not fully aware of the terms of the Prussian-Italian Treaty, feared the initiative might be taken by Italy.[3] Claiming that hostile moves had already begun just over the Venetian border, Count Mensdorff began deploying troops along the Po River to respond to the alleged Italian mobilization.[4]

This movement of Austrian troops to the Italian border was totally unexpected by either Italy or France. In fact, French diplomats as well as military observers on the scene were sure that no Italian mobilization had occurred on the Venetian frontier.[5] Napoleon III, fearful of the results of an Austrian sweep down the Italian peninsula, began to have misgivings about the war between the German powers that he

---

[1] See Mosse, *European Powers*, 235–40.

[2] Nigra to Prince Eugène de Savoie-Carignano, June 23, 1866, Ricasoli, *Lettere*, VIII, 8–18.

[3] Fletcher, *Vincent Benedetti*, 64; Alfonso La Marmora, *Les secrets d'état dans le gouvernement constitutionnel*, trans. M. M. Marcel, 5.

[4] Mensdorff to Ambassador in Berlin [*sic*], Apr. 26, 1866, *Evénements*, 189–91.

[5] Col. Schmitz to Marshall Randon, Apr. 27, 1866, FAE, Italie, Vol. 14, 332–34; Malaret to Drouyn de Lhuys, Apr. 28, 1866, *ibid.*, 335.

had originally anticipated with such complacence. According to the best military intelligence available, Austria was still strong enough in a long war to defeat the Prussian-Italian combination.[6] Now the precipitous Austrian move opened up the possibility that war might begin in Italy and perhaps be resolved there independently of the German situation, necessitating French intervention to protect Lombardy. Napoleon III in late March had vacillated over encouraging Italy to align with Prussia, envisioning then what now seemed imminent. He now tried his best, as did Drouyn de Lhuys, to persuade the Italian cabinet not to respond to the Austrian provocation.[7] La Marmora would have preferred as usual to heed French advice and delay mobilization, but on the one hand French assurances were weak and on the other he was prompted at home by the public's strong militaristic spirit.[8] Italian actionists, blindly optimistic of their military chances, were now joined by the moderates and even by the King's counselors in advocating war.[9] Finally, on April 27, La Marmora regretfully announced his decision to place the army on a wartime footing, and two days later the Camera unanimously voted unlimited credits.[10] Malaret wrote from Florence that giving advice to Italy was no longer of any use, and the Emperor feebly warned Nigra once more that if Italy attacked Austria it would be at her own risk.[11] The result in Prussia of these events was that Bismarck finally rejected the Austrian offers of mutual disarmament,[12] and the Austrian cabinet's fears of Italian-Prussian solidarity were confirmed.

Austria now sought to render ineffectual the alliance of Italy and Prussia by exploiting Napoleon's desire for peace in Italy. At this point Napoleon III assumed his position at the crossroads of the Italian and German unification movements. Over the past eight months Napoleon had gingerly explored with Goltz the possibility of some arrangement with Prussia, but negotiations had continually foundered because of France's desire for Rhineland compensations.[13] His other

---

[6] Pottinger, *Napoleon III*, 104–105; for proof and elaboration of this point see 85–104.

[7] Drouyn de Lhuys to Malaret, Apr. 28, 1866, FAE, Italie, Vol. 14, No. 29; Nigra to La Marmora, Apr. 25, 1866, *Evénements*, 185.

[8] Malaret to Drouyn de Lhuys, May 1, 1866, *OD*, VIII, 415–19; and Apr. 23, 1866, FAE, Italie, Vol. 14, No. 42.

[9] Hübner to Mensdorff, Apr. 30, 1866, HHS, Karton 208.

[10] Malaret to Drouyn de Lhuys, Apr. 30, 1866, FAE, Italie, Vol. 14, No. 350.

[11] Nigra to La Marmora, May 1, 1866, *OD*, VIII, 407.

[12] La Marmora, *Les secrets*, 5.

[13] Pottinger, *Napoleon III*, 70–71.

avenue of approach to the German crisis was an entente with Austria. Napoleon III would soon have to choose a partner, but no matter what the partnership, the contract would have to include the one constant, Venetia. Thus France's pursuit of Venetia leads us into the intricacies of the quadrangular relationship of France, Italy, Austria, and Prussia on the eve of the war of 1866.

Austria was generally considered strong enough to defeat both Italy and Prussia,[14] but the Ballplatz, not so optimistic, decided in late April, 1866, to avoid risking a two-front war, even at the cost of abandoning Venetia. This resolve brought Prince Metternich to the Quai d'Orsay on May 4 with an offer to cede the nine provinces of Venetia to France (for eventual recession to Italy) after a successful conclusion of Austria's anticipated war with Prussia. The conditions were that France and Italy had both to promise neutrality. Austria's proposal, however, included the stipulation that she would not cede Venetia unless she were able to take the Prussian territory of Silesia as compensation.[15]

There is some question concerning whether Metternich's offer of May 4, 1866, carried with it conditions over and above compensations in Silesia. Some scholars have held, for example, that Austria asked for French adherence to a plan of undoing Italian unity south of the Po River—a plan that would take away from Italy the Papal States, the Kingdom of the Two Sicilies, and the Duchies in central Italy.[16] Although no evidence of such conditions appears in the Austrian, French, or Italian sources for early May, these scholars have found clues from correspondence of a later date, between May 23 and May 30.[17] It seems indeed that Metternich and Napoleon discussed the future organization of Italy after the transfer of Venetia,[18] but there is reason to believe that in early May, 1866, the suggestion came from Napoleon III himself rather than from the Austrian representative. In reporting two sets of conversations with the Emperor, one around May 1 and another around May 8, Metternich told Mensdorff

[14] See *supra*, p. 56n6.

[15] Drouyn de Lhuys to Gramont, May 11, 1866, *OD*, IX, 95–97; Nigra to La Marmora, Paris, May 5, 1866, *Evénements*, 219–21. It is unclear in both Drouyn de Lhuys' dispatch and in Nigra's whether the offer was made on May 4 or 5, but May 4 seems more plausible.

[16] Clark, *Franz-Joseph and Bismarck*, 411–12; Barker, "Austria, France, and the Venetian Question, 1861–1866," 151.

[17] *Ibid*.

[18] Mensdorff to Metternich, May 8, 1866 (tel), Oncken I, 178.

that the destruction of Italian unity was something Napoleon might contemplate as an alternative to guaranteeing the aggrandizement of Austria in Germany. According to his long-standing instructions,[19] Metternich had to insist upon compensations in Germany.[20] Three years earlier, in March, 1863, Napoleon had made this same suggestion and Metternich had given the same answer.[21] Metternich had even more reason to remain on this course in the early part of May, 1866. Austria was doing her best at that moment to avoid a two-front war and not unduly aggravate Italy. It is not likely that she would have injected into negotiations at this time a threat of restorations in central and southern Italy. Later on, toward the end of May, there was no longer a possibility of avoiding the two-front war; it would seem logical then to have proposed restorations. Conditions concerning restorations were reported in late May; it seems preferable to leave them there.[22]

The guarantee of French and Italian neutrality, as asked on May 4, 1866, in return for Venetia was a large order in itself. Italy was already committed to Prussia; martial spirit among the Italian people was high. So it was with little hope of a favorable reply that Napoleon III passed on Austria's offer to La Marmora. The General reacted spontaneously, rejecting Austria's offer; he was bound, he claimed, by "honor and loyalty" to Prussia. Yet prospect of a peaceful settlement was still attractive; La Marmora was reminded of the possibilities inherent in the general congress already proposed by the French Emperor.[23] Meanwhile, Nigra, also becoming aware of the danger of facing Austria alone in spite of Bismarck's assurances, sat down with Napoleon III at the Tuileries to examine the Prussian-Italian Treaty to see if there were any way to justify Italy's accepting Austria's offer. The treaty itself proved to have no loophole, but Nigra suggested a possibility in something he had been discussing with Govone: the King of Prussia, still trying to stave off war with Austria, had stated that he would not be obliged to help Italy if she were attacked by

[19] Memorandum, Rechberg to Metternich, Mar. 21, 1863, given in full in Clark, *Franz-Joseph and Bismarck*, Appendix A, p. 311.
[20] Metternich to Mensdorff, May 9, 1866, Heinrich von Srbik, *Quellen zur deutschen Politik Oesterreichs von 1859 bis 1871*, Vol. 5 (Pt. 2), 628–30.
[21] See *supra*, pp. 8–9.
[22] The question of just what were Austria's conditions has importance for determining the motives for La Marmora's subsequent refusal of the offer of Venetia. See *infra*, p. 65.
[23] La Marmora to Nigra, May 5, 1866, *Evènements*, 217.

Austria.[24] Until the Prussian government decided definitely to make such a reserve on the treaty, Italy could take no action on the Austrian offer, however, and Govone returned to Berlin to keep a watchful eye on the struggle between King William and Bismarck.

THE ATTEMPTED CONGRESS

While Govone was observing the internal situation in Prussia, both the Italian cabinet and the French Foreign Office turned their attention to another solution—that offered by a general congress.[25] Napoleon III's idea of a European congress on the German and Italian questions seems first to have appeared on the diplomatic board around April 25, 1866, when Napoleon mentioned the idea in a talk with the Prussian minister in Paris.[26] A short time later this suggestion was carried to Prince Metternich; Napoleon hoped that Austria would take the initiative in calling a congress.[27] Foreign Minister Mensdorff brushed it off for the moment and offered a counterproposal on Venetia, the terms of which do not appear in the archives.[28] Even then the French Emperor preferred a congress, and so a congress and cession of Venetia in exchange for French and Italian neutrality were proposal and counterproposal during the next few weeks.

It was in answer to general feelers for a congress sent out on May 2 to Vienna, London, St. Petersburg, and Florence [29] that France received, as a counterproposal from Austria, the offer of May 4. When La Marmora received Austria's reply, he rejected the counteroffer, as we have already seen, because it implied breaking the Prussian alliance. He added in his rejection note, however, that "since the treaty [with Prussia] expires July 8 the thing can be arranged with the con-

[24] Nigra to La Marmora, May 5, 1866, *ibid.*, 219–21; Nigra to Prince Eugène de Savoie-Carignano, June 23, 1866, Ricasoli, *Lettere, VIII*, 18–28.
[25] A monographic account of this attempted congress is Adolf Kulessa, *Die Kongressidee Napoleons III im mai 1866*, modified in many details by Clark, *Franz-Joseph and Bismarck*, 404–14. These works are done from the Prussian and Austrian sides.
[26] *OD*, VIII, p. 425, n.1.
[27] Metternich to Mensdorff, Apr. 28, 1866, Oncken I, 144.
[28] Clark, *Franz-Joseph and Bismarck*, 412, in my opinion wrongly reconstructs this offer from a letter of Mensdorff to Hübner, May 25, 1866. French and Italian sources show the offer was not made in such detail at that time. See Drouyn de Lhuys to Gramont, May 11, 1866, *OD*, IX, 95–97 and 95n1; and La Marmora to Nigra, May 5, 1866, *Evénements*, 217.
[29] Drouyn de Lhuys to Diplomatic Agents, May 2, 1866, *OD*, VIII, 425–26.

gress."[30] In the meantime, word was received from Govone in Berlin that Bismarck did not consider himself legally bound to go to war against Austria if Austria attacked Italy, and it was Govone's belief that any time it seemed profitable Prussia would abandon Italy to Austria's mercy.[31] A congress then looked even more attractive to La Marmora, since such a diplomatic meeting might help him escape from his dilemma. Accordingly, he instructed his diplomatic agents to inform their respective courts that though Italy would not disarm, she looked favorably on the proposal for a congress.[32] Encouraged by such a favorable reaction from the Italian cabinet, Drouyn de Lhuys laid the full program before Nigra. France, in accord with Britain and Russia, would call a congress for the purpose of avoiding war. The basis of its discussion would be: (1) cession of Venetia, (2) the question of Schleswig-Holstein, and (3) reform of the German Constitution. Drouyn de Lhuys assured Nigra that the mere posing of the problem of Venetia implied the solution the congress should seek.[33]

Meanwhile, the French Foreign Office was struggling to keep the idea of a congress alive elsewhere. England had already expressed her less than optimistic sentiments, while Usedom's dispatches to La Marmora showed that Bismarck had no confidence in the meeting,[34] and Russia wanted previous disarmament of Prussia, Austria, and Italy.[35] But the greatest stumbling block of all was the problem of finding compensations for Austria.[36] Mensdorff had made it very clear at the outset that he would not consider sacrificing Venetia without compensation. And how could a congress offer compensation? Where could reasons like "national sentiment" gain her territory from Prussia? The Austrian Foreign Office would not admit the existence of such a thing as "the Venetian question" any more than the French would admit an "Alsatian question" or the Russians a "Polish question."[37] Moreover, Mensdorff rightly noted the secondary place given a question which really should be the primary concern of the powers, namely, Schleswig-Holstein. He felt that if a satisfactory solution here

[30] La Marmora to Nigra, May 5, 1866, Evénements, 217.
[31] Govone Memorandum, May 7, 1866, ibid., 226–33.
[32] Diplomatic Circular, May 11, 1866, ibid., 241–42.
[33] Nigra to La Marmora, May 11, 1866, Archivio Storico, Vol. 838.
[34] Evénements, 248–49.
[35] Launay to La Marmora, May 7, 1866, ibid., 238–39.
[36] France had wanted to include discussion of a guarantee for the city of Rome but dropped this because of the objections of England and Italy. Metternich to Mensdorff, May 18, 1866, HHS, Karton 82.
[37] Gramont to Drouyn de Lhuys, May 22, 1866, OD, IX, 232–34.

were assured, perhaps then the situation on the Italian peninsula could be examined. In other words, he wanted discussion of the Italian difficulties to be put in correlation with the German problem.[38]

The Austrian cabinet's objection to a proposed congress was understandable: such a gathering of the powers would prevent the one thing that could yield compensations for Austria, namely, a war in Germany. Various insignificant changes in the proposals for the congress were made. At the suggestion of Russia the powers substituted the "examination of the Italian difficulty" for the cession of Venetia in the language of the agenda.[39] It was also agreed (since neither La Marmora, Bismarck, nor Mensdorff would agree now to disarm) that disarmament should not be a condition but a desideratum of the congress and that no mention would be made of the temporal power of the Pope.[40] In order to mark off an area of compensation that could be given to Austria independently of a war in Germany, Napoleon III, sometime before May 29, went to work to set up an offer of Bosnia-Herzegovina. Large indemnities were to be offered the Sultan for the bolstering of his economy, and he was probably going to be allowed a free hand to intervene in the recent difficulties in the Danubian Principalities, in which he had already expressed interest.[41] Yet, however disguised, the Venetian question remained in top billing when the formal invitations in the name of France, England, and Russia went from the Quai d'Orsay on May 24 to Berlin, Vienna, Frankfort, and Florence.[42]

While Austrian officials were trying to express their misgivings on the question of the congress and the part Venetia would play in it, Mensdorff again attempted to push direct negotiations with France on the Venetian question. By now this line of diplomacy was being referred to as "confidential" to distinguish it from the diplomacy concerning the congress.[43] On May 25, the same day that he wrote Metternich in Paris to explain the conditions on which the Ballplatz would accept the congress, Metternich also wrote Hübner, acquainting him with the confidential offers being made to France. According to this

[38] Mensdorff to Metternich, May 25, 1866, HHS, Karton 84, No. 2.
[39] Metternich to Mensdorff, May 24, 1866 (tel), HHS, Karton 82, No. 82.
[40] Usedom to La Marmora, May 25, 1866, *Evénements*, 264.
[41] See Project of Allocution, May 29, 1866, *OD*, IX, 298–303, together with La Tour d'Auvergne to Drouyn de Lhuys, June 4, 1866, *OD*, X, 37–38; see also *OD*, IX, 320–23.
[42] Diplomatic Circular, May 24, 1866, *OD*, IX, 248–49.
[43] Cf. Gramont to Drouyn de Lhuys, May 22, 1866, *OD*, IX, 232–34.

dispatch to Hübner, Italian cooperation was now dropped as a condition and the whole bargain was based on the supposition of war with both Prussia and Italy. As Mensdorff summarized it for Hübner, it was as follows:

> In case of war between Austria and Prussia, if the attitude of France were such that she would render it easier for us to carry off complete success, Venetia could be abandoned after the peace, on condition that Austria obtain an equivalent territorial compensation in Germany, and the temporal power of the Pope be re-established on a solid basis in Italy.[44]

The clause stipulating the re-establishment of the temporal power of the Pope (here emphasized for Hübner's benefit) represents the line of negotiation between the Quai d'Orsay and the Ballplatz after it was assumed that Austria would be engaged militarily in Italy. If she had to fight in Italy, Austria planned not only to protect Venetia but also to carry the war into central Italy,[45] and she expected that spontaneous uprisings in Naples and Sicily would follow, separating these areas from Piedmont. Hübner, for example, naïvely reported in April that if war broke out, Sicily "would rise up as one man, and Vespers more bloody than that of John of Procida would exterminate in a few days the garrisons and the partisans of the Piedmontese." [46] Toward the end of May Metternich pressed Drouyn de Lhuys very strongly for French approval of a policy of restorations in Italy, similar to those proposed formerly by Napoleon III, as the current price for Venetia. Austria would indeed allow Italy to receive Venetia eventually; but as for the rest of the peninsula the Papal provinces were to be restored to the Holy See and the sovereigns of Tuscany, Modena, and Naples were to be replaced on their thrones.[47] The Ballplatz admitted quite frankly that, once engaged in a war in Italy, Austria

[44] Mensdorff to Hübner, May 25, 1866, HHS, Karton 208, No. 3. This is the first appearance of this confidential offer in the Viennese archives. Clark, *Franz-Joseph and Bismarck*, 411–12, places the actual offer in late April or early May, 1866. In the judgment of this writer the offer represents a line of negotiation that was stressed only after it was assumed that Italy could not be isolated from Prussia, and when concrete conditions had to be laid down for an order to be established in Italy after an Austrian victory there.

[45] See summary of military preparations of Austria in Clark, *Franz-Joseph and Bismarck*, Appendix C, pp. 577–79.

[46] Hübner to Mensdorff, Apr. 3, 1866, HHS, Karton 208, No. 13B.

[47] Metternich to Mensdorff, May 29, 1866 (confidential), Oncken I, 238–39.

would want to dissipate the "phantom of Italian unity"; yet Austria was prepared to work for an independent and federated Italy.[48]

Restorations as described by Metternich in these conversations were not what either the Emperor or Drouyn de Lhuys had in mind for a free and federated Italy. They were now beset by the nightmare of an Austrian invasion of the whole Italian peninsula and a possible re-establishment of Hapsburg control extending even to Lombardy.[49] Drouyn de Lhuys held before Metternich the prospect that France would not intervene if spontaneous movements took place in southern Italy and promised that she would support an entente of the Catholic powers to guarantee the present status of Papal territory and perhaps even add to the area.[50] But France could not arrange any entente based upon Austria's desires for aggrandizement in Italy after a war there, and Drouyn de Lhuys again insisted that Austria look to Germany or the Near East for compensation.[51] In effect, the federation that Austria seemed to contemplate in Italy was dangerously similar to that of 1815, and so no hope could be held out for Papal, Bourbon, or Hapsburg restorations.

Meanwhile, Napoleon III noted the responses to his invitations to the congress. England and Russia, though unenthusiastic, would come. Bismarck, around May 29, observing that the French Emperor wanted peace at any price,[52] gave up hope of interesting him in armed co-operation and agreed to come to the congress himself.[53] At the same time Nigra, viewing the situation around Paris, saw some hope for a congress but advised Italy to wait calmly "with weapons in hand."[54] On the thirtieth La Marmora sent word that he would be present. There were even encouraging signs from Vienna.[55] Yet Austria's attitude toward the congress had not really softened, and she was encouraged to hold out against it not only by her hope for success in secret diplomacy but also by the hesitant attitudes of Great Britain and Russia. Britain, besides attaching little importance to the congress, feared the possibility of a diplomatic triumph for Napoleon III, and Gorcha-

---

[48] Mensdorff to Metternich, June 1, 1866, *ibid.*, 247–48.
[49] Metternich to Mensdorff, May 29, 1866, *ibid.*, 237–38.
[50] *Ibid.*, 237–39.
[51] *Ibid.*
[52] Barral to La Marmora, May 29, 1866 (tel), *Evénements,* 269.
[53] Barral to La Marmora, May 30, 1866, *ibid.,* 270.
[54] Nigra to La Marmora, May 29, 1866 (tel), *ibid.,* 269.
[55] Mosburg to Drouyn de Lhuys, May 29, 1866, *OD,* X, 314–15.

kov secretly but directly encouraged Austria in her refusal.[56] Gorchakov was probably still afraid that Ottoman territory might be distrib-
uted as compensation.

Although the conversations between Metternich and Drouyn de
Lhuys on restorations in Italy did not promise great success for the
confidential diplomacy, Mensdorff decided that it was time to put an
end to hopes for a congress. He formulated his answer so as to shut
the door firmly but noiselessly:

> We accept the invitation to the congress on condition that it be
> agreed in advance that there be excluded from deliberations all
> combinations which would tend to give to one of the states in-
> vited today a territorial aggrandizement or an increase of
> power.[57]

There was no doubt what this message meant. If no territorial aggrandizement were allowed certainly Venetia could not be discussed,
and if Venetia were excluded from discussion there was no reason
why Napoleon III should continue to push for the congress.[58] Mensdorff admitted that his reply sealed the fate of the proposed meeting
but explained that Austria had no hope of gain from it. The suggested
indemnifications in the Ottoman Empire were not enough; and to cede
Venetia, thus admitting the pretentious claims of nationalities, would
be suicidal for Austria, a state comprising a dozen different peoples.
Thus she would fall back on her rights as established by previous
treaties.[59] Metternich was instructed to continue the confidential
offers, since if war came with Prussia and Italy, French neutrality
would be vital for Austria.[60]

The sudden collapse of the congress diplomacy endangered La
Marmora's position both militarily and politically. He had somehow
managed to keep the Garibaldians in hand and under the prodding of
the French Emperor had braved the opposition of the Party of Action
in the Camera in order to put his hopes in the congress. Now the
Garibaldian movement reached such a crescendo that Garibaldi was

[56] Anna Augusta Ramsay, *Idealism and Foreign Policy*, 200–208. These are
sound conclusions based on documents from the British Foreign Office.
[57] Mensdorff to Metternich, May 31, 1866 (tel), HHS, Karton 84, n.n.
[58] See Mosbourg to Drouyn de Lhuys, June 1, 1866, *OD*, IX, 358–62; *Evénements*, 276.
[59] I.e., Zurich. Mensdorff to Metternich, June 1, 1866, HHS, Karton 84, No. 2.
[60] Mensdorff to Metternich, May 31, 1866 (tel), HHS, Karton 84, n.n.

presenting a plan of attack on Venetia to the Italian ministry.[61] Militarily, since the Italian armies had been held back from the Mincio and Po frontiers while hope lasted for a congress, La Marmora felt that Austria, master of Peschiera and Mantua, could with impunity cross over, cut off the Italian railroad, and put Lombardy in danger.[62] Convinced that war was imminent, La Marmora obtained the King's permission to move the four Italian corps up to the Mincio and Po.[63]

THE SECRET CONVENTION WITH AUSTRIA

With Italy's intentions clarified by her refusal to break with Prussia and with the last chances for a congress fading, the Emperor awaited the next diplomatic move from Austria. Up to the present, unofficial negotiations with that country had consisted of vague feelers for an entente with France in case of war with Prussia. These feelers were traceable as far back as April 21, 1866, when Metternich asked the Emperor if there were any engagement that barred an understanding with Austria in case of war. Napoleon answered somewhat vaguely but indicated that he was entirely free and that an entente with Austria would be very agreeable provided it stay secret and be as extensive as possible.[64] Such a desire for an entente with France was implicit in Austria's propositions of May 4, May 23 (circa), and May 29, which had been presented as counterproposals to Napoleon's proposal for the congress. The Emperor, while preferring the congress, did not explicitly reject the idea of an entente with Austria. He continued to maintain the position he had outlined to Metternich on April 21 and confirmed on April 23—that he would scrutinize every proposition coming from Austria.[65]

---

[61] Dieudé Defly to Drouyn de Lhuys, June 2, 1866, *OD*, IX, 17.

[62] La Marmora to Nigra, June 5, 1866, *Evénements*, 295–96.

[63] *Evénements*, 294; Dieudé Defly to Drouyn de Lhuys, June 2, 1866, *OD*, X, 17.

[64] Metternich to Mensdorff, Apr. 21, 1866 (tel), Oncken I, 139.

[65] Metternich to Mensdorff (tel), Apr. 23, 1866, HHS, Karton 82, No. 59. *Note:* The story of the following negotiations with Austria can be found briefly in Clark, *Franz-Joseph and Bismarck*, 433–38, and in Heinrich von Srbik, "Der Geheimvertrag Oesterreichs und Frankreichs vom 12 juni 1866," *Historisches Jahrbuch*, Vol. LVII (1937), 454–507, published in Italian as "La convenzione segreta tra Austria e la Francia del 12 giugno 1866," *Rivista storica italiana*, Series V, Fasc. 12 (December, 1937). (References will be to the Italian edition.) Both Clark and Srbik have studied the question almost exclusively from the Austrian side. Here the treaty is restudied adding French and Italian documentation.

After the congress failed Napoleon did not have long to wait. On June 3 Metternich sought an audience with him and gave him a dispatch from Mensdorff explaining why Austria could not have accepted a European congress: The proposed discussion of territorial aggrandizement would have become embarrassing. The dispatch did not tell Napoleon anything he did not already know. Then Metternich produced three more dispatches from his superior containing modifications of the May 29 offer. When Napoleon asked what it all came to in the way of propositions, Metternich produced a note which he himself had drawn up which stated what he called the "maximum" of Austria's concessions.[66] This note is not in the Austrian archives, but its content might be surmised from one of Mensdorff's dispatches. Among the new offers was a promise that if left free in Italy, Austria would not seek to re-establish Austrian domination of the peninsula and that she desired a federation of states as a new order in Italy.[67] Another dispatch from Mensdorff shows that some kind of action was asked from France which would allow the Austrian army to be freed in the south in order to permit Austria to employ all her force in the north.[68] The Emperor thought it a good proposition but not complete because it was necessary, said he, "that we discuss the Venetian question frankly." [69] The Emperor then opened his desk drawer and, producing a prepared note, said: "Here is a little project short and simple, which I submit to you." [70] Metternich took the paper and after a few melancholy moments could only comment that the proposal amounted to putting a knife at Austria's throat.[71]

To use threat in his negotiations was unusual for Napoleon III, but circumstances forced him to do so in this instance. He was still in a position of strength with regard to Austria, yet he had just (unknown

[66] Metternich to Mensdorff, June 6, 1866, HHS, Karton 83, No. 30B.

[67] Metternich's note is not to be found in the archives, but its content can be inferred from one of Mensdorff's dispatches. Mensdorff to Metternich, June 1, 1866, Oncken I, 247–48. There was much in this dispatch about the distinction between Italian independence and Italian unity. Mensdorff felt that France and Austria could agree on Italian independence but not unity. Unity, the dispatch noted, menaces the interest of Catholic people in the Roman question. It endangers Austria's Tyrol, Istria, and Dalmatia, cutting off her outlet to the sea. Thus Austria had to subordinate all Italian arrangements to this—that Italian unity be abandoned. As for Venetia itself, it is an interior question—the army, patriotic feeling, etc.—so Venetia could not be given away without a war.

[68] Hübner to Mensdorff, June 2, 1866, HHS, Karton 208, No. 22B.

[69] Metternich to Mensdorff, June 6, 1866, HHS, Karton 83, No. 30B.

[70] Ibid.

[71] Ibid.

to Austria) seen the alternative to an alliance with Prussia move beyond his grasp. It was clear to him by June 1 that he could not obtain sufficient compensation from Bismarck to justify a pro-Prussian policy, the last hope having passed with the failure of the "Kiss mission" in late May.[72] After hopes for a congress faded and the Kiss mission proved bootless, Napoleon III called an extraordinary session of his Council of Ministers to take a last look at the policy of alliance with Prussia. Schemes proposed by both Prince Jerome and Jean Gilbert Persigny, former minister of the interior, failed to gain endorsement.[73] Finally, knowing that Bismarck could still not barter German soil on the Rhineland, Napoleon III decided to maintain strict neutrality, hoping for later fulfillment of Bismarck's promise that should Prussia be successful in the war, she would proceed to no new arrangements in Europe without the French Emperor's agreement.[74] A further step was to demand of Austria the price of his German ambitions. After clarifying his relations with Prussia Napoleon drew up the "little project" and placed it before the Austrian Minister with the confidential assurance that he had given up his Rhineland ambitions. Metternich again saw the knife that he had earlier felt at his throat when the Emperor closed the interview with the words, "If you feel you must refuse, *I am going to have to arm and intervene before long.*" [75]

What was in the "little project"? The note given to Metternich is not in the archives, but its substance can be inferred from the instructions issued Gramont for his mission to Vienna the next week. The Austrian government was asked to cede Venetia, not to Italy but to France at the conclusion of peace whatever the results of the war, whether Austria won or lost, against Italy or Prussia. France also asked Austria for a promise similar to the one extracted from Bis-

[72] This mission represented an attempt initiated by Bismarck to use the offices of a Hungarian expatriate, Kiss de Nemeskér, to seek a last-minute entente with the French. The terms Kiss brought Bismarck from Napoleon III foundered on the same rock as virtually every other attempt at such an arrangement, namely, Rhineland compensations. Pottinger, *Napoleon III,* 137–41. Paul Bernstein, "The Economic Aspects of Napoleon III's Rhine Policy," *French Historical Studies,* Vol. I, No. 3 (Spring, 1960), 342, suggests that Napoleon III's designs on the Rhineland are related to acquisition of the Saarbrücken coal mines, but it would appear from Pottinger's study that the Rhineland economic resources had their value mainly in attracting public opinion.

[73] Ollivier, *L'empire libéral,* VIII, 176–80.

[74] *Ibid.,* 180; Drouyn de Lhuys to Gramont, June 19, 1866, *OD,* X, 216; Drouyn de Lhuys to Benedetti, July 2, 1866, *OD,* X, 303–304.

[75] *Sic* in the dispatch of Metternich to Mensdorff, June 6, 1866, HHS, Karton 83, No. 30B.

marck, namely, that if any postwar adjustments calculated to disturb
European equilibrium were to be made, they should not be made
without first consulting France. In return, France would preserve absolute neutrality. But as for restraining Italy, France promised no
more than to make all efforts to persuade her to remain neutral.[76]

Other considerations that came up in the interview between Metternich and the Emperor pointed the way to additional important
agreements to be formally negotiated later. The main item of concern
was Italy's future political conformation, and in these discussions Napoleon spoke with unusual candor to the Austrian diplomat. He intimated that "if he could sleep tranquilly" knowing that Austria did
not want to efface the results of the war of 1859, he had just as soon
have the Austrians defeat the Italians if Italy continued her movements to the frontier or attacked. Napoleon would not look with dis-
favor upon Austrian victories [77] even should such triumphs lead to
internal changes in the Italian peninsula and finally cause the collapse of Italian unity.[78] Thus Napoleon would permit anything
short of Austrian occupation of the south or violation of Lombardy. In
a conversation with Metternich on May 29, the Emperor had already
been at the point of admitting that his policy of promoting Italian
unity had been a mistake:

> Perhaps I was wrong in allowing the Italian revolution to
> triumph. I did it—and to aid you, Austria, to completely reverse
> it would be a ridiculous negation of a policy of ten years' stand-
> ing.[79]

[76] "*Art. I:* If war breaks out in Germany the French government undertakes with
respect to the Austrian government to preserve an absolute neutrality and make all
efforts to obtain the same attitude on the part of Italy.

"*Art. II:* Whatever be the results of the war, the Austrian government undertakes to cede Venetia to France at the moment when it concludes peace.

"*Art. III:* If the events of war should change the relations of the German powers
among themselves in a manner to upset the European equilibrium, the Austrian
government undertakes to reach agreement with the French government before
sanctioning the adjustments of territory."—Annex Drouyn de Lhuys to Gramont,
June 4, 1866, FAE, Autriche, Vol. 71, Négotiation Secret No. 1; also in *OD*, X,
27.

[77] See Hübner to Mensdorff, Apr. 3, 1866, HHS, Karton 208, No. 13B, for long
discussion of the possibilities of revolt in Sicily and Naples if war is declared between Italy and Austria.

[78] Hübner in Rome was urging anticipation of Italian attack allowing Austria
in perhaps one decisive defeat over the Italian army to overthrow the "phantom
of the kingdom of Italy" and at the same time checkmate French interference.
Hübner to Mensdorff, June 2, 1866, HHS, Karton 208, No. 22A.

[79] Metternich to Mensdorff, May 29, 1866, HHS, Karton 82, No. 29B.

Now, as at Villafranca, he was willing to distinguish between Italian unity and Italian independence and settle for the latter in a deal with his main competitor in that field of diplomacy and intrigue.

Gramont returned to Vienna with the "little project" formulated in three articles.[80] He was also given oral instructions to offer a number of assurances to the Austrian cabinet making explicit and formal the Emperor's confidential words to Metternich in their June 3 conversation. Such assurances had again to do with the future of Italy. If Austria were to be victorious in and over Italy, she should yield up Venetia. If France then gave Venetia to Italy, Italy would stipulate as a condition of the transfer the recognition of the temporal sovereignty of the Pope and the inviolability of his present territory. In such a contract there should also be due guarantees of indemnities and frontiers and special restrictions on the port of Venice. The agreement would also contain a stipulation that France would not intervene in southern Italy if revolutions broke out there.[81]

Gramont arrived in Vienna on June 6 and presented the text of the proposed convention to Emperor Francis Joseph that evening. The reactions of the Emperor and his counselors were predictable: the price was too high. They objected particularly to the phrase "whatever be the results" of the war and maintained that Austria could not yield Venetia if she were defeated in Germany.[82] Gramont saw the difficulty, and at his suggestion Drouyn de Lhuys allowed the cession of Venetia to be contingent upon Austria's victory over Prussia. But he required of Austria a pledge that if she were successful in Italy she would not change the status quo ante bellum except in concert with France.[83] Now Francis Joseph had another objection, namely, that if the victory over Prussia were not decisive Austria might be unable to get equivalent compensation, in which case she could not yield Venetia.[84] Drouyn de Lhuys refused Francis Joseph's proposed modification, however, since he saw in it a loophole by which Austria might refuse to cede Venetia after having profited by French neutrality.[85] Despite Gramont's opinion that providing equivalent compensation for Austria

---

[80] See *supra*, pp. 70–71.

[81] Annexed to Gramont to Drouyn de Lhuys, June 7, 1866, *OD*, X, 65–67.

[82] Gramont to Drouyn de Lhuys, June 6, 1866, *OD*, X, 59; and June 7, *OD*, X, 65–67.

[83] Drouyn de Lhuys to Gramont, June 7, 1866, *OD*, X, 60.

[84] Gramont to Drouyn de Lhuys, June 9, 1866, *OD*, X, 96–97.

[85] Gramont to Mensdorff, June 10, 1866, *OD*, X, 108–109.

was reasonable and safe,[86] Drouyn de Lhuys, undoubtedly at the Emperor's insistence, stood firm, demanding immediate acceptance of the secret convention as drafted.[87]

June 10 and 11 were indeed decisive. By June 10 Emperor Francis Joseph had indicated his expectation of war and needed France's commitment.[88] The next day Bismarck had succeeded, as he put it, in pushing his "old horse" across the ditch, for on June 11 the Prussian King finally called a council of war.[89] In both camps the big question was the attitude of the mysterious French Emperor. Bismarck, making one last attempt, rerouted to Paris the Hungarian General Türr, who had come to Berlin seeking funds to promote a revolution against the Hapsburgs in Hungary in concert with the Italians. Türr later claimed that he had been authorized to offer to the Emperor, through Prince Jerome, the prospect of Rhineland territory, plus Belgium and Luxemburg, in return for active participation.[90] If Türr brought from Bismarck an offer of Rhineland compensations, it was a case of too little, too late. The mission only strengthened the position of Napoleon III, who was able to demand a speedy agreement to his "little project." Agreement was forthcoming on June 11 when Francis Joseph withdrew his proposed modification of the second article and accepted the convention as presented on June 7.[91]

The secret convention with Austria was initialed on June 12 in expectation of later ratifications. In its final form it contained three articles and an additional note. France first guaranteed her own absolute neutrality and promised to try to keep Italy neutral. Secondly, Austria agreed to cede Venetia to France in the event of success in Germany, and she pledged herself to consult France before changing the status

[86] Gramont to Drouyn de Lhuys, June 10, 1866, *OD*, X, 110.

[87] Drouyn de Lhuys to Gramont, June 11, 1866, *OD*, X, 119.

[88] Ollivier, *L'empire libéral*, VIII, 171; Gramont to Drouyn de Lhuys, June 11, 1866, *OD*, X, 115.

[89] Ollivier, *ibid.*, 172.

[90] Türr offered this information in a letter from Vienna on August 2, 1870, and published in the Hungarian paper *Reform;* Ollivier, *ibid.*, VIII, 172–73, reproduces portions of the letter. In this contest for French aid on the part of Prussia, Italy, and Hungarian revolutionaries, Prince Jerome no doubt played a big part. However, the story is yet to be told. Perhaps it will be revealed by the researcher who is able to obtain access to Prince Jerome's yet unpublished papers about 1958 transferred from the Imperial Villa Pringins in Switzerland to the Parisian town house of the present Prince Napoleon. The present writer attempted to gain such access but received word from the Prince that the documents were as yet unclassified and *"incommunicables."*

[91] Gramont to Drouyn de Lhuys, June 11, 1866, *OD*, X, 119.

quo ante bellum in Italy. Thirdly, Austria would not make territorial changes in the German confederation after the war without prior consultation with France. The assurances to be given Austria were set down in an additional note and in large part conformed with the verbal instructions given Gramont at the time of his original mission. This important addition to the treaty provided that when ceding Venetia to Italy the French government would stipulate the maintenance of the temporal sovereignty of the Pope and the inviolability of his present territory. It also guaranteed the inviolability of the new frontiers to be established between Italy and Austria. As to the details of the retrocession, Italy would pay Austria an indemnity for the erection of fortresses to guard her new frontier. The Kingdom of Italy was to assume a part of the public dette of the Austrian Empire prorated according to the population of the province of Venetia.[92] Restrictions were to be placed on the port of Venice so that as an Italian port it would not be a menace to the Austrian Adriatic coastline or the Austrian navy.

Other important clauses in the additional note applied to the political order to prevail in Italy after Austrian victory. Here France agreed to what extent she would permit exploitation of an Austrian military victory in the Italian peninsula. It was again stressed that Austria was not to change the status quo in Italy except by agreement with France. Since it was clear that France would never permit the return of the Hapsburg princes in central Italy, Francis Joseph insisted on an additional note reserving Hapsburg rights in Germany.[93] Nothing was said in the convention about restricting the military operations of Austria in the Italian peninsula except that Austria should not interfere in whatever internal revolutions took place there. The one real concession to Austrian desires to undo Italian unity was that France would not intervene if "spontaneous movements are produced in Italy of such a nature as to undo Italian unity." [94] Obviously, there would be no restorations in the sense that Metternich had proposed toward the end of May. The status quo, i.e., as of June, 1866, of the

[92] " ... une part de la dette publique de l'Empire d'Autriche, au prorata de la population de cette province," OD, X, 147. This was not in Gramont's first instructions.

[93] The purpose of this clause was principally to safeguard the rights of Francis Joseph's cousin, Archduke Ferdinand, Grand Duke of Tuscany, in order to re-establish his sovereignty in some German principality. Gramont to Drouyn de Lhuys, June 12, 1866, OD, X, 142–48.

[94] The text of the Convention together with the "Additional Note" and the "Explanatory Note" are to be found in OD, X, 258–60, as ratified on June 23. See Appendix A, infra.

city of Rome, was definitively to be maintained. The first draft of the convention guaranteed "recognition" of the temporal sovereignty of the Pope, but this term was altered at the insistence of Drouyn de Lhuys before final ratification on June 23 to read "maintenance." "Maintenance" would not imply (as would "recognition") that the Italians must make a declaration in principle—a declaration that was not demanded by the September Convention.[95]

Thus France had assumed but two obligations: to maintain absolute neutrality in the ensuing conflict and to make every effort to obtain the same from Italy. An Austrian victory was clearly foreseen in Germany, and it was assumed that France would not be successful in keeping Italy neutral. At a time when such pledges were honored, giving up her "jewel of empire" and abandoning her hopes to be reestablished in Italy were a considerable price for Austria to pay. Yet she had returned to her original policy, whereby she was ready to yield Venetia in exchange for considerable increase of power in Germany. It was perhaps this gamble that drew from one of her own eminent historians, Heinrich von Srbik, the accusation that by signing this convention with France, Austria "stands before the tribunal of history as having . . . merited the loss of her mission in Germany.[96] Above all, the convention is proof of the strong position held by the French Emperor on the eve of the war of 1866.

ITALY DECLARES WAR

On June 12, as soon as the convention was assured, Napoleon III, in a public letter to Drouyn de Lhuys, declared to all the courts of Europe that his policy in face of the coming struggle in Germany was one of neutrality and that he had but two interests: the equilibrium of Europe and the preservation of his work in Italy. Naturally he did not here reveal the full commitment that was in the secret convention with Austria, for the letter circulated called his policy one of "watchful neutrality" and avowed that France remained poised to intervene if necessary.[97]

Making "every effort" to obtain Italian neutrality consisted for the

[95] Drouyn de Lhuys to Gramont, June 18, 1866, *OD*, X, 212–14.
[96] Srbik, "La convenzione segreta tra Austria e la Francia del 12 giugno, 1866," 59.
[97] The document was a letter addressed to his foreign minister, circulated with all diplomatic agents and published in the *Moniteur*. Napoleon to Drouyn de Lhuys, June 11, 1866, *OD*, X, 120–22.

Emperor of offering the weak suggestion to Nigra on June 12 that perhaps during the campaign "it could happen that it might be useful if Italy did not push the war with too much vigor." [98] Indeed the Emperor knew that Italy could not be restrained from entering the war, and from the time of the collapse of the proposed congress he seemed to have become more and more indifferent about Italy's military activity. Thus he made no protest when General La Marmora declared himself obliged to move his troops to a defensive position on the Venetian border.[99] Nor did Napoleon protest the gathering of Italian volunteers on the Tyrolean frontier to wait for Garibaldi, whom the Italian government had authorized to come to the continent from his exile on the island of Caprera.[100]

That Italy did not heed Bismarck's urging to advance immediately upon the Quadrilateral [101] was due largely to Nigra's knowledge from the beginning of negotiations for the secret convention. As early as June 5, he had learned the details of the French government's proposals.[102] On the basis of this information, Nigra advised restraining the volunteers and scrupulously avoiding anything that would allow Austria to come swooping down on Italy before the war began in Germany.[103] Nigra felt that if Italy did not provoke war, she had nothing to lose from the negotiations going on in Vienna. If France remained neutral, a victory for Austria was foreseeable, but with Austrian victory Italy would receive Venetia as a gift from France. It would be better to take it by conquest but only after fighting had begun in Germany and when Austrian armies were concentrated else-

[98] Nigra to La Marmora, June 12, 1866, Passamonti, Constantino Nigra ed Alfonso La Marmora dal 1862–1866," 459–61.

[99] Malaret to Drouyn de Lhuys, June 8, 1866, FAE, Italie, Vol. 15 (tel). See telegrams from Nigra to La Marmora, June 8, Evénements, 307–08; a note penciled on Malaret's June 8 dispatch in the handwriting of Drouyn de Lhuys shows that Drouyn himself advised Nigra against this movement of the troops.

[100] Malaret to Drouyn de Lhuys, June 10, 1866, FAE, Italie, Vol. 15 (tel); Evénements, 307.

[101] La Marmora to Count Barral, June 5, 1866, OD, X, 44; see also Barral to La Marmora, June 3, 1866, Evénements, 291.

[102] Metternich to Mensdorff, June 12, 1866, HHS, Karton 83, No. 31A. It is not unlikely that the Emperor himself, either directly or indirectly, had the information leaked to Nigra. He told Metternich he was convinced that his cousin Prince Jerome had committed "the indiscretions"; and June 17, 1866, ibid., No. 32A. But Nigra declared to La Marmora that he had some of the information from the Emperor's own mouth; by June 12 Nigra knew that Austria promised Venetia and respect for the status quo in Italy in return for French neutrality. June 12, 1866, Passamonti, "Constantino Nigra ed Alfonso La Marmora dal 1862–1866," 459–61; Nigra to Prince Eugène, June 23, 1866, Ricasoli, Lettere, 8–18.

[103] Nigra to La Marmora, June 5, 1855, Evénements, 299–300.

where.[104] All Italian plans had to be based ultimately on a war of liberation, for public passions had risen to a wartime level.[105]

Thus events from the collapse of the congress to the signing of the convention between France and Austria gradually shaped a war policy in Italy and strengthened lines with Prussia. But these events also caused Italy to be wary of provoking Austria before hostilities began in Germany. On the day the French convention with Austria was signed, a chain reaction set in. Sure of French neutrality and the cooperation of many of the secondary German states, Austria broke off diplomatic relations with Prussia in protest against her sending General Edwin Manteuffel, the Prussian governor of Schleswig, into Holstein.[106] On June 14 the Frankfort Diet on Austria's motion voted federal mobilization against Prussia because of its violation of the Treaty of Vienna and the Gastein Convention. Awaiting the opening of hostilities, Victor Emmanuel II relieved General La Marmora from his ministerial duties and sent him to take command of the army facing the Quadrilateral. The General was replaced, following the changing temper of the nation, by the anti-French Ricasoli as president of the Council and by Visconti-Venosta as foreign minister.[107]

Francis Joseph, though he had secured federal sanction against Prussia, did not want to repeat the mistake of 1859 by being the one to fire the first shot. Bismarck was even more reluctant to commence hostilities, but he finally persuaded King William to order Prussian troops into Saxony on June 15. Even at that point Francis Joseph did not attack though Prussian troops were on the Austrian border.[108] Then Bismarck called urgently upon the Italians to begin hostilities. He told the Italian representative, Barral, that Austria and Bavaria were charged with carrying out the order of federal sanction passed at Frankfort. This, he said, constituted a declaration of war between Austria and Prussia, and he asked that Italy now begin war against Austria.[109] Receiving this communication not only as chief of staff but

[104] See Nigra to La Marmora, June 8, 1855, *ibid.*, 308.

[105] Bigelow Lawrence, American ambassador to Florence, compared enthusiasm for war in Italy to the spirit with which the "loyal states" took up the American Civil War. Bigelow Lawrence to Secretary of State Seward, June 11, 1866, Howard R. Marraro, "American Documents on Italy's Annexation of Venetia (1866)," *Journal of Central European Affairs,* Vol. VI (January, 1946), 358–59.

[106] Gramont to Drouyn de Lhuys, June 12, 1866, *OD*, X, 133.

[107] Malaret to Drouyn de Lhuys, June 20, 1866, FAE, Italie, Vol. 15 (tel); La Marmora remained Minister without Portfolio.

[108] Clark, *Franz-Joseph and Bismarck,* 472.

[109] Barral to La Marmora, June 17, 1866, *Evénements,* 350.

as the still officially presiding president of the cabinet,[110] La Marmora immediately got in touch with Victor Emmanuel II, who replied on June 19, ordering the General to send a declaration of war to Austria.[111] On the morning of June 20, La Marmora forwarded the declaration, not to Vienna but to Archduke Albert, commander of the Austrian forces at Mantua. The document cited Austria's massing of armaments on the border, despite the protests of "the three great Powers," as the reason for the declaration.[112] Victor Emmanuel II that same day wrote to Napoleon III that he had just declared war on Austria and had confidence in his army. He was grateful to the Emperor, he wrote, and added, "J'ai le coeur gai et beaucoup de foi dans l'avenir." [113]

It was not until June 21, however, that Prussia officially declared war against Austria. Even then the declaration was only a notification sent by the Prussian Crown Prince commanding Prussian troops in Saxony to the nearest Austrian officer that a state of war existed. After sending the note, the Prussian Prince invaded the Austrian territory of Bohemia.[114]

Italy had formally declared war, indeed a day earlier than her ally, and was preparing to enter the field against Austria. La Marmora as chief of staff with 120,000 men under his immediate command advanced from Cremona and took a position along the Mincio River on the western border of the Venetian provinces; General Enrico Cialdini with 80,000 men lined up along the Po; and Garibaldi was poised at Como with 30,000 volunteers ready to enter the Trentino region.[115] After the Prussians had entered Bohemia, La Marmora on June 23 led his army across the Mincio and occupied a few small towns on the right bank of the river.[116] Thus in the formality of their declarations and in their readiness for military action, the Italians were already deeply committed to a war against Austria.

[110] La Marmora claimed that his replacement by Ricasoli had not yet officially taken place, *ibid.*, 354.
[111] Victor Emmanuel II to La Marmora, June 19, 1866, *ibid.*, 354.
[112] Text of declaration, June 20, 1866, *ibid.*, 355.
[113] Victor Emmanuel II to Napoleon III, June 20, 1866, *OD*, X, 230.
[114] Clark, *Franz-Joseph and Bismarck*, 472; Taylor, *Struggle for Mastery*, 166. According to Gordon Craig, *The Battle of Königgrätz*, 39–40, Prussia did declare war on Hanover, Saxony, and Hesse on June 15.
[115] Marraro, "American Documents on Italy's Annexation of Venetia (1866)," 354. The two armies—because of poor organization and jealousies between La Marmora and Cialdini—operated in almost complete independence of each other. See also Mack Smith, *Italy*, 79.
[116] Malaret to Drouyn de Lhuys, June 23, 1866 (tel), FAE, Italie, Vol. 15, p. 98.

FRENCH OPINION ON NEUTRALITY

For a complete understanding of the policy of Napoleon III during these months, it is necessary to take into consideration the severe limitations placed upon him by public opinion in France. It might be said that he had to work within the framework of a policy of neutrality because he had no other choice, sensitive to and dependent upon public opinion as he always was. Napoleon III was in the habit of keeping his finger on the pulse of the nation through a system of reports regularly sent to the Ministry of Justice from all the judicial districts in France by agents called the *procureurs généraux*. These reports during the Polish and Danish crises had told him that the French people, despite their strong emotional leanings toward the Poles and Danes, wanted peace.[117] Again, in the early weeks of the German crisis, the reports of the *procureurs généraux* registered alarm at the suggestion of war and positive opposition to French participation in the conflict.[118] News items and editorials in the French press tended to corroborate the reports of the *procureurs généraux*.[119]

The French Bourse also carried a great deal of weight with the Emperor. France, the Second Empire, the wealthiest nation on the continent,[120] by 1865 carried more than 40 per cent of the public debt of the Italian Kingdom [121] and virtually all the Papal debt.[122] On April 10, 1866, Baron de Rothschild and M. Péreire, representing the two leading banking houses in France, personally appealed to the French Emperor to throw his enormous influence on the side of peace. Their fear was that war would send the stock market and business in general into acute distress.[123] This sentiment persisted in financial circles through the month of May.[124]

A striking example of the power of the French bondholders, the

[117] Lynn M. Case, *French Opinion on War and Diplomacy During the Second Empire*, 6–7.
[118] *Ibid.*, 197.
[119] *Ibid.*, 198.
[120] Rondo E. Cameron, "French Finance and Italian Unity: The Cavourian Decade," *American Historical Review*, Vol. LXII (April, 1957), 552.
[121] Rondo E. Cameron, "French Foreign Investment, 1850–1880" (unpublished Ph.D. dissertation, University of Chicago, 1953), 45; see also his *France and the Economic Development of Europe, 1800–1914*, 451.
[122] See Cameron, "French Foreign Investment," 134; and Cameron, *France*, 433.
[123] Case, *French Opinion*, 198.
[124] Metternich to Mensdorff, May 16, 1866, HHS, Karton 83, No. 25F; Hübner to Mensdorff, June 2, 1866, HHS, Karton 208, No. 22B.

rentiers, came in the middle of May when the Italian Camera voted an 8 per cent tax on all annuity coupons paid to foreign investors. The French Ministry of Foreign Affairs ordered Malaret in Florence to protest energetically against this impost on behalf of the French holders of such annuities.[125] This protest, strengthened by a threat from the Stockbrokers' Syndicate in Paris to bar the quotation of all future loan obligations of the Italian government,[126] was apparently effective. The Italian Senato, when it received the tax bill from the Camera, rejected it out of hand.[127]

During May sentiment for peace was further reinforced by a great wave of anti-Prussian feeling in France. This was evidenced in the press, in the official corps of the government (except for the group around Prince Jerome Napoleon), and in the army.[128] Public sentiment against both Prussia and Italy was aroused by a masterful speech delivered during the interpellation in the Corps législatif on Imperial foreign policy on May 3. In this speech the old warrior Thiers warned against any action that would promote the unification of either Germany or Italy. He foretold of encirclement by another combination such as that devised by Charles V. A united Italy and a united Germany, he cautioned, could join hands across the Alps to crush France.[129]

Sensing that public opinion had been aroused against Prussia by Thiers,[130] the Emperor wanted to test out further the temper of the French people. On May 6 in a rather enigmatic speech at the town of Auxerre he stated that in loyalty to the policies of the first Napoleon, he held in utter detestation the treaties of 1815 and suggested that he would like to return to the boundaries granted in 1814. The difference between the boundaries of 1814 and 1815 was essentially the areas of Saarlouis and Saarbrücken. Thus the French people could see here if they so wished designs to seek compensations out of a war in Germany.[131] The Auxerre speech produced little short of a sensation

[125] Drouyn de Lhuys to Malaret, May 16, 1866, FAE, Italie, Vol. 14 (tel), p. 417.

[126] Drouyn de Lhuys to Malaret, May 18, 1866, *ibid.*, 427.

[127] Malaret to Drouyn de Lhuys, June 19, 1866, FAE, Italie, Vol. 15, No. 17. The above incident also demonstrates the anti-French feeling in the Italian nation at large.

[128] Metternich to Mensdorff, May 16, 1866, HHS, Karton 82, No. 25.

[129] Excerpts reproduced in Oncken I, 153–59.

[130] Gustave Rothan, *La politique française en 1866*, 158.

[131] *Moniteur*, May 7, 1866, reproduced in Oncken I, 165.

in Italy, convincing the Italians that France would aid them in acquiring Venetia.[132] Napoleon III soon had his answer, too, from the French nation. First reply, naturally, came from the stock market (Rothschild was alarmed); the second reaction came from the press, which almost universally resented the warlike implications of the speech; and, finally, four-fifths of the *procureurs généraux* reported that the people were opposed to the speech.[133] He saw much the same sentiment reflected when he tested the reaction to his public letter to Drouyn de Lhuys of June 12.[134] France wanted to remain at peace.[135]

PRIMACY OF THE ITALIAN QUESTION

It was quite logical for Napoleon to sell France's neutrality at the highest possible price. That Venetia was that price, exacted from Austria in the June 12 convention, tends to lend meaning and credibility to certain statements made to Prince Metternich in May, 1866. In conversations of June 20, 21, 22, and 23, the Emperor repeatedly assured the Austrian envoy that he had totally abandoned interest in Germany for the pursuit of Venetia, even if it meant Austrian defeat of Italy or settlement of the German question short of war. He said on May 21:

> I have but one interest in all this; it is to be finished with the Italian question by means of the cession of Venice. If this cession can be achieved by peace I will do all I can to contribute to it; if not I shall profit from the chances that war between Austria and Prussia will offer me on this.[136]

Again on May 23 he confided to Metternich, "with Venetia I can finish once and for all with the Italians and get an enormous weight off my chest."[137] And Benedetti—with whom the Emperor communicated more intimately than with his foreign minister—assured Barral, the Italian ambassador in Berlin, that the Emperor's only interest in Ger-

---

[132] Dieudé Defly to Drouyn de Lhuys, May 11, 1866, *OD*, IX, 102–103; Nigra to La Marmora, May 7, 1866 (tel), *Evénements*, 235.
[133] Case, *French Opinion*, 200–201.
[134] See *supra*, p. 79.
[135] Case, *French Opinion*, 200–201.
[136] Metternich to Mensdorff, May 21, 1866, Oncken I, 218–21.
[137] Metternich to Mensdorff, May 23, 1866, *ibid.*, 227–30.

man hostilities was Venetia and that he had no interest in stopping quarrels among the German powers.[138]

Venetia might have come by way of the Prussian-Italian Treaty, thus rendering the pact with Austria unnecessary, but the unexpected mobilization on the Italian border immediately following the treaty of April 8 gave another complexion to the situation. If war began in Italy instead of Germany, it might force Napoleon III to take up the unpleasant task of intervening in that theater to save his work in Lombardy. His constant "risk and peril" warnings were repeated expressions of his fears on that score. It was in response to this danger of having to participate in Italy and not because of any desire for peace in Germany that he attempted to call a congress in May. For both Napoleon III and General La Marmora the congress would have brought a welcome delay, and it might have even been able to arrive at some solution to the Italian problem. The prominent place of Venetia in the agenda of the congress, and the dogged efforts to obtain compensation for Austria, make plans for a congress point primarily and directly at the Italian question. The Emperor would have given up his hopes of war in Germany for a peaceful solution of the Venetian question.

Napoleon III also believed that he might gain a favorable resolution of the German question by way of the Italian question. Benedetti had suggested this to him back in January. The envoy to Berlin reasoned that if Austria were disengaged from Venetia, necessitating complete withdrawal from Italy, she could turn her full attentions to Germany and assume there her proper importance as a counterbalance to Prussia's growing power.[139]

When the congress failed, the inevitability of war, even in Italy, had to be taken as grounds for further policy. To help Prussia was now out of the question. Not to help her was to assure an Austrian victory, according to Napoleon's calculations of the relative military strength of each.[140] Leading from what was yet an apparently strong position, the Emperor literally forced Austria to concede to France maximum benefit of an Austrian victory: cession of Venetia and a voice in any new arrangements in Germany or Italy. The "little project" the Emperor drew from his desk the morning of June 3 was

[138] Barral to La Marmora, May 23, 1866, *Evénements*, 260.
[139] Quoted in full by Fletcher, *Vincent Benedetti*, 78.
[140] See Ollivier, "L'entrevue de Biarritz, 1865," 513–14; *Evénements*, 301–302.

backed up by what in reality was merely an empty threat. Yet it guaranteed the French Emperor almost complete control of the postwar situation, liquidation of his obligations to the September Convention, and an end to his work in Italy. Perhaps the Rhineland was the focus of more traditional French foreign policy, but it was not the primary interest of Napoleon III. And the convention of June 12, but for the capricious turn of military fortune, would be recorded as one of the great diplomatic feats of the whole career of Napoleon Bonaparte's nephew.

CHAPTER IV

Sadowa, Venetia, and the Unredeemed Trentino

NAPOLEON III "ACCEPTS" VENETIA

DECISIONS now left to the field of battle were not long in coming. Four days after Italy's declaration of war the forces of General La Marmora and Victor Emmanuel II, impatiently making for the fortress of Peschiera, were caught by Archduke Albert in the same military trap that was the undoing of a Sardinian army in 1848. Although Custozza was a defeat more embarrassing than disastrous,[1] Napoleon III in the presence of Prince Metternich rejoiced at the news, expressing the thoughts that the loss would make the Italians reflect on their desires for independence from him and that the battle's outcome augured well for the war against Prussia.[2]

Since Austria's military objectives in Germany lay in Silesia, General Ludwig von Benedek advanced his forces, which were the main Austrian army, through Bohemia toward the Silesian border, while Archduke Albert remained to guard the Quadrilateral. General Benedek, however, besides having to face the needle-gun, was surprised by large concentrations of Prussian troops stationed near Silesia,[3] apparently in anticipation of his attack, and was in such immediate trouble that by July 1 he was forced to wire Vienna for permission to negotiate an armistice on the field. The Austrian cabinet ordered Benedek to continue fighting but gave him permission to retreat while Vienna attempted to obtain the release of Archduke Albert and his troops from Venetia to come to his assistance.[4] At this point the French Emperor began to play his role in the war.

[1] It was due largely to lack of coordination by the three leaders, La Marmora, Cialdini, and Garibaldi, and to the ineptitude of the officer corps. Malaret to Drouyn de Lhuys, July 4, 1866, FAE, Italie, Vol. 15, No. 79; La Marmora to Ricasoli, June 28, 1866, Ricasoli, *Lettere*, VIII, 27–28; Hübner to Mensdorff, June 30, 1866, HHS, Karton 208, No. 27B.
[2] Metternich to Mensdorff, June 27, 1866 (tel), HHS, Karton 83, p. 115; and June 29, *ibid.*, No. 35A.
[3] Gramont to Drouyn de Lhuys, July 5, 1866, *OD*, X, 326–28.
[4] *OD*, X, 314–15n3.

On July 2 the Austrian Minister at the Tuileries, acting on instructions sent him by telegraph, approached Napoleon III to seek French mediation in obtaining a military armistice in Italy, without, however, revealing to him the gravity of the situation. Austria would conclude with him immediately—independently of further chances in Germany—the definitive treaty of the cession of Venetia. The French were to be asked immediately, but provisionally, to occupy the Quadrilateral fortresses and all military positions in Venetia. In addition, urgent entreaties were to be made to the French Emperor for outright military aid in Germany as the only way to avert Prussia's otherwise inevitable domination of Europe.[5] Metternich, as he spoke with Napoleon, who was still elated over the Battle of Custozza, laid before him a somewhat doctored picture of the military situation in Germany, and then presented the requests and propositions contained in his instructions. Probably sensing that there was some important battle yet to be decided, Napoleon III said he needed twenty-four hours to think over the Austrian propositions. The next day, July 3, Metternich returned to the Tuileries, where he found both the Emperor and his Foreign Secretary waiting for him. The Emperor greeted him with the assurance that he had found a way. "Cede to me Venetia," he said, "and I will offer my mediation to Prussia as well as Italy." The three of them, that historic afternoon while the Battle of Sadowa was waging, discussed this new project of Napoleon's which Metternich might well have again characterized as involving a knife at one's throat. The Emperor then wrote out both the proposition Austria was to make to France and the response the Emperor was to give.[6] As sent to Mensdorff that evening, the counterproposal was to appear as a response by France to an offer of Venetia in return for French mediation for an armistice at both Berlin and Florence. The response to be made by the Emperor was as follows: "The Emperor accepts the cession of Venetia and proposes at Berlin and Florence mediation on bases indicated by an armistice." [7] Thus Venetia was to pass directly into French hands, nothing being said about occupation of the fortresses or armed intervention in Germany.

[5] Mensdorff to Metternich, July 2, 1866 (tel), HHS, Karton 84.

[6] Metternich to Mensdorff, July 7, 1866, Oncken I, 315–19; Gramont to Drouyn de Lhuys, July 5, 1866, *OD*, X, 326–28.

[7] Metternich to Mensdorff, July 3, 1866, Oncken I, 298–99. See also summary of negotiations by Drouyn de Lhuys in which the impression is given that France is accepting an offer of Venetia made by Austria; Drouyn de Lhuys to Malaret, July 23, 1866, FAE, Italie, Vol. 15, No. 51.

At eight-thirty the next evening Mensdorff's answer arrived. Metternich immediately took it to the Tuileries, where the Emperor, aware of the outcome at Sadowa, received the affirmative answer with visible satisfaction. In the presence of the Austrian Minister he immediately drew up a note for the *Moniteur* to explain his démarche to the French people, and then two telegrams, one to the King of Italy, the other to the King of Prussia.[8] All three documents were written so as to give the impression that the Austrian Emperor took the initiative in offering Venetia to the French in return for Napoleon's mediation for peace in Germany and Italy. The telegram to the King of Prussia read: "The Austrian Emperor informs me that he cedes Venetia to Italy and that he is ready to accept my mediation to put an end to the conflict which has arisen between Austria and Prussia."[9] To Victor Emmanuel II, Napoleon described himself as recipient of Venetia: "The Austrian Emperor acceding to the ideas expressed in my letter to M. Drouyn de Lhuys *cedes to me* Venetia and declares himself ready to accept my mediation."[10] The King of Italy was exhorted to accept an honorable peace and prevent further useless effusion of blood since the Italian army had already shown its valor.

Considering the reactions of the Italians during the past two months, the answer Victor Emmanuel II wired to Napoleon III on July 5 should not have been surprising. He thanked the French Emperor for his interest in the Italian cause but said that the present proposition was of such gravity that he had to consult both his government and his ally Prussia.[11] This reply poorly veiled the host of reservations and hesitations the Italians had about the latest French proposition. Nigra feared, for instance, that the latest agreement between Austria and France contained a guarantee on the Roman question and that such a cession of Venetia would preclude for the Italians possession of the Trentino, which they had hoped to obtain by conquest.[12] La Marmora called it an "insupportable humiliation" to receive Venetia now as a gift from France.[13] Visconti-Venosta saw this snatching of a military conquest from Italy's grasp as harmful to Italian prestige at home and abroad.[14] Ricasoli, the most outraged of

[8] Metternich to Mensdorff, July 7, 1866, Oncken I, 315–19.

[9] Napoleon III to King William I of Prussia, July 4, 1866, *OD*, X, 314–15.

[10] Napoleon III to Victor Emmanuel II, July 4, 1866, *ibid.*, 315. (Italics added.)

[11] Victor Emmanuel II to Napoleon III, July 5, 1866 (tel), Ricasoli, *Lettere*, VIII, 37.

[12] Nigra to Visconti-Venosta, July 6, 1866, Archivio Storico, Vol. 838, No. 351.

[13] La Marmora, *Les secrets*, 7.

[14] Malaret to Drouyn de Lhuys, July 5, 1866, *OD*, X, 322–24.

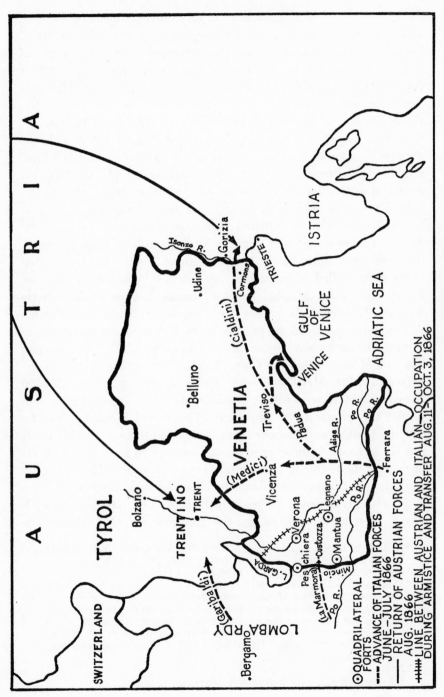

Military Movements, June–October, 1866

them all, later called July 5 a day of "very unhappy memory" because
Italy was then at the point of resuming attack to erase the infamy of
Custozza.[15] This disappointment also registered among the people of
Italy and was quickly reported by the French consuls in Italy.[16]
Italy's reaction was one of extreme frustration and anger. Her con-
sternation would have been even greater had she known that Na-
poleon III had all but forced Austria to cede Venetia to France.

Before July 5 was out Napoleon found himself faced with the
greatest decision of his life—whether or not to intervene against Prussia. Noting the evasiveness of Victor Emmanuel's reply, the Emperor
panicked at the thought that what he had done might get him involved in a war with both Prussia and Italy. Postponing a trip to
Vichy, he immediately initiated studies to determine how long the
fleet of Toulon would take to get to Venice and how many regiments
he could send immediately to the German frontier.[17] Finally, that
evening he called a council of his advisers,[18] including Eugénie,
Drouyn de Lhuys, Marshal Jacques Randon, Eugène Rouher, Pierre
Baroche, Charles de la Valette, and others. The Minister of Foreign
Affairs came prepared to present a resolution for energetic action
against Prussia by sending an observation corps of 80,000 troops into
Alsace and summoning the Corps législatif for an emergency session
to vote credits. Marshal Randon spoke of adding another 250,000
troops within three weeks.[19] Eugénie, as might be expected, supported the proposals of Drouyn de Lhuys and Randon while La
Valette, Rouher, and Baroche strongly opposed them. Opposing views
did not so much indicate pro-Prussian leanings as fears of the effects
of war on the economy and the adverse reaction of public opinion.[20]
La Valette was concerned about the effects of such intervention upon
Italy, which had signed the treaty with Prussia on Napoleon III's advice.[21] Despite the opposition, the Emperor accepted Drouyn de

[15] Ricasoli to Buoncompagni, Sept. 5, 1866, Ricasoli, *Lettere*, VIII, 160–64.

[16] Dieudé Defly to Drouyn de Lhuys, July 6, 1866, *OD*, X, 336.

[17] Metternich to Mensdorff, July 7, 1866, Oncken I, 315–19.

[18] Metternich to Mensdorff, Sept. 27, 1866, HHS, Karton 83, No. 57A. Metternich mentions the calling of the council but gives no record of the meeting.
Rouher kept notes on the meeting which can be found in the Archives Nationales,
Paris, but a full account of the meeting is possible only after much analysis of
other records, such as has been done by Pottinger, *Napoleon III*, 156–62; see
also Ollivier, *L'empire libéral*, VIII, 415–31; Rothan, *La politique française*, 111.

[19] Pottinger, *Napoleon III*, 157.

[20] *Ibid.*

[21] Friedjung, *Struggle for Supremacy*, 240–41.

Lhuys's resolution and signed a decree convoking the Corps législatif, giving a copy of the decree to the *Moniteur* for publication in the following morning's edition. Napoleon apparently had made his decision, though, indicative of the stress created by such a momentous move, he withheld from signing the mobilzation orders.[22]

During the evening and through the night of July 5 every chink in the wall of this decision was probed. Prince Jerome, apparently not present at the meeting, learned of the proceedings and hastened to the Tuileries to plead the Prussian-Italian cause.[23] That night Napoleon III saw Rouher and La Valette, who reinforced their arguments by painting a vivid picture of the total war that might result.[24] As a result of this night of agonies, the notice intended for the morning edition of the *Moniteur* was withdrawn, and the mobilization order remained unsigned. Further meetings and discussions served little purpose other than to dissipate the Emperor's remaining energies. Then, toward the end of the next day a telegram came from King William of Prussia saying somewhat ambiguously that he accepted French mediation,[25] further convincing Napoleon III that his decision was premature.

According to a distinguished French historian, Pierre Renouvin, the reversal of this decision was the "focal point of the whole crisis" and the "great political error of the reign" of Napoleon III.[26] Another scholar has reflected painfully that "a gesture would have sufficed" to dissipate the threat, even as it would have in 1936.[27]

The close observer of this event is tempted to cling to a first impression, that Napoleon III simply cringed before a decision he knew he should make and, like many a man, went down just having missed greatness. Yet there were profound considerations that may well have caused his resolution to slacken. The arguments of Rouher and La Valette concerning the hardships of war were influential, but thoughts of war's effect upon the French public had been in Napoleon's mind all

[22] Pottinger, *Napoleon III*, 158.
[23] *Ibid.*, 158–59.
[24] Friedjung, *Struggle for Supremacy*, 241.
[25] Malaret to Drouyn de Lhuys, July 7, 1866, *OD*, X, 340; Drouyn de Lhuys to Benedetti, July 6, 1866, *OD*, X, 329. Malaret said that the acceptance of Napoleon III's mediation by King William took place July 6 at 9:30 P.M.
[26] Pierre Renouvin, "La politique extérieure du Second Empire" (mimeographed), 149.
[27] Pierre Rain, "Sadowa," *Revue des deux mondes*, Vol. 14 (July, 1966), 190–98, esp. 196–97.

through the spring of 1866. Drouyn de Lhuys expressed the Emperor's concern tersely a few days after the meeting at St. Cloud: "His Majesty is resolved not to impose upon the French people the misfortunes and sacrifices of war." [28] Eugénie added for Metternich's benefit that the most important of all the reasons for the decision of July 5 was the "economic consideration which was acting forcefully upon all spirits from the beginning of the year," causing in the Corps législatif and with the public an "immoderate desire of peace, a desire of which the rapidity of military events could not change." [29]

Drouyn de Lhuys's and Eugénie's statements might have been rationalizations of their own personal defeat, but there was in both their statements a basic truth which could not have been difficult to observe. Since May, when the Emperor was attempting to formulate a policy on the eve of war, the trend of public opinion was decidedly against war.[30] In May public opinion prevented an active pro-Prussian policy; now in July it prevented a pro-Austrian one. But the common denominator was the same: fear of precipitating a more general European war.[31]

Desire for peace was nearly universal in France just before the war. The bourgeoisie wanted peace because war would slow commerce and especially endanger the Italian loans.[32] This was certainly the burden of Rouher's arguments both in the council meeting and at the Tuileries; he is known to have been under a great deal of pressure from French financiers and industrialists.[33] This reluctance to disturb the tempo of French life was shared by other classes who realized the importance of peace for the continuation of economic and cultural progress. Only in peace, according to liberal political thinkers, could the dictatorial aspects of the Empire be mitigated and personal liberties achieved.[34] All this was reflected on the one hand in the disturbing effect of the news of Sadowa on the people of Paris, and on the

[28] Drouyn de Lhuys to Gramont, July 12, 1866, *OD*, XI, 8.

[29] Eugénie to Metternich, Aug. 13, 1866, copy annexed to Metternich to Mensdorff, Aug. 13, 1866, HHS, Karton 83, No. 173.

[30] See *supra*, 79–81.

[31] First suggested by Lynn M. Case in "French Opinion and Napoleon III's Decisions after Sadowa," *Public Opinion Quarterly*, Vol. XIII, No. 3 (Fall, 1949), 441–61, the decision from the point of view of popular pacifism is elaborated in André Armengaud, "Opinion française au moment de Sadowa et la crise nationale allemande" (unpublished Ph.D. dissertation, University of Paris, 1958).

[32] Armengaud, "Opinion française," 58–60.

[33] Robert Schnerb, *Rouher et le Second Empire*, 186.

[34] Armengaud, "Opinion française," 58–60.

other in the universal enthusiasm with which they received the announcement in the *Moniteur* on July 5 that Napoleon III had rescued
Venetia out of the conflict and that Austria had asked him to medi-
ate.[35] Although opinion changed later in July, desire for peace was
the unmistakeable temper of feeling when the Emperor faced the decision the night of July 5.[36] There was also the easy reasoning that
military neutrality was actually consistent with the Emperor's position
before the war, and it may well be that a basic sympathy with German nationalism as promoted by Prussia was the deciding factor.[37]
Yet the post-Sadowa days were hardly moments of cold rationality. As
Rouher himself said afterward, "The decision we had to make would
fix the future for centuries, and we had minutes to decide." [38] Perhaps
the impressions of Professor Pierre Rain, writing on the centenary of
the event, deserve the most serious reflection: "Time has but a fore-
lock; he [Napoleon III] was not able to seize it." [39]

There was now left the precarious road of peaceful mediation.[40]
The day after the St. Cloud meeting some hope of dealing successfully
with Italy appeared in King William I's reply that he accepted the
French offer of mediation though he could not yet set the conditions
of an armistice. Benedetti and Malaret, both at their posts, were instructed to insist upon an immediate armistice.[41] Meanwhile telegrams flew back and forth between Napoleon and Victor Emmanuel.
The Austrian Emperor gave the impression that since Prussia had accepted mediation and the Italian King was disposed to do the same,
he would accept the armistice, at least in principle. In these communications the points of negotiation were discussed: direct cession of
Venetia, the giving over to Italy of the Venetian fortresses at the

[35] *Ibid.*, 92–95.

[36] "For the desire of peace was such, before Sadowa, that the government had
it wished, without doubt would not have been able to make acceptable to the
French people military measures of precaution."—*ibid.*, 202.

[37] Pottinger, 203–10, finds the argument from public opinion inadequate and
prefers to look at the failure to intervene as consistent with the Emperor's deeply
rooted "principle of nationalities," here represented by the Prussian reorganization
of Germany.

[38] Schnerb, *Rouher*, 186.

[39] Rain, "Sadowa," 196.

[40] See the thorough study of the Emperor's mediation in the war, emphasizing
the Prussian side, in Pottinger, *Napoleon III*, 167–80. The present study will
pursue the negotiations with Italy, though the two strains cannot really be
separated.

[41] Drouyn de Lhuys to Benedetti, July 6, 1866, *OD*, X, 329. The council met
July 5, and King William's acceptance was sent July 6 at 9:30 P.M.; Marlaret to
Drouyn de Lhuys, July 7, 1866, *OD*, X, 340.

armistice, inclusion of the Tyrol in ceded territory, and exclusion of the Roman question from all discussion.[42] Actually Victor Emmanuel did not want an armistice; or at least he wanted to delay it as long as possible. The Italian King told Bismarck that he was delaying the armistice, and he held off the French under the pretext of seeking concerted action with his ally.[43] The Prussians gave the same excuse to Benedetti in Berlin.[44] Malaret sought out Ricasoli the morning of July 6 and plied him with all arguments and offered every possible guarantee if only he would accept Venetia on the terms proposed. But Ricasoli was adamant, and the interview ended in an exchange of threats.[45] Unable to appreciate fully the real reason for Italy's obstinacy, the French did not seem to suspect that the Italians were fighting a delaying action until they could resume their invasion of Venetia, while Austria was battling for the defense of her capital. It was probably for this reason that a second meeting of the council, on July 7, ruled out armed intervention against Italy but left hanging the question of intervention in Germany.[46] Nevertheless, the Emperor expressed to Ricasoli his extreme irritation at the latter's attitude and threatened to call the Corps législatif and announce the retrocession of Venetia to Austria.[47] Ricasoli had apparently anticipated armed intervention from France at least to the extent of enforcing the latter's temporary sovereignty over Venetia, for he dispatched a special emissary, Demetrio Diamilla-Müller, to Napoleon III to ask him not to take actual possession of Venetia even pro forma.[48]

---

[42] Victor Emmanuel II to Napoleon III (tel), July 6, 1866, Bortolotti, *La guerra*, 242–43; Metternich to Mensdorff, July 7, 1866 (tel), HHS, Karton 83, No. 128.

[43] Visconti-Venosta to Usedom, July 6, 1866, Ricasoli, *Lettere*, VIII, 329; Ricasoli to La Marmora, July 8, 1866, *ibid.*, 332; Visconti-Venosta to Ricasoli, July 4, 1866, *ibid.*, 330; see also excerpt from Ricasoli's letter to Barral, July 9, 1866, in which he tells Barral to tell Bismarck that the cabinet did not want an armistice, Bortolotti, *La guerra*, 247; Malaret to Drouyn de Lhuys, July 9, 1866, *OD*, X, 374.

[44] Drouyn de Lhuys to Malaret, July 7, 1866, *OD*, X, 344–45.

[45] *Ibid.*, 354–57.

[46] Pottinger, *Napoleon III*, 162. The conclusion on Italian intervention is taken from Rouher's notes.

[47] Ricasoli to Nigra, July 8, 1866, Castellani, *La Marmora*, 39–40.

[48] D. Diamilla-Müller, "Il riscatto della Venezia," *Gazzetta di Venezia*, July 29–30, 1890. It is not clear what arguments Diamilla-Müller was to use on Napoleon III, but Ricasoli told him, either for his own benefit or the Emperor's, that if the French flag went up over Venice and the Quadrilateral fortresses, Italian troops could not "keep their agreement with the King of Prussia." See *infra*, p. 94, for the results of this mission.

Italy "Conquers" Venetia

Before Napoleon III had made his first move to meet some of Victor Emmanuel II's conditions,[49] the Italians had recommended hostilities on land and sea. Ignoring the fact that Venetia was now French territory, General Cialdini crossed the Po River on the southern border on July 9, and on the same day thirty-five Italian vessels loaded with marines left their base for the Dalmatian Coast.[50] Cialdini marched on literally unopposed,[51] primarily because Archduke Albert, at Napoleon's request, was ordered to withdraw behind the Mincio in order to facilitate the concluding of an armistice,[52] and secondly because the Austrians had already decided to abandon the defense of open territory in Venetia. By July 10 evacuation of troops to the northern front for the defense of Vienna had begun. Between July 10 and July 24 the bulk of Austrian manpower was withdrawn from all sectors in Venetia. About 70,000 troops and 15,000 horses went to support Benedek in defending Vienna against the Prussians. The general headquarters of the Austrian army of the south left for Vienna on July 12.[53] The French made no attempt to defend their newly ac-

---

[49] On July 9 Prince Jerome was commissioned to go to Florence to negotiate an armistice with his father-in-law on the basis of immediate surrender of the fortress of Verona. See Instructions for Prince Napoleon, July 10, 1866, FAE, Italie, Vol. 15, p. 170.

[50] Malaret to Drouyn de Lhuys, July 9, 1866, OD, X, 374. Prince Jerome's mission was postponed when this was learned. See the dispatch together with Drouyn de Lhuys to Malaret, July 14, OD, XI, 32–34.

[51] There is some evidence that the French took steps to protect the city of Venice by sea or even to come to the assistance of the Austrian navy in the Adriatic. On July 9 Napoleon III scribbled on a letter Eugénie was writing to Metternich: "I am sending the fleet to Venice. N."—Eugénie to Metternich, July 9, 1866, Oncken I, 327. Metternich, perhaps misinterpreting this note, wired Mensdorff that "the [French] fleet" had already left for Venice—Metternich to Mensdorff, July 9, 1866, Oncken I, 328. The archives of the French Ministry of the Navy have no record of fleet or squadron movements such as are suggested in these documents. There is only a set of instructions for Captain de Surville of the frigate La Provence, given July 10, to proceed to Venice with another vessel to act in the peaceful role of intermediary in the transfer of Venice to the Italians. France, Archives du ministère de la Marine, Mouvements de la Flotte, 1866. French ships were sighted passing through the Straits of Messina on July 13, a week before the battle of Lissa between the Austrian and Italian navies; Malaret to Drouyn de Lhuys, July 14, 1866 (tel), FAE, Italie, Vol. 15, p. 172.

[52] Mensdorff to Metternich, July 8, 1866 (tel), HHS, Karton 84.

[53] Col. Merlin, French military attaché in Vienna, to Minister of War, Aug. 25, 1866, France, Archives du ministère de la guerre, Archives historiques, Mission du Col. Merlin en 1866.

quired territory. The two frigates, *La Provence* and *L'Eclaireur,* sent from Toulon on July 10, caused speculation as to their mission,[54] but when they arrived in Venice on July 17,[55] as far as can be ascertained, they merely lay at anchor in the harbor awaiting developments.[56] Whether or not the Diamilla-Müller mission was successful in changing the original orders of these ships is open to question.[57] Even before the Italians resumed hostilities, Napoleon III intimated to Metternich that he was going to let Italy take Venetia. He would intervene, however, if they attempted to extend their military activities beyond its confines. To reassure the Austrian envoy of this, he showed him a telegram he had sent to Victor Emmanuel II: "After you take Venetia, you will find me across your path if you ever think of going farther." [58]

Yet complications would arise out of Napoleon's permissiveness toward Italian military operations in Venetia. Although the Italians did not dare as yet attack any of the Quadrilateral fortresses, it was already clear that they meant to have the Trentino.[59] La Marmora had brought up the question of the Trentino during the negotiation of the treaty with Prussia, but Bismarck was reluctant to put in writing anything that would compromise him with the members of the Ger-

[54] Diamilla-Müller ("Il riscatto della Venezia," July 29–30, 1890) claimed that the frigates carried orders to disembark troops in Venice and run up the French flag in the city and over the Quadrilateral fortresses.

[55] Pilet to Drouyn de Lhuys, July 17, 1866, *OD,* XI, 88–89.

[56] The sources are silent on any activity of the ships until after the retrocession to Italy was enacted.

[57] Diamilla–Müller ("Il riscatto della Venezia," *Gazzetta di Venezia,* Aug. 9–10, 1890) claimed that he actually prevailed upon Napoleon III to change the orders originally issued to the ships and that on the following day (July 16), the Emperor relayed messages to them via semaphores along the shore telling them to await new orders in Venice. Once in the harbor they were told not to do anything "to jeopardize the Italian aspirations." It is possible that secret orders were originally given to the squadron, but none such as Diamilla-Müller suggests appear in the instructions given to Captain de Surville on July 10, preserved at the Archives de la Marine, Paris. Nor can such a supposition be reconciled with Prince Jerome's original orders, which were to offer to hand over the fortress of Verona to Italian forces as a pledge of the rest of them. See instructions for Prince Napoleon, July 10, 1866, FAE, Italie, Vol. 15, p. 170.

[58] Mensdorff to Metternich, July 8, 1866 (tel), HHS, Karton 84. It is difficult to see where beyond Venetia the French were able to stop the Italians except in their known ambitions to cross the Adriatic and cut across the Dalmatian Coast toward Vienna to concert with the Prussians. See Ricasoli to Visconti-Venosta, July 10, 1866, Ricasoli, *Lettere,* VIII, 53–54. This is possibly why in this conversation Napoleon III said something to Metternich that led him to believe that the French Mediterranean fleet had departed for Venice.

[59] See Appendix B, *infra.*

manic Confederation to which the Trentino belonged.[60] But he did intimate verbally that perhaps during or after the war the Trentino might be permitted to come under Italian control.[61] The question came up in the very first days of the present crisis, for Nigra on July 4 (when there was question of accepting Venetia from France) made it clear that the Trentino had to be included.[62] It was a condition of any discussion of an armistice in the telegram from Victor Emmanuel II to Napoleon III a few days later.[63] At any rate it was the clear understanding of the Italian government during the post-Sadowa crisis that they had Bismarck's oral agreement that the Trentino was to be included in the term "Venetia." [64] Militarily, the sector had been the special preserve of Garibaldi and his youthful volunteers. They had made a first unsuccessful attack upon the fully guarded approaches around the time of the Battle of Custozza. Just prior to Cialdini's crossing of the Po (July 8), the Garibaldians resumed their hammering at the outposts of the region [65] but were driven back.[66] The Garibaldians, numbering some 38,000, were certain to have greater effect after Archduke Albert's withdrawal from the south. General Franz Kuhn, the Austrian commander in the Tyrol, with only about 12,000 infantry and a troop of cavalry, had up to now only to protect the southwest passages.[67]

While Prussia was successfully holding up the armistice, Ricasoli planned to make good use of the time. He wanted to support the volunteers with regular troops so that the region could be successfully and firmly occupied before negotiations began.[68] He wanted Garibaldi then to be freed to lead troops across Croatia into Austrian Fiume—a move to be synchronized with Prussian moves in Serbia and

[60] Barral to La Marmora, Mar. 30, 1866, Chiala, Ancora, 99.
[61] Ibid.
[62] Nigra to Visconti-Venosta, July 5, 1866, Archivio Storico, Vol. 838, No. 351.
[63] Victor Emmanuel II to Napoleon III (tel), July 6, 1866, Bortolotti, La guerra, 242–43.
[64] Verbale della deliberazione del Concilio degli Ministri, I, 12 Junio 1861–30 Maggio 1867, Session of July 26, 1866, p. 130. Archivio Centrale Roma, Archivio di stato. Manuscript notes taken verbatim from those archives by Professor Norbert Miko were used.
[65] Pilet to Drouyn de Lhuys, July 8, 1866, FAE, Venise, Vol. 27, No. 49.
[66] Friedjung, Der Kampf um die Vorherrschaft im Deutschland, 1859 bis 1866, II, 402. For a detailed account of the whole campaign in the Tyrol see this volume, 400–408. (The German edition is cited here because military history is omitted in the English translation.)
[67] Ibid., 402–403.
[68] Ricasoli to Visconti-Venosta, July 8, 1866, Ricasoli, Lettere, VIII, 51–52.

Hungary.[69] It is probable that the attack on the Adriatic shore by the fleet had something to do with this plan. Meanwhile Visconti-Venosta continued the regular negotiations with Napoleon III for an armistice, holding firmly to the condition that the Italian Tyrol be included in the annexation of Venetia.[70] Ricasoli again came under the attack of the French Minister in Florence, who tried to get him to listen to reason; but Ricasoli fended him off until Malaret once more became exasperated with this man whom Cavour once called "the civilian Garibaldi." [71] Malaret blamed his lack of success with Ricasoli upon the latter's utter irresponsibility, his complete lack of "political sense . . . intelligence . . . or suppleness." He despaired of the cabinet President's ability ever to control the agitated Italian people and press. Yet Malaret did divine just what Ricasoli was about—delay of the armistice until the Italian regular army could secure the Trentino so that this territory could be demanded in the negotiations.[72] Ricasoli was supporting this policy by instructing his agent in Berlin to encourage Bismarck to make ever more exorbitant demands upon Austria so that the Italian government would not bear full responsibility for delaying the armistice.[73]

DEBACLE

In face of the uninterrupted march of the Italians into Venetia and their subsequent stand on the Tyrol question, another important decision was made at the Tuileries by July 11. This was to support the preliminaries of peace which Bismarck held out as a *sine qua non* of armistice, so as to achieve a quick peace in Germany, thereby isolating Italy's action.[74] Whereupon Drouyn de Lhuys finally gave final and official notice to Metternich that France could not go to war, leaving Austria the choice of accepting ejection from the Confederation as demanded in the preliminaries, or continuing the war *à outrance*.[75] Thus, with the last hope of French intervention dissipated and with the Prussians five or six days from Vienna, the Austrian position quick-

[69] Ricasoli to Visconti-Venosta, July 10, 1866, *ibid.*, 53–54.
[70] Visconti-Venosta to Nigra, July 9, 1866, *ibid.*, 50.
[71] Malaret to Moustier, Oct. 17, 1866, FAE, Italie, Vol. 16, No. 122.
[72] Malaret to Drouyn de Lhuys, July 10, 1866, FAE, Italie, Vol. 15, No. 82.
[73] *Ibid.;* Ricasoli to Barral, July 10, 1866, Ricasoli, *Lettere*, VIII, 331–32.
[74] Metternich to Eugénie, July 11, 1866, HHS, Karton 83, No. 37B.
[75] Drouyn de Lhuys to Metternich, July 12, 1866 (copy), *ibid.*, No. 38.

ly deteriorated. By July 14 both Vienna and Berlin received from the French Foreign Office a list of six conditions—Bismarck's preliminaries of the peace modified by the French Emperor—which if accepted by both parties would signal the end of hostilities in that sector of the war. The provisions were: (1) integrity of the Austrian Empire save Venetia, (2) dissolution of the Germanic Confederation, (3) formation of a Northern Confederation under Prussia, (4) freedom for the South German states to form their own union, (5) annexation of the Elbe Duchies by Prussia.[76]

Malaret was to try to coordinate the mediation in Germany with more pressure on the cabinet in Florence, but the Italians were already out of reach. Ricasoli had gone off to general headquarters, and Visconti-Venosta was incommunicado. Moreover, people in Florence were speaking of Istria, Friuli, and Trieste.[77] When, however, the French government noticed on July 17 that Mensdorff's resistance to the peace terms was breaking down,[78] a new mission was formed to pursue the Italian cabinet to general headquarters at Ferrara. Napoleon's special negotiator in Italy, Prince Jerome, headed the new mission, with terms that were to make more honorable the transfer of Venetia to Italy—(by plebiscite), and to discuss the Tyrol question under the title of frontier rectification.[79] Benedetti at the same time went to Prussian general headquarters to press for acceptance of the six points by King William I.

Before Prince Jerome reached Ferrara, Benedetti achieved success in his mission. On July 20 both Prussia and Austria accepted the six points and a five-day truce as preparation for a full armistice.[80] In accepting this truce Prussia stopped her military advance when she was at the point of taking the city of Vienna. This was not entirely due to Benedetti's diplomatic skill and the pressure brought to bear by the French Emperor. Nor was it merely another instance of Bismarck's habit of wisely limiting his objectives. The fact is that by July 17 the

---

[76] Drouyn de Lhuys to Benedetti and Gramont, July 14, 1866, *OD*, XI, 30–32.

[77] Malaret to Drouyn de Lhuys, July 14, 1866, FAE, Italie, Vol. 15, No. 83.

[78] Mensdorff to Metternich, July 17, 1866, Oncken I, 361–62.

[79] Nigra to Visconti-Venosta, July 18, 1866, Archivio Storico, Vol. 838. Text of letter to Victor Emmanuel II in Giuseppi Govone, *Mémoires*, 508.

[80] Mensdorff to Metternich, July 20, 1866 (tel), HHS, Karton 84. Gramont to Drouyn de Lhuys, July 21, 1866, *OD*, IX, 137. Prussia was to recognize the integrity of Austria save Venetia. Austria recognized the dissolution of the Germanic Confederation and would not oppose the formation of another arrangement of which she would not be a part. See also Drouyn de Lhuys to Malaret, July 21, 1866, *OD*, X, 138.

military picture had changed quite radically. By that time the Austrians were able to bring to the defense of Vienna the greater part of their forces previously assigned to the Italian theater. Some 70,000 additional troops and 3,000 cavalry had come from Italy to support Benedek.[81] Moreover, Bismarck stopped hostilities without consulting or warning his ally.[82]

Meanwhile, the Italian military advance had gone just far enough to be compromised by the truce in Germany. Cialdini, having crossed the Po on July 8, made rapid progress, marching northward and eastward to the city of Venice unopposed by the skeleton force left in the Quadrilateral by Austria. By July 17 he was in possession of Padua, Vincenza, and Treviso and had begun to surround Venice,[83] while another army began to move along the Mincio River to break communications among the forts of the Quadrilateral.[84] Simultaneously, the Italian fleet, equipped with land forces, was on its way from Ancona across the Adriatic to the Dalmatian Coast,[85] where on the nineteenth it began to bombard the island-fortress of Lissa. There the Austrian fleet challenged the Italian vessels and defeated and drove them off the next day.[86] During that naval battle on the Adriatic the Italians were preparing to launch another strategic move. On July 21 a detachment from Cialdini's army under General Giacomo de Medici veered off westward toward the Tyrol to support Garibaldi's still un-

---

[81] Col. Merlin to Minister of War, July 17, 1866, France, Archives du ministère de la guerre, Archives historiques, Mission du Col. Merlin en 1866. See the Govone dispatch to Visconti-Venosta, July 26, 1866 (tel), Bortolotti, *La guerra*, 255, which records a conversation between Govone and Bismarck. Bismarck admitted that the presence of Austrian reinforcements had a part in his decision.

[82] Usedom to Ricasoli, July 17, 1866, Ricasoli, *Lettere*, VIII, 73–75. Visconti-Venosta to Nigra, July 17, 1866, Italy, Ministero degli affari esteri, *Documenti diplomatici e negoziati commerciali, 1866. Documenti diplomatici presentati al Parlamento, dal Ministero degli affari esteri il 21 dicembre, 1866*, 733–34. (Hereafter cited as *Documenti presentati*.)

[83] Pilet to Drouyn de Lhuys, July 17, 1866, FAE, Venise, Vol. 27, No. 52.

[84] Dieudé Defly to Drouyn de Lhuys, July 15, 1866, *OD*, XI, 65–66.

[85] Consul of France at Ancona to Drouyn de Lhuys (tel), July 16, 1866, FAE, Italie, Vol. 15, p. 188.

[86] The attack on Lissa was obviously meant to precede a landing on the Austrian-held Dalmatian Coast, with the idea of cutting across Croatia toward Hungary or Vienna. More evidence that the Italians were supporting Prussian military strategy in the east was the fact that on July 16 Cialdini sent a detachment of troops to Vienna. Col. Schmitz to the Minister of War, Ponte Lagosuro, July 17, 1866, France, Archives du ministère de la guerre, Archives historiques, Mission du Col. Schmitz en Italie, 1862–67.

successful efforts from the other side.[87] Medici was surprisingly successful against the battle-fatigued forces of General Kuhn through July 22 and 23; it looked as though the latter would have to withdraw into the city of Trent.[88] On land, therefore, the Italian war machine appeared strong enough to take both Venetia and the Trentino.

In Florence, however, where the news of General Medici's success had not yet arrived, Ricasoli was visibly shaken by the defeat at Lissa and what he regarded as the treachery of Prussia in accepting the truce. When Malaret saw him on July 21, Ricasoli spoke as if he had seen the writing on the wall, saying that Italy could not possibly hold out against an armistice. In effect, he had dropped all conditions except that of the Trentino, and this was now put in the more subdued tones of "national boundaries"—a compromise no doubt resulting from his talks with Jerome at Ferrara.[89] On July 22 both Malaret and Ricasoli went to Ferrara, where Victor Emmanuel II and Visconti-Venosta were holding talks with Prince Jerome. Victor Emmanuel huddled briefly with his ministers on July 23, and the decision was made to suspend arms without previous conditions.[90] Establishing solidarity with France, Italy was on the point of breaking with Bismarck, who still did not want her to sign an armistice but to continue fighting.[91]

Yet the cessation of hostilities was not to come so quickly. Just twenty-four hours after issuing the order to suspend arms, the Italian cabinet received word that General Medici had broken through and taken a position a few kilometers from the city of Trent, with the result that the greater part of the Trentino region was now in Italian hands. When Ricasoli and Visconti-Venosta learned of this develop-

[87] Malaret to Drouyn de Lhuys, July 26, 1866, *OD*, XI, 229–32. Friedjung, *Die Kampf um die Vorherrschaft*, II, 405, says that Garibaldi was actually in retreat when Medici made his appearance.

[88] Friedjung, *Der Kampf um die Vorherrschaft*, II, 405–406.

[89] Malaret to Drouyn de Lhuys, July 21, 1866, FAE, Italie, Vol. 15, No. 85. On July 21 or 22 Victor Emmanuel II sent his conditions for armistice to Napoleon III: No discussion of Rome; Austria should be in agreement with the principle on which the cession is made; the Trentino should be allowed to be brought up at peace talks. Nigra to Drouyn de Lhuys, July 22, 1866, *OD*, XI, 152.

[90] Malaret to Drouyn de Lhuys, July 24, 1866, FAE, Italie, Vol. 15, No. 86. General Medici in the Trentino did not get word of cease fire until July 25. Friedjung, *Der Kampf um die Vorherrschaft*, II, 407.

[91] Malaret to Drouyn de Lhuys, July 26, 1866, *OD*, XI, 229–32; and July 31, 1866, *OD*, XI, 315–19.

ment, they regretted their decision to suspend arms. Going to Prince
Jerome, who was still at Ferrara, they presented him with the old conditions—no armistice without the Trentino, the Quadrilateral, and a
plebiscite in Venetia. If Austria accepted this, Italy would negotiate a
separate peace treaty with her and break with Prussia.[92] Prussia, on
the other hand, was on the point of signing a definitive armistice
without Italy but wanted all agreements to rest in suspense until Prussia could declare to Italy that Venetia was hers and that the Prussian-
Italian Treaty had been honored and fulfilled.[93] Ricasoli recognized
the delay at Nicholsburg as indicating that hostilities might still be resumed—a possibility of which he would take advantage.[94] Prince
Jerome then had to devise ways to meet the demands of the Italians
on the basis of their military position in the Trentino. Time was of the
essence since to settle affairs at Nicholsburg the Venetian question
had to be resolved.

As the Austrians and Prussians were approaching the end of their
five-day truce, Prince Jerome on July 26 proposed to the Italians an
attractive compromise on the Trentino question. He offered an armistice on the basis of a military *uti possidetis,* a provision allowing military forces to remain in possession of occupied territory during the
armistice and peace talks. Since Italy would thus be left in possession
of the greater part of the Trentino territory, she would be in a very
advantageous position to annex the area at the peace table. The Emperor, as he had often said, would not support annexation of the
whole Italian Tyrol, but he would offer his good offices if Italy could
clearly distinguish certain economically and strategically essential
areas in the Tyrol and bring them up under the title of rectification of
frontiers. As for Venetia proper, Austria was to surrender it without
further conditions except for assumption of its public debt by the an-
nexing power and its transfer by means of a plebiscite. It is not clear
whether Jerome made these proposals on his own initiative or received the first instructions from the foreign minister. No instructions
appear in the French archives but the diary of Jerome's mission is in
the Italian archives. The diary reveals that he had held detailed discussions with the Italian cabinet on July 26 concerning the *uti possidetis,* the manner of transfer of the fortresses, and the rectification of

[92] Malaret to Drouyn de Lhuys, July 26, 1866, *OD,* XI, 229–32.
[93] Benedetti to Drouyn de Lhuys, July 25, 1866, *OD,* XI, 214–15.
[94] Visconti-Venosta to Nigra, July 29, 1866, Ricasoli, *Lettere,* VIII, 86–87.

boundaries in the Tyrol.[95] The proposals as wired to Malaret on July 29 were somewhat different and in more diplomatic form; Jerome may have proposed them originally and referred them to the home office for approval and modification.[96]

The day the *uti possidetis* was offered to Italy, Austria and Prussia arrived at an armistice agreement at Nicholsburg, the agreement to be contingent on Italy's response.[97] Anticipating a favorable response, Benedetti had been authorized to give assurance that Venetia would be ceded to Italy thus allowing Bismarck to be disengaged from his ally and to sign a separate peace.[98] Furthermore, Bismarck had refused to support the Trentino claims at Nicholsburg. So the Italian cabinet, rather than continue the war under danger of military and diplomatic isolation, on July 28 accepted the armistice as proposed by the French,[99] obviously relying on the hope held out by the *uti possidetis*.

During the next week progress was made on working out the details of the armistice. On August 2 Nigra accompanied Napoleon III and Drouys de Lhuys to Vichy, where they discussed (under the supposition of the *uti possidetis*) the details of the boundary question, the attitude to be taken on the Italian Tyrol, and an honorable manner of transferring Venetia to Italy.[100] General Barral, the Italian representative at Nicholsburg, told the Prussian and Austrian plenipotentiaries that Italy was declaring an armistice; but he did not say anything about the *uti possidetis*.[101] On the fighting front, Generals Cialdini and La Marmora were informed of the terms agreed upon. Finally, the Italian general staff sent General Bariola to Cormons to conclude the armistice on the field with the Austrian authorities.[102]

When Bariola met the Austrian generals on August 5, the great shock came. The generals demanded, threatening resumption of hostilities, that the Italians evacuate the Tyrol and all Venetia east and

[95] Compte-rendu by Prince Jerome, annexed to Nigra to Visconti-Venosta, Aug. 2, 1866, Archivio Storico, Vol. 838. See also Marsh to Seward, July 31, 1866, Marraro, "American Documents on Italy's Annexation of Venetia (1866)," 362–64.

[96] Malaret to Drouyn de Lhuys, July 29, 1866, *OD*, XI, 283; and July 30, 1866, *OD*, XI, 301–302.

[97] Usedom to Visconti-Venosta, July 29, 1866, *Documenti presentati*, 756–57.

[98] Gramont to Drouyn de Lhuys, July 28, 1866, *OD*, XI, 278–80.

[99] Napoleon III to Drouyn de Lhuys, July 29, 1866, *OD*, XI, 283.

[100] Nigra to Visconti-Venosta, Aug. 4, 1866, Archivio Storico, Vol. 838.

[101] Barral to Visconti-Venosta, Aug. 5, 1866, *Documenti presentati*, 767–70.

[102] Visconti-Venosta to Nigra, Aug. 5, 1866, *ibid.*, 764–65.

south of the Isonzo River by August 10. Having no instructions for such an unexpected contingency, Bariola had to return to General Headquarters.[103] What had happened? Drouyn de Lhuys, now in almost full control of foreign policy, because of the Emperor's illness had failed to mention anything of the *uti possidetis* to the Viennese cabinet until August 4,[104] at which time the cabinet had rejected it and refused to continue negotiations at Cormons.[105]

The slip—or finesse—was Drouyn's, but the embarrassment was the Italians'. Since the armistice with Prussia was confirmed by an armistice in Italy, the Austrian general staff had been able to begin returning to the Italian front the troops that had left some four weeks before to defend Vienna. Accordingly, on August 4 they started to redeploy not only troops of the army of the south but a large portion of Benedek's corps as well. While the Italian army was quiescent during the cease fire, these troops were being carried across Carinthia by rail to the Tyrol at the rate of 20,000 per day. It was evident that they were to bring pressure upon the Italians in negotiations for the new frontiers.[106] Now not only did Austrian forces hopelessly outnumber General Medici in the Trentino, but Cialdini, faced with superior numbers in the eastern sector, could not move.[107] When Drouyn de Lhuys tried to break this deadlock by urging Austria to accept the *uti possidetis*, Mensdorff stood firmly on the agreement with Prussia that the Austrian Empire was to remain intact save Venetia;[108] in turn the Italian government insisted on their agreements made with France and reminded Drouyn de Lhuys that the whole situation was of his making.[109]

[103] Visconti-Venosta to Nigra, Aug. 6, 1866, Ricasoli, *Lettere*, VIII, 93; Nigra to Drouyn de Lhuys, Aug. 6, 1866 (tel), FAE, Italie, Vol. 15, p. 284.

[104] Drouyn de Lhuys to Gramont, Aug. 4, 1886, *OD*, IX, 372. On August 1 Drouyn de Lhuys presented to the Austrian government a convention of three articles which was to settle the armistice between Italy and Austria, but it does not mention the *uti possidetis* or the Trentino. Drouyn de Lhuys to Gramont, Aug. 1, 1866, *OD*, XI, 331–33. This convention was the one the Austrians accepted on August 4, 1866. Gramont to Drouyn de Lhuys, Aug. 4, 1866, *OD*, XI, 379.

[105] Gramont to Drouyn de Lhuys, Aug. 5, 1866, *OD*, XI, 386–87.

[106] Col. Merlin to Col. Colson, Aug. 7 and 25, 1866, Archives du ministère de la guerre, Archives historiques, Mission du Col. Merlin en 1866, Correspondance particular avec Col. Colson. Col. Merlin here noted that the Austrian troops were being carried on "our railroads."

[107] La Marmora to Ricasoli, Aug. 6, 1866, Ricasoli, *Lettere*, VIII, 336. Drouyn de Lhuys to Malaret, Aug. 7, 1866 (tel), FAE, Italie, Vol. 15, p. 292.

[108] Gramont to Drouyn de Lhuys, Aug. 5, 1866, *OD*, XI, 386–87; Mensdorff to Metternich, Aug. 5, 1866 (tel), Karton 85, n.n.

[109] Nigra to Drouyn de Lhuys, Aug. 6, 1866, Archivio Storico, Vol. 838.

Another crisis was mounting for the tired and sick Emperor as he prepared now to leave Vichy, where he had repaired a fortnight before in a state of severe strain and exhaustion.[110] The new fear that beset the Emperor and his cabinet was that revival of war in Italy would rekindle hostilities in Germany.[111] There was always the possibility that Bismarck would use the unsettled conditions in Venetia as a pretext to nullify his agreements at Nicholsburg if it were to his advantage; or, what was equally undesirable to the Emperor, Bismarck would make a private convention with Austria on Venetia excluding France as intermediary.[112] Meanwhile Bismarck sat back complacently, refusing to support either Italy's claims in the Tyrol or the *uti possidetis*.[113] France's tenuous ties with Austria were under strain because, having accepted harsh terms under French mediation at Nicholsburg, Austria returned to find that her abandonment of Venetia to France had only resulted in humiliating invasion by an unopposed Italian army. Also, Austria's previously inaccessible position in the Tyrol had been outflanked and the Italians were on non-Venetian territory.[114] Having now recovered this military position, she was unwilling to relinquish it and kept pouring troops into the Tyrol. Such was the attitude of Austria that Eugénie, emerging from a Council meeting at St. Cloud on August 9, had regretfully to tell Nigra that the French government could not even ask Austria to withdraw her troops.[115] French mediation was stymied and embarrassed.

As the August 10 deadline approached, it was clear to the Italian government that the whole question of peace in Europe hung upon Italy's decision to withdraw from the Trentino. Since August 6 the Italian council had been sitting in solemn deliberation over the ques-

[110] Nigra to Visconti-Venosta, Aug. 6, 1855, Ricasoli, *Lettere*, VIII, 95; Metternich to Mensdorff, July 26, 1866, Oncken I, 377–79. Prince Metternich had much to say around this time about the health of the Emperor. He saw him as a man pale, hesitant, defeated, "whose will power has yielded before the state of complete exhaustion." Metternich to Mensdorff, July 26, 1866, Oncken I, 377–79. Metternich attributed his condition to the crisis he had suffered since Sadowa, whereas Eugénie traced the disintegration back to the time of his scandalous love affair with Marguerite Bélanger two years before. Metternich to Mensdorff, July 26, 1866, Oncken I, 379–81.

[111] Drouyn de Lhuys to Gramont, Aug. 6, 1866, *OD*, XI, 390–91.

[112] Metternich to Mensdorff, July 26, 1866 (tel), HHS, Karton 83, No. 158.

[113] Govone, *Mémoires*, Appendix, Note V, pp. 503–508; Barral to Visconti-Venosta, Aug. 7, 1866, Ricasoli, *Lettere*, VIII, 336–337.

[114] Mensdorff to Metternich, Aug. 8, 1866, HHS, Karton 85, n.n.

[115] Eugénie to Nigra, Aug. 9, 1866, copy annexed to Nigra to Visconti-Venosta, Aug. 10, 1866, Archivio Storico, Vol. 838.

tion of resuming military action on all fronts. For three days they weighed their own admitted numerical inferiority and lack of coordination against the humiliation of withdrawal and a weakened position at the peace conference. Ultimately, on August 9, on the basis of a realistic report of General Menabrea, the council decided that Italy could not meet the concentration of troops in the Tyrol. They gave the army permission to withdraw "for strategic reasons" and ordered La Marmora to conclude a military armistice and to withdraw from the Trentino and Istria.[116] Ricasoli instructed Nigra to announce this in Paris and to ask for assurances that the other conditions of the armistice be honored.[117] At home the Italian cabinet attempted vainly to save face by giving the withdrawal the appearance of a strategic concentration of forces to meet the Austrian attack.[118] Then, compounding Italy's humiliation, Austria excluded the Italian plenipotentiaries from the final peace negotiations at Prague. Robbed of her hopes of standing with her ally in a tripartite treaty, Italy had to accept a separate peace with Austria under French mediation.[119]

The armistice was signed on August 11. As arranged on the field, Austrian troops for the duration of negotiations were to occupy territory from Lake Garda to the Po, and from the Po to Legnano, a clearly defined territory around the Quadrilateral. Italy remained in possession of all the rest of the administrative confines of Venetia except the city of Venice.[120] (See map, p. 87.)

AFTERMATH

"Una Pace Miserabile" was the bitter comment of Nigra in reporting to Visconti-Venosta.[121] The King, the army, and the nation at large were deeply distressed and felt they had been deceived, humiliated, and robbed of glory. The left bitterly denounced the man they

[116] Verbale della deliberazione del Concilio, pp. 133–35. Italian forces had also penetrated into Istria as far as the territory of Gorizia just beyond the Venetian border.

[117] Nigra to Visconti-Venosta, Aug. 10, 1866, Archivio Storico, Vol. 838, No. 361.

[118] Malaret to Drouyn de Lhuys, Aug. 9, 1866, OD, XII, 43–44.

[119] Barral to Visconti-Venosta, Aug. 10, 1866, Ricasoli, Lettere, VIII, 337; Malaret to Drouyn de Lhuys, Aug. 11, 1866, OD, XII, 69.

[120] Convention of the Armistice annexed to Visconti-Venosta to Nigra, Aug. 13, 1866, Documenti presentati, 772–74.

[121] Nigra to Visconti-Venosta Aug. 18, 1866, Ricasoli, Lettere, VIII, 110–15; Ricasoli to Carlo Buoncompagni, Sept. 5, 1866, Ricasoli, Lettere, VIII, 160–64.

accused of "having turned to ashes the golden fruits of opportunity," while the right, which had favored the French alliance, were embarrassed by the complications introduced by their patron the French Emperor.[122] Even the great and patriotic La Marmora paid the price of his French sympathies, being replaced as chief of staff by General Cialdini.[123]

This reaction was not caused exclusively by the affair of the *uti possidetis*, for the feeling of wounded pride, called exaggerated by Malaret, was prevalent in Italy from the time Napoleon first accepted Venetia from the Austrians.[124] The American ambassador to Florence, George Marsh, on July 11 marked the "cool arrogance" with which Napoleon III accepted Venetia from Austria and presumed to negotiate on behalf of the Hapsburgs with Italy. He also noted the deeply wounded pride of all European courts concerned and said he would not be surprised if a coalition formed to wage a "war of nationalities" against the second Bonaparte.[125] Ricasoli, reflecting on the whole period of French mediation since July 5, called it a "violence" of which there was no explanation except in the "grand egoism" of the French. Napoleon III's interference robbed the Italians and Prussians of the strength of united action, which was particularly painful for Italy since, as Ricasoli claimed, she had been ready to resume war ever since July 5 to wipe out the memory of Custozza.[126]

Especially galling to the Italians and to Ricasoli in particular, was the failure of the French to appreciate the genuine feeling of the Italian government and people in the Trentino question. Malaret continually described it as an interior question—the surrender of a weak liberal government before the public clamor for glory and new victories. More surprisingly, he called it an entirely "new" question, raised for the first time amid the circumstances of the armistice.[127] What he probably did not know was that a conservative and pro-French cabinet, as far back as the signing of the Prusso-Italian Treaty in April,

[122] Green Clay to Secretary Seward, Aug. 13, 1866, Marraro, "American Documents on Italy's Annexation of Venetia (1866)," 356n10.

[123] Malaret to Drouyn de Lhuys, Aug. 17, 1866, FAE, Italie, Vol. 15, No. 98.

[124] See dispatches of Malaret from July 5 on, esp. Malaret to Drouyn de Lhuys, July 31, 1866, OD, XI, 315–19; Malaret to Drouyn de Lhuys, July 7, 1866, FAE, Italie, Vol. 15, No. 81.

[125] Marsh to Seward, July 31, 1866, Marraro, "American Documents on Italy's Annexation of Venetia (1866)," 363–64.

[126] Ricasoli to Buoncompagni, Sept. 5, 1866, Ricasoli, *Lettere*, VIII, 160–64.

[127] Malaret to Drouyn de Lhuys, July 31, 1866, OD, XI, 315–19.

considered the Trentino to be a part of Venetia. Bismarck at the time would not honor this in writing lest he compromise himself with the Germanic Confederation, but he did recognize the claim to the extent of giving his verbal assent.[128] Furthermore, the Emperor himself should have been aware of the longstanding nature of this problem since the Italian intermediary, Count Arese, let him know unofficially, without revealing the agreement with Bismarck, that the Italian government considered the Italian Tyrol included in the Venetian question.[129]

The stunned reaction in Italy had an understandable basis: the French government had broken out of its predicament at the expense of the weakest of the four participants. Yet it was hardly the arrogance that Marsh reported nor the violence by which Ricasoli characterized the incident. One reads expressions of Italian sentiment at the time with sympathy but not without feeling that Italy was painfully conscious that her military weakness had been exposed and that this caused her to be oversensitive about the Trentino and eager to blame it and previous embarrassments on the perfidy of her allies.

For the Emperor the past month had been both physically and morally trying. His present state of exhaustion and incapacity, which was to plague him for the rest of his reign, was due largely to the strain of these days.[130] It may well be that July 5, as Metternich remarked, was the beginning of all the "hesitations and tergiversations" of his career.[131] He had not got the Italians off his hands, he had not prevented a colossus from rising in Germany. The war that he had counted on to solve all his problems in Germany and Italy had ended by creating new ones, and he must have reflected bitterly that perhaps Thiers was right when he warned that Italy and Germany, united by his help, would one day join hands across the Alps and encircle him —not in an embrace but in a strangle hold.

What blame his Foreign Minister must bear for the debacle of the last days is not clear. Certainly, Drouyn de Lhuys had fuller charge than ever of Imperial policy at least from July 26 to the armistice, but he never left his chief's side even at Vichy. While the two consulted occasionally, it is clear that the Emperor was *hors de combat* during those days. Ricasoli felt, perhaps rightly, that the *uti possidetis* affair

---

[128] Verbale della deliberazione del Concilio, p. 130.
[129] *Ibid.*
[130] See *supra*, p. 103n10.
[131] Metternich to Mensdorff, July 7, 1866, Oncken I, 315–19.

was a finesse attempted by Drouyn de Lhuys on his own initiative to prevent peace talks from failing at Nicholsburg. The Austrian cabinet did fear that the suspension of arms between Prussia and Austria due to expire July 27 would not be renewed because of the suspended state of affairs in Venetia. Austria even contemplated dealing directly with the King of Prussia for the transfer of Venetia.[132] It is not inconceivable, therefore, that Drouyn de Lhuys with the double purpose of getting Austria "off the hook" and keeping the Venetian question in French hands made the compellingly attractive offer to Italy. How can we reconcile this with the evidence that Prince Jerome initiated the idea of the *uti possidetis?* [133] We can only surmise that Jerome, in trying every possibility to interest Italy, offered the *uti possidetis* with the understanding that it would be referred to Paris and finally cleared with Vienna. That the Austrian government was not immediately consulted was partly the responsibility of the Ambassador at Vienna, who told Drouyn he thought Austria would have no objections.[134] *Adhuc sub judice lis est!*

The conflict of interested parties at court had been responsible more than once for ambivalence in the foreign policy of the Second Empire. The past month of crisis, complicated by the Emperor's illness, saw a denouement in the drama. Rouher, the minister of state, and the violent-tempered Prince Jerome led the pro-Italian faction, while Drouyn de Lhuys, strongly seconded by the Spanish-born Empress who distracted herself with politics after the Emperor's love cooled, did his best to favor Austria. The battle for control went on not only for the council meetings but also for the press. On July 18 Prince Metternich obtained permission from his home office to borrow 500,000 francs from the Crédit Foncier to outbid the Prussians and Italians in bribing the French press.[135] He wanted also to compete in this way for the support of Jerome Napoleon, whom Metternich claimed was being paid handsomely by Bismarck.[136] The conserva-

---

[132] Rouher to Napoleon III, July 26, 1866, FAE, Italie, Mémoires et documents, Papiers Rouher, Section I, Allemagne.
[133] See *supra,* p. 100 and p. 101n95.
[134] Gramont to Drouyn de Lhuys, July 31, 1866, *OD,* XI, 326.
[135] Metternich to Mensdorff, July 18, 1866, Oncken I, 366–67; and July 14, 1866, *ibid.,* 366n 1.
[136] Metternich to Mensdorff, July 18, 1866, HHS, Karton 83, No. 39A. He claimed to have had information about letters of exchange "in very high figures" destined for one of the principal aides-de-camp of Prince Jerome. As to the press, charges of bribery are especially leveled at *La Liberté, Le Siècle,* and *L'Opinion nationale.*

tive, pro-Catholic, pro-Austrian party never gave up the struggle for armed intervention, while the liberal, anticlerical, pro-Prussian "Italianissimes," as Metternich dubbed them, opposed any military action. To favor the former group, hope had constantly to be held out to the Viennese cabinet for armed intervention—a factor that helped put Austria in a false military position.[137]

At any rate, Napoleon III was able to stop the war of 1866 because he still had enough power to give the impression that anyone who did not deal with him as a friend must ultimately face him as an enemy. Yet he did so at great expense to his prestige and especially to his relations with Italy and Austria. When hope of an Austrian victory vanished, the Emperor made a frantic effort to stop the war and to salvage Venetia quickly before peace was made. The *uti possidetis* incident is related to this. An Austro-Prussian armistice signed on July 26 still remained dependent for its efficacy upon armistice in Italy. This armistice was not forthcoming, however, because Italy had sought not only to take Venetia but also to obtain the coveted Trentino. It was on July 26 that Drouyn de Lhuys promised Italy all she wanted in order to secure—if our hypothesis is correct—the peace at Nicholsburg. He also wanted to keep the cession of Venetia coming from the Emperor's hands. Austria had already paid half the price of French mediation; Italy paid the other half with the sacrifice of her military ambitions and national pride.

[137] See Metternich to Eugénie, July 10, 1866, Oncken I, 332, in which he expresses hope for armed mediation by France.

CHAPTER V

The Transfer of Venetia to Italy

THE PROBLEM OF THE VENETIAN DEBT

AFTER the armistice was concluded, Italy not only was in a weak position because of the *uti possidetis* debacle but, excluded from a tripartite treaty at Prague, had to face Austria alone over the peace table. She dreaded this encounter because her budget was in critical condition and she feared that Austria would use her advantage to magnify the financial indemnity involved in transferring Venetia.[1] The Italian cabinet was thus forced to overcome its irritation with the French Emperor and again ask his help. Visconti-Venosta expressed his desire that the peace negotiations be held under the auspices of the French Emperor.[2] Napoleon III, however, either because of the persistent influence of the pro-Austrian faction at court[3] or because the role of mediator had grown distasteful to him, was unwilling to accept the responsibility of seeing Italy through the making of the treaty. He discouraged the Italians in their attempts to have the conferences held in Paris[4] and counseled them to accept Vienna as the site. Gramont, the French ambassador, would merely assist at the negotiations as the Emperor's commissioner.[5]

Of more vital interest to the Emperor was the formula to be followed in the transfer of Venetia to Italy. Since early August he had wanted on the one hand to clarify and define his own legal position as true recipient of the rights to Venetia from Francis Joseph, and on the other to see that Venetia was returned to Italy by means of his favorite principle of nationalities, ultimately by means of a plebiscite.

[1] Malaret to Drouyn de Lhuys, Aug. 22, 1866, FAE, Italie, Vol. 15, No. 102; Nigra to Visconti-Venosta, Aug. 23, 1866, Ricasoli, *Lettere*, VIII, 120–25.
[2] Malaret to Drouyn de Lhuys, Aug. 13, 1866, *OD*, XII, 85–86.
[3] Metternich to Mensdorff, Aug. 18, 1866 (tel), HHS, Karton 83, No. 179.
[4] Nigra to Visconti-Venosta, Aug. 18, 1866, Ricasoli, *Lettere*, VIII, 100–15; Drouyn de Lhuys to Gramont, Aug. 20, 1866, *OD*, XII, 142.
[5] Nigra to Visconti-Venosta, Aug. 23, 1866, Ricasoli, *Lettere*, VIII, 120–25; La Valette to Gramont, Sept. 3, 1866 (tel), Vol. 12, p. 10.

To achieve such a formula, on August 1, 1866, the Emperor had submitted to Francis Joseph an outline of a convention to be concluded between them. Besides making the cession of Venetia to the French Emperor formal, this proposal would provide for the subsequent transfer of the rights of possession to a commission of Venetian citizens who would deal with the French and Austrian authorities and conduct the plebiscite. The agreements made between Italy and France were also to be honored; no conditions should be added to the transfer of the territory except that the public debt remaining applicable to Venetia should be assumed by Italy.[6]

The Austrian cabinet had only minor modifications to make in Napoleon's formula but found it necessary to clarify one item—the debt—and it was on this point that Napoleon would be drawn willy-nilly into the negotiations between Italy and Austria. In a redraft of the proposed convention of transfer, the Austrian cabinet required that the public debt applicable to the provinces of Venetia must be based on the debt of the whole Austrian Empire prorated according to the population of the annexed provinces.[7] This interpretation of the debt question was perfectly in accord with the wording of the Secret Convention of June 12, 1866, between France and Austria (see Appendix A), but it was certain to impose heavy financial burdens on Italy. Since Napoleon was eager to have Austria accept the rest of the formula of transfer as he proposed it, he accepted the pro rata specification together with Austria's whole redraft of the formula.[8]

When a copy of this redraft was sent to Florence for approval, the Italian cabinet, far from endorsing it, immediately dispatched a special representative, General Menabrea, to Paris and asked that everything be held up until he could talk with the Emperor.[9] The Italian cabinet was about to point out another stupendous misunderstanding in these tortuous relations among France, Italy, and Austria. Italy had thought that, since the Treaty of Zurich of November 10, 1860, was the precedent, the basis of calculation would not be the public debt of the whole Empire but the special debt adhering to Venetia proper from

[6] Drouyn de Lhuys to Gramont, Aug. 1, 1866, *OD*, XI, 331–33.

[7] Project annexed to Gramont to Drouyn de Lhuys, Aug. 5, 1866, *OD*, XI, 387–89. At the dissolution of the Napoleonic Kingdom of Italy, the precedent was established that the component parts of that kingdom when annexed to other states should carry with them the public debt applicable to them at the time of transfer.

[8] Malaret to Drouyn de Lhuys, Aug. 13, 1866, *OD*, XII, 81–82.

[9] *Ibid.*

the time it became part of the Napoleonic Kingdom of Italy. The point was of some importance since according to Visconti-Venosta's quick estimates the transferable debt under the pro rata principle would run as high as 500,000,000 francs.[10] Furthermore, the limitation of the debt to the special and absolute sum adhering to Venetia was the meaning of the phrase "without previous onerous conditions" in the language of Prince Jerome on the memorable July 26 when the *uti possidetis* was offered;[11] and it was understood in this way by the Italians when they accepted the armistice on July 29.[12]

After hearing the objections of General Menabrea, Drouyn de Lhuys had to backtrack again. He now had to ask Austria not to use the words "pro rata" but to substitute the vague phrase "debt applicable to the Lombardo-Venetian Kingdom," leaving to a committee of financial experts the task of determining it further.[13] But the Austrian response promised another clash. The most they could do was modify the term "pro rata" to read "proportional," which still prejudged, according to the French, any decision of the committee of experts.[14]

By August 21 this had become such an issue with the Austrians that members of the cabinet threatened to resign rather than accept the French proposal on the debt.[15] It looked to the wearied Austrians as if their difficult situation vis à vis Prussia was being exploited once again. Bismarck had agreed around August 10, as a consolation to Italy for his having made a separate peace, that he would include in the final treaty between Prussia and Austria a satisfactory article on Venetia.[16] To cash in on this promise Visconti-Venosta now recommended that the Italian interpretation of the Venetian debt question be written into such an article. He suggested that the treaty stipulate that Venetia be given over without conditions other than "the liquida-

[10] Malaret to Drouyn de Lhuys, Aug. 13, 1866, FAE, Italie, Vol. 15, No. 97.
[11] Compte-rendu by Prince Jerome, annexed to Nigra to Visconti-Venosta, Aug. 2, 1866, Archivio Storico, Vol. 838.
[12] Malaret to Drouyn de Lhuys, July 30, 1866, OD, XI, 301–302. Here Malaret shows that in the conditions agreed upon for armistice, Italy understood that "without conditions" meant without onerous financial conditions except for the debt according to the precedent of Zurich.
[13] Drouyn de Lhuys to Gramont, Aug. 15, 1866, OD, XII, 109.
[14] Drouyn de Lhuys to Gramont, Aug. 18 (tel), FAE, Italie, Vol. 15, p. 360; Austria's idea in any case was to have passed on to Italy a part of the Austrian debt which would equitably represent Venetia's participation in the Empire and not merely the strictly localized "Venetian debt." Drouyn de Lhuys to Gramont, Aug. 19, 1866, OD, XII, 140–41.
[15] Gramont to Drouyn de Lhuys, Aug. 21, 1866, OD, XII, 156–59.
[16] Note from Govone's *Mémoires* in OD, XII, 135n3.

tion of the debt applicable to the territory ceded on the basis adopted at Zurich." [17] Bismarck welcomed this chance to acquit himself of his obligations to his ally. He presented to Austria a formula which paid deference to the precedent of Zurich but left room for its interpretation. His version read "the liquidation of the *debt which shall be recognized as applicable to* the territories ceded conformably to the precedent of the Treaty of Zurich." [18] Prussia's ability to threaten renewed hostilities always gave her the power to hasten agreements, but it may well have been that Bismarck's formula seemed preferable to Austria. At any rate, the Austrian cabinet as a *pis aller* accepted Bismarck's formula for inclusion in the forthcoming treaties.[19] In view of Bismarck's claim that the preliminary cession of Venetia to France was a "fiction," and his threat to bring in a new intermediary such as England or Russia, Drouyn de Lhuys quickly accepted this formula for the convention.[20] Thus the Treaty of Prague between Prussia and Austria, signed August 23, and the Treaty of Cession of Venetia to France, signed August 24, contained identical wording on the Venetian debt. Italy would assume "the debts which will be recognized as applicable to the Lombardo-Venetian Kingdom conformably to the precedents of the Treaty of Zurich." The Treaty of Cession between Austria and France (see Appendix D, p. 140, for text of treaty) added that the amount of the debts applicable to Venetia would be further determined by a special commission.[21]

Thus Prussia, Austria, Italy, and France found basic agreement on the financial question, and it would seem that the last hurdle had been passed in establishing peace among all four. General Edmund Le Boeuf, the Emperor's aide-de-camp, was dispatched to Venice to act as French commissioner for the transfer of the territory; and General Menabrea and Count Wimpffen, the Italian and Austrian plenipotentiaries, began talks at Vienna for the definitive peace.[22]

[17] Barral to Visconti-Venosta, Aug. 17, 1866, Ricasoli, *Lettere,* VIII, 340. See also Benedetti to Drouyn de Lhuys, Aug. 18, 1866, *OD,* XII, 134–36, in which he says he thought Italy indicated this clause in the Treaty of Prague and in accepting it Prussia would feel justified in making a separate peace.

[18] Benedetti to Drouyn de Lhuys, Aug. 18, 1866, *OD,* XII, 134–36. The clause "which shall be recognized" leaves open the question concerning the nature of the precedent at Zurich. (Italics added.)

[19] Gramont to Drouyn de Lhuys, Aug. 22, 1866, *OD,* XII, 162. This was done before signing the Treaty of Prague.

[20] Gramont to Drouyn de Lhuys, Aug. 21, 1866, *OD,* XII, 156–59.

[21] Text of treaty, *OD,* XII, Appendix II, 395–400.

[22] Drouyn de Lhuys to Gramont, Aug. 24, 1866, *OD,* XII, 178.

We shall defer until later in this chapter a report on General Le Boeuf's mission to Venice so we may fix attention on the peace conference at Vienna, where on the very first day the debt question reappeared. Having obtained leave of the French Emperor to deal directly with the Italians,[23] Count Wimpffen got right to this most important problem.

The Austrian experts had worked out a defense of their original position on the debt by taking full advantage of a vague clause in the Austro-Prussian Treaty: "which shall be recognized as applicable to the territories ceded." Wimpffen's argument was based on the fact that at precedent-creating Zurich three-fifths of a loan contracted by Austria in 1854 was applied to Lombardy when it passed to Sardinia in 1859. This, it was claimed, was a pro rata or proportional sum, not a localized or absolute one. Therefore, the precedent was created at Zurich for the proportional sharing of debts for a ceded territory. This Wimpffen supported with an argument from equity saying that a province which shares in the benefits of the Empire should share in its expenses, a principle recognized in the Secret Convention between France and Austria on June 12, 1866.[24]

Thus Austria repeated her original demand, that Italy assume a portion of all the outstanding debts contracted by the Austrian Empire since 1859, prorated to the population of the Venetian provinces. Specifically this meant participation in three large loans, one made in 1860 and two in 1864, amounting in all to 386,938,000 florins.[25] The proportion of the population of Venetia to the whole Empire being 24 to 350, the debt applicable under this heading was to be 26,532,946 florins. Besides this portion of the debts contracted by the Empire since 1859, Italy, according to the Austrian authorities, had to assume that part of the aforementioned loan made in 1854 which still remained applicable to Venetia, roughly 26,600,000 florins. Thirdly, and about this there was no dispute, the charge originally upon Venetia from a defunct bank of the Napoleonic Kingdom of Italy called the Monte Lombardo-Veneto was to be transferred to Victor Emmanuel's

---

[23] Gramont to La Valette, Sept. 2, 1866 (tel), FAE, Autriche, Vol. 493, p. 5.
[24] Report of Count Wimpffen, HHS, P.A. XI, Italien, Krieg und Freidausverhandt, Karton 157; Mensdorff to Metternich, Sept. 2, 11, 1866, HHS, Karton 85; Malaret to La Valette, Sept. 5, 1866, FAE, Italie, Vol. 16, No. 107.
[25] The Austrian unit, the florin, will be used whenever reference is made to the negotiations since it was the unit used. A florin at the time was equal to 2.5 francs.

Italy.[26] The total debt to be assumed by Italy under these three headings was 75,250,000 florins, about 200,000,000 francs.[27] This was considerably below Visconti-Venosta's first estimates but still a formidable
sum.

General Menabrea flatly denied that Zurich set a general precedent for the pro rata sharing of debts by a ceded possession. The stipulation at Zurich on the debt of 1854 was purely an exception granted
out of many others which Austria tried unsuccessfully to affix at the
time. Menabrea claimed that like the Monte Lombardo-Veneto, the
debt of 1854 was affixed specifically upon Lombardy and Venetia at
the time the loan was made. Therefore, it did not establish that Italy
should not have to assume a pro rata portion of all debts contracted
by the Austrians since 1859.[28]

The French Empire was interested in the partition of the Venetian
debt—and Napoleon III had spelled out this interest in notes to both
Gramont and Malaret before the conferences began. The French
treasury had been creditor of the original Monte Lombardo–Veneto
bank for some 77,000,000 francs, a sum that was reduced in the negotiation of the Treaty of Zurich to 20,000,000 francs. Of this sum, in
1860 Austria assumed 5,000,000 francs debt by reason of retaining
possession of Venetia, while Italy assumed 7,500,000 francs by reason
of obtaining Lombardy. The remaining 7,500,000 francs should have
been applied to Parma, Modena, and those parts of the Papal States
that were included in the old Kingdom of Italy, but France could not
get Sardinia to assume such debts formally at the time. In addition to
this, French private investors held certain credits on the Austrian government which were as yet unpaid. They claimed that when Austria
was liquidating the debts she assumed from the Napoleonic Kingdom

---

[26] The "Monte Lombardo–Veneto" was a name used to designate this lump
sum of money which became part of the public debt of the Napoleonic Kingdom
of Italy. When this kingdom was dissolved in 1815, the debt passed to Austria
since Lombardy and Venetia came into her possession at the Treaty of Vienna,
and was henceforth designated as the Monte Lombardo–Veneto. Obviously,
three-fifths of it had already been assumed by Italy in 1860.

[27] The above reconstruction of Austrian claims is put together from the follow-
ing reports: Summary for use of Ambassador, FAE, Autriche, Vol. 493, pp. 39–44;
Mensdorff to Metternich, Sept. 11, 1866, *ibid.*, pp. 55–59; Gramont to La Valette,
Sept. 11, 1866, *ibid.*, No. 124.

[28] Menabrea's brief included in HHS, P.A. XI, Italien, Kreig und Freidausver-
handt, Sept. 14, 1866, Karton 157n.n.; unsigned letter possibly from Visconti-
Venosta to Nigra, Sept. 10, 1866, FAE, Autriche, Vol. 493, p. 45; Malaret to
La Valette, Sept. 12, 1866, FAE, Italie, Vol. 16, No. 109.

of Italy at its dissolution in 1815, she paid off those held by Austrian nationals but not those held by private investors in France.

Napoleon III instructed Gramont and Malaret to find an opportune time to have these claims inserted in the treaty. Specifically, he wanted to have the debt of 5,000,000 francs applicable to Venetia duly transferred to Italy, and if possible some recognition of the 7,500,000 francs due from Parma, Modena, and the Papal States. Finally, Gramont was to request some sort of protocol to reserve the rights of French private investors who held claims upon Austria in the above way.[29]

The French Empire had another, somewhat more subtle, interest in all this. Italy and France were at this very time in the midst of negotiations for the transfer of the Papal debt applicable to the lost states of Romagna, the Marches, and Umbria. According to a major provision of the September Convention, the Italian government was to assume the public debt of these provinces.[30] Since virtually all of the foreign debt of Pius IX was held in France, some 142,425,000 francs under care of the Rothschilds,[31] and since the Papal government in its reduced state was now incapable of paying this debt by itself, it was of the greatest interest to France to have the financial clause of the September Convention duly carried out. On the other hand, the Italian economy was at the time in critical condition; the budget had been out of balance even before the war.[32] The Italian treasury consequently would be in no position to bear the full weight of the Pontifical debt if another huge sum were added by the Venetian debt. Therefore, it was of equal interest to the French government, continually besieged by the Bourse in matters where the investments of Frenchmen were concerned, to see that Italy not be crippled by debts coming from the Venetian transfer.

[29] A letter to Malaret signed N. (I take this to mean "Napoleon III" from its recurrence elsewhere), Aug. 31, 1866, FAE, Italie, Vol. 15, pp. 404–407. For the history of this claim see Mensdorff to Metternich, Sept. 25, 1866, HHS, Karton 85; see also Gramont to La Valette, Sept. 15, 1866, FAE, Autriche, Vol. 493, No. 126.

[30] For the negotiations of the transfer of the Papal debt, see Malaret to Drouyn de Lhuys, Aug. 24, 1866 (tel), FAE, Italie, Vol. 15, p. 386; for a short summary of the negotiations, see OD, XII, 384, FAE, Italie, passim, May, 1866—December, 1866.

[31] Rondo E. Cameron, "Papal Finance and the Temporal Power, 1815–1871," Church History, Vol. XXVI (June, 1957), 134. See also his France and Economic Development, 433.

[32] Cochut, "La situation financière en Italie," 231–34.

FRENCH MEDIATION

After less than a week of negotiations at Vienna between the Austrian and Italian representatives, it seemed certain that the French Emperor would be called into the discussions. Caught in a deadlock, about September 11 both sides began to cast sidelong glances at France,[33] but it was the Italian cabinet that made the first formal request. They had already enlisted the help of their erstwhile ally, Prussia, for this particular stage in the negotiations, and on September 13 Nigra asked La Valette, the acting minister of foreign affairs, to lend support to the Prussian minister, Baron Karl von Werther, whom Bismarck dispatched to Vienna immediately.[34] Faced again with the threat of rupture with Prussia,[35] Austria too was forced to request Napoleon III's intervention. She asked him to support her figure on the debt, which she now reduced to about 60,000,000 florins (150,000,000 francs) for all three debts.[36]

Needless to say, the French cabinet could not work up sympathy for Austrian demands. La Valette and Gramont would have liked to see the Italian figure accepted then and there or have the question deferred to a special commission after the signing of the peace.[37] At any rate, La Valette decided to support the Italian cause with a view to getting the best possible terms for Italy in the most expeditious way possible. Since Austria would not reconsider Italy's figure, Gramont proposed on September 20 that Mensdorff accept the same conditional clauses as were inserted in the Treaty of Prague and the Treaty of Cession of Venetia so that the treaty could be signed immediately.[38]

After Austria refused to defer consideration of the debt question, Gramont invited Werther and Menabrea to his apartment in Vienna to work out an ad hoc compromise. All three agreed that the Monte Lombardo–Veneto and the debt of 1854 should be paid and that the pro rata sharing of Imperial debts contracted since 1859 be rejected

---

[33] Mensdorff to Metternich, Sept. 11, 1866, HHS, Karton 85, n.p; Nigra to La Valette, Sept. 12, 1866, *OD*, XII, 286–87.

[34] Nigra to La Valette, Sept. 13, 1866, FAE, Autriche, Vol. 493, pp. 72–75.

[35] Goltz to La Valette, Sept. 14, 1866, *ibid.*, 80–81.

[36] Mensdorff to Metternich, Sept. 18, 1866, HHS, Karton 85, n.n.; Metternich to La Valette, Sept. 19, 1866, *OD*, XII, 310.

[37] La Valette to Gramont, Sept. 14, 1866, *OD*, XII, 295.

[38] Gramont to La Valette, Sept. 20, 1866, FAE, Autriche, Vol. 493, No. 127.

on principle. If, therefore, Austria would waive this latter claim, perhaps Italy would meet Austria's figure of 39,000,000 florins as Venetia's part of the loan of 1854—a figure some 12,000,000 above the Italian calculation.[39] When this plan was presented at the peace conference, some progress was seen. Vienna was finally willing to drop the pro rata principle, but the Italian government would go no higher than 32,000,000 florins on the debt of 1854—a figure Wimpffen could not get his government to meet.

A few bold strokes then from the hand of the very able La Valette cut through the maze of proposition and counterproposition. He got permission from the Italian cabinet to advance the Italian figure as high as 36,000,000 florins. Then on September 22 he proposed to Mensdorff to split the difference, offering 35,000,000, a figure that included indemnification for nontransportable war matériel in Venetia.[40] After an anxious forty-eight hours during which the Austrian cabinet held a special meeting, Mensdorff wired Metternich to accept.[41] The French Emperor answered a last request to guarantee payment of the 35,000,000 florins, saying he would give efficacious moral support but no guarantee.[42]

The settlement of the debt question removed the last obstacle to the conclusion of the Treaty of Vienna between Austria and Italy, which was signed on October 3, 1866. General Menabrea more than once had introduced the question of the rectification of frontiers in Venetia, i.e., drawing an exact line along the Isonzo River and Lake Garda, and had prepared by much research to present the economic, political, and strategic arguments.[43] But neither Werther nor Gramont would support him in view of the pressure already being brought to bear on Austria in the debt question.[44] Italy had to accept as her frontier the then existing administrative confines of Venetia. As for the retrocession of Venetia to Italy, Austria left the transaction to France entirely. The treaty merely mentioned that the Emperor of

[39] *Ibid.*

[40] La Valette to Gramont, Sept. 23, 1866, *OD*, XII, 323–24; Visconti-Venosta to Nigra, Sept. 21, 1866 and Nigra to Visconti-Venosta, Sept. 21, 22, 23, 25, 1866, Ricasoli, *Lettere*, VIII, 201–208; Gramont to La Valette, Sept. 21, 1866, *OD*, XII, 318.

[41] Mensdorff to Metternich, Sept. 24, 1866, HHS, Karton 85, n.n.

[42] Napoleon to La Valette, Sept. 25, 1866, *OD*, XII, 326.

[43] Menabrea to Visconti-Venosta, Oct. 2, 1866, *Documenti presentati*, 817–25; Malaret to Drouyn de Lhuys, Aug. 28, 1866, FAE, Italie, Vol. 15, No. 105.

[44] Menabrea to Visconti-Venosta, Oct. 16, 1866, *Documenti presentati*, 845–62.

Austria consents to this reunion, and evacuation of territory was to
be carried out by special commissions. The rest of the rather lengthy
document concerns noncontroversial and administrative matters such
as transfer of railroads, return of the Venetian archives removed during the war, and future negotiations on a commercial treaty.[45] (See
Appendix D, p. 140, for text of treaty.)

To have Venetia without onerous conditions was a great relief to
the Italians. Boundary rectification and the Trentino were sacrificed to
a quick solution of the debt problem, which in light of Italy's perilous
economic condition was necessary. No brilliant victory, it was sufficient to soothe some of the recent irritation. When Menabrea, who
had handled the Italian cause with admirable realism, wrote Ricasoli
the day of the signing, he gave the French at least secondary credit.
"The prompt arrival of Signor Baron de Werther, Minister of Prussia,"
he wrote, "was efficacious enough to hasten the thing [the peace] and
I must say also that the ambassador of France helped wonderfully to
remove the difficulty." [46]

The French gained a little in their relations with Italy and much
with respect to the Bourse. First of all, Italy, one of the major fields of
the French investor, was not only saved from ruin but brought more
securely into financial bondage to France. The Emperor's government
could now with less scruple press upon Italy's assumption of the Pontifical debt—ultimately to amount to some 400,000,000 francs.[47] In addition, the Treaty between Austria and Italy stipulated that the 87,000,-
000 francs (35,000,000 florins) that Italy was to pay Austria for the
debt of 1854 were to be in drafts or treasury notes payable at Paris,
adding that much more to Italy's debt in France. Finally Gramont
was able to have two protocols added to the same treaty honoring the
two most important claims put forth by French financial interests.[48]
The first stipulated that Italy would assume the 5,000,000 franc Monte
Lombardo–Veneto debt and begin to pay the French government interest on it. By a second protocol a reluctant Austria finally agreed to
recognize the credits of private French investors due from the Austrian Empire for debts assumed but not liquidated in the Napoleonic

---

[45] Copy of the Treaty of Vienna, Oct. 3, 1866, can be found in *OD*, XII,
400–407. *OD*, however, omits the two protocols on French reserves. These can
be found in FAE, Autriche, Vol. 493, pp. 174–90. See Appendix D, *infra*.
[46] Menabrea to Ricasoli, Oct. 3, 1866, Ricasoli, *Lettere*, VIII, 250–51.
[47] Cameron, "French Foreign Investment, 1850–1880," 43.
[48] See *supra*, p. 115.

Kingdom of Italy.[49] The Treaty of Vienna between Austria and Italy was duly signed October 3, 1866.

DIFFICULTIES OVER THE TRANSFER

By an act of July 4, 1866, sealed and confirmed in a treaty on August 24, Austria had formally ceded Venetia to the Emperor of the French and, except for the evacuation of Austrian troops from the fortresses, would leave the matter there. Francis Joseph, though forced to consent to the "rejoining" of Venetia to the Kingdom of Italy in the Treaty of Prague (with Prussia),[50] withheld mention of such consent in the treaties with either France or Italy [51] and expressed indifference about what was done with Venetia after cession to France. It was therefore up to France and Italy to work out an agreeable mode of transferring Venetia to Italy. There were two elements in the problem: (1) to transfer in a proper manner the rights of the territory to Italy, and (2) to have the Quadrilateral and other fortresses (i.e., Pastrengo, valley of the Adige, Palmanova, and the city of Venice) [52] evacuated of Austrian troops and turned over to the Italian military.

The difficulty of carrying out these two seemingly simple steps brought into play a conflict between two fundamental concepts of the transaction. Napoleon III received Venetia by contract from another sovereign. He fully intended to turn it over to Italy, but he held to the position that the right of possession had to pass to Italy from his hands. He was unalterably opposed to direct cession from Austria, but

[49] Actually the latter question, that of credits on Austria, was to remain formally "reserved," that is, undecided but with the rights of the parties involved recognized, as was done in a convention of September 9, 1860, preliminary to the Treaty of Zurich. The protocols mentioned above do not appear in the version of the treaty given in *OD*, XII, 400–407, but appear in manuscript in both French and Austrian archives: FAE, Autriche, Vol. 493, p. 189; HHS, Italien, Krieg und Friedensvorhandl, Karton 157. They are also referred to in Moustier to Gramont, Oct. 19, 1866, FAE, Autriche, Vol. 493, No. 106. See Appendix D, *infra*, for text.

[50] Text of the Treaty of Prague, *OD*, XII, Appendix II, 395.

[51] Text of the Treaty of Cession of Venetia, *OD*, XII, Appendix II, 398–400. The French Foreign Office tried to have Austria include in the Treaty of Cession this same formula of consenting to the rejoining of Venetia to Italy. Austria insisted, however, that the transaction here be considered a "retrocession," i.e., avoiding acknowledgment of the principle of nationalities, and she withheld formal consent. Drouyn de Lhuys to Gramont, Aug. 16, 1866, *OD*, XII, 114–15; Gramont to Drouyn de Lhuys, Aug. 15, 1866, *OD*, XII, 112–14.

[52] Project of Special Convention drawn up by the Commission for evacuation and transfer of the fortresses, FAE, Venise, Vol. 27, pp. 401–406.

he did promise Italy during the recent armistice negotiations that transfer could be accomplished by a plebiscite and that it should be considered not a "retrocession" but a "rejoining," as in the case of Nice and Savoy.[53] Yet even here it would be he, Napoleon III, who would free the Venetian populations "to dispose of themselves." [54] The Italian cabinet, on the other hand, once its troops were in possession of seven-eighths of the territory of Venetia, considered that the territory had already come under the sovereignty of Victor Emmanuel II.[55] Indeed six out of the nine provinces were immediately placed under the royal administration after their "conquest" by Italian armies. Mantua and Verona, dominated by Austrian forces in the Quadrilateral and the city of Venice were the only areas not considered by the Italians under their sovereignty.[56] Thus the Italians ultimately denied the French Emperor's right to cede the six occupied provinces and therefore denied the need of any plebiscite in that area.[57] Ricasoli wanted all French mediation eliminated.[58] In other words, the Italians claimed Venetia by title of conquest—a title they believed to be confirmed by the Treaty of Prague.

It will be recalled that on the very day of the Treaty of Cession (August 24) Napoleon III gave General Le Boeuf instructions to carry out the double task involved in placing Venetia into Italian hands. These instructions directed Le Boeuf to receive the Lombardo-Venetian territory in the name of the Emperor [59] from an Austrian plenipotentiary and in the same way to take possession of the forts still in Austrian hands. Then Le Boeuf was to draw up proceedings of the transfer and give both the land and the fortresses into the hands of the local Venetian authorities. It was his primary political task, in

[53] Nigra to Visconti-Venosta, Aug. 4, 1866, Archivio Storico, Vol. 838, n.p.; note verbali, Nigra to Drouyn de Lhuys, July 30, 1866, Archivio Storico, Vol. 838; Compte-rendu by Prince Jerome, annexed to Nigra to Visconti-Venosta, Aug. 2, 1866, Archivio Storico, Vol. 838. Lombardy also passed through French hands in the Treaty of Zurich of 1859, but there was no plebiscite and it was considered a "retrocession." See text of Treaty of Turin, Mar. 24, 1866, Pierre Albin, Les grands traités politiques (Paris: Felix Alcan, 1923), 87–88.

[54] Nigra to Visconti-Venosta, Aug. 4, 1866, Archivio Storico, Vol. 838.

[55] Le Boeuf to Moustier, Oct. 19, 1866, FAE, Venise, Vol. 27, pp. 447–50.

[56] Le Boeuf to Napoleon III, Sept 15, 1866, OD, XII, 298–301.

[57] Ibid.

[58] Malaret to Drouyn de Lhuys, July 24, 1866, FAE, Italie, Vol. 15, No. 86.

[59] Venetia was still referred to legally as the Lombardo-Venetian Kingdom. Lombardy with exception of Peschiera and Mantua, was carved out of it in 1860 but the legal form of Lombardo-Venetian Kingdom was left intact. See text of Treaty of Zurich, Albin, Les grands traités, 64–72.

cooperation with Pilet, French consul at Venice, to create a legal depository for the rights being transferred by Napoleon III. Hence, immediately upon his arrival there on August 30, Le Boeuf set about creating a commission of Venetian citizens—not the Venetian municipal authorities as such—representing all the people of the territory. This commission, so he thought, could legally receive the rights of possession and then conduct a plebiscite to consult the will of the people. In this ingenious way Venetia would be "rendered back unto itself." [60] As for the fortresses, Le Boeuf could deliver them over to the local municipal authorities who would in turn summon in the Italian army.[61]

Up to the time of Le Boeuf's arrival the Italian cabinet, preoccupied with the debt question at Vienna, knew nothing about the above instructions. They had supposed that the Treaty of Prague, giving as it did Francis Joseph's consent to the annexation of Venetia to Italy, was sufficient; any intervention of a French commission in Venetia would be superfluous.[62] At least the Italians thought that once Le Boeuf had arrived he would limit his activities to those parts of Venetia not yet under Italian control. They assumed that the fortresses could pass directly into Italian hands and that Le Boeuf could be persuaded to play down as much as possible the idea of the plebiscite.[63] Before knowing just what Le Boeuf was about, Visconti-Venosta in early September began to instruct Nigra on handling the transfer. A simple declaration to the city of Venice that it was *sui juris* and a telegram to each of the fortresses that they might be turned over to the Italian army might be a direct and expeditious way of effecting the transfer. Visconti-Venosta wanted his sovereign to be able to march triumphantly into Venice after the peace and not be forced to wait for his rights at the gates of the city.[64]

[60] Drouyn de Lhuys to Le Boeuf, Aug. 23, 1866, FAE, Venise, Vol. 27, pp. 356–58; instructions and powers for General Le Boeuf from Napoleon, annexed to above dispatch. The correspondence to and from Le Boeuf relative to his mission in Venice is found at the end of Vol. 27, FAE, Venise, "The Mission of General Le Boeuf." See also Drouyn de Lhuys to Pilet, Aug. 23, 1866, FAE, Venise, Vol. 27, No. 5.

[61] Drouyn de Lhuys to Pilet, Aug. 23, 1866, FAE, Venise, Vol. 27, No. 5.

[62] Malaret to La Valette, Sept. 3, 1866, FAE, Italie, Vol. 14, No. 106; Nigra to Ricasoli, Aug. 23, 1866, Ricasoli, *Lettere*, VIII, 121–25.

[63] Visconti-Venosta to Nigra, Sept. 4, 1866, Ricasoli, *Lettere*, VIII, 158–59; Malaret to Drouyn de Lhuys, Sept. 7, 1866, *OD*, XII, 269–70.

[64] Nigra to La Valette, Sept. 5, 1866, FAE, Autriche, Vol. 493, pp. 19–21; Visconti-Venosta to Nigra, Sept. 7, 1866, *OD*, XII, 269–70.

When Nigra conveyed these ideas to La Valette in Paris, however, he found that the French Foreign Ministry was quite serious about the ritual Le Boeuf had set up. In every case France was to be the intermediary. The declaration of transfer was to be made not directly to municipal authorities in Venice but to a commission or to the assembled syndics of the principal cities of Venetia.[65] Malaret assured Visconti-Venosta that this was nothing more than the required procedure for putting the Venetian provinces "in full possession of themselves" and the rendering of homage to a principle both states cherished.[66] Ricasoli sensed that there lurked in the idea of this commission a dangerous principle,[67] but apparently other members of his cabinet disagreed; by September 10 Victor Emmanuel accepted a compromise worked out between Nigra and La Valette. As to the evacuation of the fortresses, that would proceed according to Le Boeuf's instructions, but an Italian commissioner could be appointed and would be put in touch with the Austrians as need required. The French representative could make declaration of transfer to a commission at Venice as arranged. But the commission would have only three members: one, the syndic of the city of Venice, the other two representing the rest of Venetia. Le Boeuf's mission would end there since the commission in cooperation with municipal authorities would conduct the plebiscite.[68] This seemed to camouflage French mediation sufficiently to satisfy Visconti-Venosta. Nigra helped sell this compromise to his chief by suggesting that once the Italian army had the Quadrilateral it could control the whole situation.[69]

Ricasoli did not like this compromise. He was under great pressure from the Party of Action, which he leaned on for support and which was even now causing great agitation in the city of Venice against French mediation.[70] Ricasoli, therefore, began a campaign to convince Victor Emmanuel II that the commission must be formed

---

[65] Nigra to Visconti-Venosta, Sept. 7, 1866, Ricasoli, *Lettere,* VIII, 173.

[66] Malaret to La Valette, Sept. 9, 1866, FAE, Italie, Vol. 16, No. 108.

[67] Visconti-Venosta to Nigra, Sept. 8, 1866, Ricasoli, *Lettere,* VIII, 176.

[68] The substance of the note Nigra drew up in concert with La Valette is dated Sept. 7, 1866, FAE, Italie, Vol. 16, p. 39, and annexed to La Valette to Malaret, Sept. 12, 1866, *ibid.,* No. 67. It was approved by the Italian cabinet on September 12, 1866, La Valette to Malaret, Sept. 10, with postscripts dated Sept. 12, 1866, *ibid.,* No. 57. This note is explained and supplemented by information given in Nigra to Visconti-Venosta, Sept. 10, 1866, Ricasoli, *Lettere,* VIII, 181–82; Visconti-Venosta to Nigra, Sept. 11, 1866, *ibid.,* 186.

[69] Nigra to Visconti-Venosta, Sept. 11, 1866, Ricasoli, *Lettere,* VIII, 187.

[70] Le Boeuf to Napoleon III, Sept. 15, 1866, *OD,* XII, 298–301.

and the plebiscite conducted in such a way as to preserve the principle of the King's already existing sovereignty by conquest. He had other objections to the plebiscite: consulting the population might be a dangerous precedent when it came to taking the city of Rome; also such voting seemed to jeopardize the monarchical principle.[71] Victor Emmanuel II finally gave way and sent Count Ottaviano Vimercati as an envoy to Venice to tell Le Boeuf that he understood the plebiscite would be limited to the territory not yet in Italian hands and that the fortresses were to be handed over without a French intermediary.[72] The press and contrived public agitation in Venetia, setting to work immediately, attacked the idea of the commission so effectively that Le Boeuf could not find Venetian citizens brave enough to affix their names to the document being drawn up for the cession.[73]

On September 26 Le Boeuf received new instructions that eliminated the interval of French possession of the fortresses and allowed the Italian representative now in Venice to have a say in selecting the commission. But Le Boeuf's instructions did not reduce the principal irritant—the idea of the plebiscite.[74] It was then that Ricasoli and Victor Emmanuel II decided to press their advantage and take matters into their own hands. Around October 1, contrary to the advice of their ambassador in Paris, they prepared a decree on the King's authority to convoke the Venetian communes to a plebiscite immediately after the signing of the peace in Vienna.[75] On October 7, four days after the Treaty of Vienna, this decree was issued in Venetia designating this plebiscite for October 21 and stating its mode of execution.[76] It was clear now that the Italian cabinet was going to conduct their own plebiscite and frustrate all further French intervention in Venetia. On October 10 another decree came forth from Victor Emmanuel II extending the Constitution he had already established for the six conquered provinces to the remaining sections such as Mantua, Verona, and Venice proper.[77] Five days later plans were so definite that the

[71] Ricasoli sent Nigra a long letter airing his views on the plebiscite (Sept. 15, 1866, Ricasoli, *Lettere*, VIII, 189–93).

[72] Pilet to La Valette, Sept. 17, 1866, FAE, Venise, Vol. 27, pp. 249–53.

[73] Le Boeuf to Napoleon III, Oct. 26, 1866, *ibid.*, 457–61.

[74] Drouyn de Lhuys to Le Boeuf, Sept. 26, 1866, *ibid.*, 417–18; see also Nigra to Visconti-Venosta, Oct. 6, 1866, Ricasoli, *Lettere*, VIII, 206–207.

[75] Nigra to Visconti-Venosta, Oct. 1, 1866, Ricasoli, *Lettere*, VIII, 201.

[76] Pilet to La Valette, Oct. 17, 1866, FAE, Venise, Vol. 27, p. 282; and Oct. 18, 1866, *ibid.*, 283.

[77] Decree of Oct. 10, 1866, annexed to Pilet to Moustier, Oct. 24, 1866, *ibid.*, 299–306; see also Pilet to Moustier, Oct. 23, 1866, *ibid.*, 295–97.

Italian government published in the *Gazzetta ufficiale* the formula upon which the Venetian people were to vote.[78] Moreover, at this same time the Italian troops, ignoring the French, attempted to gain entrance into the fortresses before evacuation by Austria. Le Boeuf, on October 9, then at Peschiera and Legnano transferring the fortresses, refused the Italian soldiers admittance, but Napoleon III told him by telegraph to let them in.[79] The General obeyed and continued on his rounds of the fortresses accompanied by General Karl Moering, the Austrian commissioner, evacuating Mantua on October 11, Palmanova on October 13, Verona on October 15 and 16.[80] He returned to Venice on October 17.

In Venice Le Boeuf reached the peak of exasperation. There he realized that the Italian government, its troops already in control of the fortresses, had set a date for a plebiscite and were going to run it themselves, completely circumventing the French. He wired the Emperor at Biarritz and the foreign minister at Paris for information, but neither knew anything of Victor Emmanuel's decrees.[81] The General thereon took the initiative. After making a threatening protest to General Thaon di Revel, the Italian commissioner,[82] he issued orders for Captain de Surville of the French frigate *La Provence* (which had lain at anchor off the Venetian harbor since its mission in July). He directed that if the complaint were not answered satisfactorily, de Surville should run up the French flag over one of the forts outside the city of Venice and bring a sufficient number of marines ashore to occupy the city. The purpose of this action, as he later declared to the Emperor, was to enforce his threat of holding up the retrocession of Venetia. The Emperor, however, wanted no trouble. Again he refused to support his aide de camp and ordered him on October 18, the evening before the ceremony of transfer, not to protest further but to proceed to the ceremony as scheduled.[83]

Meanwhile, di Revel had referred Le Boeuf's threat to Florence

[78] "We declare ourselves united to the Kingdom of Italy, under the constitutional, monarchical government of King Victor Emmanuel II and his successors."— *Gazzetta ufficiale*, annexed to Malaret to La Valette, Oct. 15, 1866, FAE, Italie, Vol. 16, No. 127.

[79] Moustier to Le Boeuf, Oct. 10, 1866 (tel), FAE, Venise, Vol. 27, p. 435.

[80] Le Boeuf to Napoleon III, Oct. 26, 1866, *ibid.*, 457–61.

[81] Napoleon III to Minister of Foreign Affairs, Oct. 18, 1866, *ibid.*, 284; Minister of Foreign Affairs to Pilet, Oct. 18, 1866, *ibid.*, 286.

[82] Di Revel to Ricasoli, Oct. 17, 1866, Ricasoli, *Lettere*, VIII, 295; see also Ollivier, *L'empire libéral*, VIII, 616.

[83] Le Boeuf to Moustier, Oct. 19, 1866, FAE, Venise, Vol. 27, pp. 447–50.

where a hasty solution to the conflict of views in the cabinet was reached. Ricasoli told Visconti-Venosta there was no official decree but only an announcement of the plebiscite. This answer, relayed to di Revel, was dressed up with explanations about the embarrassment of the Italian government in face of the impatience and protestations of the Liberal party.[84] Le Boeuf accepted this explanation from di Revel and withdrew his threat.[85] It is probable that the directive from the Emperor had arrived first and motivated his acceptance, since the Italian reply was contrary to the facts and could not have satisfied the conscientious Le Boeuf.

Obediently the General re-established relations with di Revel and planned the ceremony of retrocession. Le Boeuf wanted to have the protocol performed with dignity in the Ducal Palace following a public procession in front of the Venetian civic guard in Piazza di San Marco. But di Revel warned him that the people might shower him with insults if he appeared thus in public. Perhaps losing confidence in his support from Paris, the General yielded, repairing on the morning of October 19 to a nearby inn with only the Austrian plenipotentiary, General Karl Moering, and the three-membered Venetian Commission present.[86] After receiving the cession from Moering, Le Boeuf made the following declaration to the three Venetians: "We declare Venetia remitted to itself so that the populations, masters of their destinies, can express freely by universal suffrage their wishes on the annexation of Venetia to the realm of Italy." [87]

Count Michiel, Podestà of Venice, responded for the Venetian committee by acknowledging—not receiving—the declaration and was further mandated to carry out the plebiscite in cooperation with the Venetian municipalities. Besides giving a brief address expressing homage to the principle of popular sovereignty, according to the in-

[84] Ricasoli to Visconti-Venosta, Oct. 17, 1866, Ricasoli, Lettere, VIII, 295–96; di Revel to Le Boeuf, Oct. 17, 1866, FAE, Venise, Vol. 27, pp. 442–43; Le Boeuf to Moustier, Oct. 17, 1866, FAE, Venise, Vol. 27, p. 439; Ollivier, L'empire libéral, VIII, 617.

[85] Le Boeuf to di Revel, Oct. 18, 1866, FAE, Venise, Vol. 27, p. 457; Le Boeuf to Napoleon III, Oct. 26, 1866, ibid., 457–61.

[86] The commission had been selected by October 4; Count Michiel, Podestà of Venice, was president; Chevalier Beppa, Podestà of Verona, and Emi Kelder of Mantua were the other two members. Le Boeuf to La Valette, Oct. 4, 1866, ibid., 427–28. The fact that these men were selected from the provinces still under Austrian control signifies another concession to the Italian point of view on the cession.

[87] Procès-Verbal de la remise de la Vénétie, ibid., 293–94.

structions Le Boeuf was supposed to declare *urbi et orbi* the Emperor's policy in his whole intervention in Venetia by a solemn reading of His Majesty's letter to Victor Emmanuel II of August 11, 1866. Although Le Boeuf read his prepared speech, it is unlikely that in the confines of the local tavern he took the trouble to read Napoleon's letter. The letter, now resting silent in the archives, shows how the French Emperor still hoped the world would view his actions over the past three months:

> Your majesty knows that I have accepted the offer of Venetia in order to preserve it from all devastation and prevent a useless spilling of blood. My purpose always has been to give it [Venetia] to itself so that Italy might be free from the Alps to the Adriatic. . . . Your majesty recognizes that in these circumstances the action of France is again exercised in favor of humanity and the independence of peoples.[88]

It is reminiscent of Napoleon III's address at the outset of the War of 1859, in which he said:

> I do not want conquest. . . . The purpose of this war is to render Italy to herself. . . . We are not going to foment disorder in Italy or disturb the power of the Holy Father but remove her [Italy] from all foreign pressures.[89]

The scene now enacted was sad fulfillment of the Emperor's words. General Altmann, who had been the Austrian governor of the province of Venetia the morning of October 20, after signing the proceedings of the transfer immediately went to the pier where an Austrian corvette awaited him. A large crowd of people at the pier parted respectfully to let him pass, and as he embarked the few hisses from Garibaldians were drowned out by a peal of genuine applause. Immediately the Italian flag with the cross of Savoy was hoisted in Piazza di San Marco and the city resounded with "vivas" of all sorts but yet, the French consul standing by heard no word of gratitude, as he

---

[88] Project of Allocution annexed to Minister of Foreign Affairs to Le Boeuf, Oct. 1, 1866, *ibid.*, 423. The allocution given in the instructions of Oct. 1, 1866, is the same as in the Procès-Verbal of the retrocession. The letter, however, does not appear with the instructions or the allocution.

[89] Ernest Lavisse, *Histoire de France contemporaine (depuis la Révolution jusqu'à la paix de 1918)*, VII, 109.

said, "for the benefactors to whom Italy and Venice owe their independence." [90] At noon the Italian troops were admitted to the city of Venice at the western entrance, and they proceeded by boat to the Piazza di San Marco. As they made their way up the Grand Canal, they passed the consulate general of France. Someone at the head of the flotilla began to cry "Vive la France," but his timid cries were soon lost in the furious bursts coming from the boats along the quay, "Viva Italia," "Viva l'Unità d'Italia." [91] Pilet, the consul general, blamed the anti-French atmosphere upon Garibaldians and other agitators directed from Florence, but the significance of the events remains. Especially revealing is a letter that di Revel wrote Ricasoli the day of these demonstrations. He boasted that the action of Le Boeuf and Pilet in the transfer of Venice had been completely stifled ("... a été étouffée entre deux portes").[92]

The plebiscite was held on the day following the entry of troops into Venice, October 21, and results were announced on the twenty-seventh—641,758, yes; 70, no—and a salvo of artillery from the turrets of the Italian warship in the harbor announced the annexation of Venetia to Italy.[93] On November 7, Victor Emmanuel II made an elaborate, solemn entry into Venice in the garlanded royal gondola, a ceremony planned by Ricasoli.[94] Ricasoli had planned for the King a triumphal march beginning, as he said, at Turin, "the cornerstone, . . . the home of the idea of independence, where your August Dynasty and Your Majesty have initiated and pursued the great work which has its fulfillment in Venice." [95] No position of honor was accorded the French diplomatic corps present for the King's entry. They listened to the Te Deum rather perfunctorily and left.[96] Total acknowledgment of the French role was a one-line notice in the October 19 edition of the *Gazzetta ufficiale:* "This morning in a room of the Hotel of Europe the cession of Venetia was carried out." [97]

[90] Pilet to Moustier, Oct. 20, 1866, FAE, Venise, Vol. 27, No. 70.
[91] *Ibid.*
[92] Di Revel to Ricasoli, Oct. 20, 1866, Ricasoli, *Lettere*, VIII, 298–99.
[93] Pilet to Moustier, Oct. 27, 1866, FAE, Venise, Vol. 27, No. 74. The total population of Venetia (1871) including Mantua was close to three million. *Enciclopedia italiana*, XXXV, 81.
[94] Pilet to Moustier, Nov. 7, 1866, FAE, Venise, Vol. 27, No. 77; Ricasoli to Victor Emmanuel II, Oct. 13, 1866, Ricasoli, *Lettere*, VIII, 278–79.
[95] Ricasoli to Victor Emmanuel II, Oct. 13, 1866, Ricasoli, *Lettere*, VIII, 278–79.
[96] Pilet to Moustier, Nov. 6, 1866, FAE, Venise, Vol. 27, No. 76.
[97] Ollivier, *L'empire libéral*, VIII, 618; see also di Revel to Ricasoli, Oct. 8, 1866, Ricasoli, *Lettere*, VIII, 269–70.

Aftermath: Back to the Roman Question

There was here an element of aggression which the French met for the first time in their relations with Italy. Goaded by the enraged Ricasoli, Victor Emmanuel II for the first time seemed to be treating Napoleon III as a fellow sovereign, not a patron, and he had won his first little victory. The Italian King had virtually forced capitulation in the very principle of French mediation. For one thing the celebrated commission as finally formed did not represent the whole of Venetia but only the provinces of Mantua, Verona, and Venice—areas not under Italian military occupation. The ceremony was not an effective transfer of the rights of possession but a mere declaration certified by three Venetian citizens. Finally the plebiscite came directly from Victor Emmanuel II. Thus the principle of French intervention was, if not compromised, at least obscured. Di Revel boasted a victory and Ricasoli was elated,[98] whereas the loyal Le Boeuf returned from his mission to a cool reception from his Emperor.[99]

Obviously the Italian government preferred to have Venetia by title of conquest rather than by annexation. Why did the Emperor refuse this? At least three reasons are clear. First, he had obtained Venetia for Italy in the only way it could have been disengaged from Austria, i.e., under contract between sovereigns, not under the principle of nationalities; he could not nullify this act. Secondly, Venetia, from having been the principal French prize to be won from the German conflict, was now going to be the only prize. Napoleon III had to have a tangible victory to show those who reproached him for allowing a war that was disadvantageous to France. Finally, the Emperor was not happy about aiding and abetting the power of such a party as was behind Ricasoli with its avowed radical tendencies and poorly veiled intentions to have *Roma Capitale* despite the September Convention. This latter reason becomes ever more convincing in light of what followed and brings this study full circle back to the Roman question.

Immediately after the annexation, elections were held in Venetia

---

[98] Ricasoli to Buoncompagni, Oct. 28, 1866, Ricasoli, *Lettere*, VIII, 314–17.

[99] Ollivier, *L'empire libéral*, VIII, 619. Ollivier says that later, when Napoleon learned more facts about Le Boeuf's mission, he apologized and gave the General the ribbon of the Legion of Honor.

to select deputies from the nine new provinces to the Camera in Florence. These elections were dominated by the strenuous efforts of the Party of Action to second the efforts of the government's party in obtaining votes. The objectives of this coalition were revealed in the anticlerical demagoguery that marked the campaign. Opposition candidates were condemned as "devotees of the Papacy and slaves of France." The leaders from Florence preached at banquets and patriotic meetings that Rome should now be taken and the Pope expelled.[100] It was significant that after all this, four-fifths of the deputies elected in Venetia were from Ricasoli's Moderate Liberal Party.[101]

In Florence Malaret noted that there was much less hope for a solution of the Roman question now than at the time of the September Convention.[102] This was because the government and Camera at Florence seemed neither willing nor able to hold the radical elements in check. A great francophobia had built up in previous months, with the consequent weakening of conservative forces. It was a different government from that to which Napoleon III promised Venetia in September, 1864. The misunderstanding engendered by the Venetian question, as it turned out, instead of closing the road to Rome had opened it.

This was precisely the fear of the clerical party in Rome when it learned Austria had given up Venetia. They predicted in July that the cession of Venetia would remove the last rampart that separated the Eternal City from the Italy of Victor Emmanuel II.[103] With the withdrawal of the French troops imminent, Pius IX sorely regretted the removal of Austria from Italy and saw the cession of Venetia as "Rome's sentence of death and . . . the end of the temporal power." [104] Nor was the weakening of defenses considered to be only the removal of Austria. Monsignor Berardi, acting Papal secretary of state, declared in August, to Sartiges, French chargé d'affaires at Rome, that after seeing Italy shake loose from its dependence on France in the question of Venetia, no one any longer believed "in the moral barriers between Italy and Rome." [105]

---

[100] Pilet to Moustier, Dec. 8, 1866, FAE, Venise, Vol. 27, No. 84; and Nov. 26, 1866, *ibid.*, No. 82.
[101] Malaret to Moustier, Nov. 29, 1866, FAE, Italie, Vol. 16, No. 138.
[102] Malaret to Moustier, Oct. 24, 1866, *OD*, XII, 10–16.
[103] Sartiges to Drouyn de Lhuys, July 7, 1866, *OD*, X, 361.
[104] Hübner to Mensdorff, July 31, 1866, HHS, Karton 208, No. 29B and C.
[105] Sartiges to Drouyn de Lhuys, Aug. 7, 1866, *OD*, XII, 3–8.

It was doubtless with such things in mind that after the cession of Venetia Napoleon III became intransigent on the Roman question. He was not able to stipulate with Italy, as his June 12 treaty with Austria had required, the maintenance of the temporal sovereignty of the Pope or the integrity of his present territory. But he made it as clear to Victor Emmanuel as he could that he would be unmovable on the Roman question. During a visit of Count Arese, the Italian special envoy, he made the following statement: "Now there remains the affair of Rome, but let it be known that as for me I will yield nothing and that I am completely decided on executing the September Convention to support the temporal power of the Pope by every means possible." [106] At the same time he commissioned his own special envoy, General Emile Fleury, to Florence to begin the new phase of negotiating the transfer of the Pontifical debt. Besides settling this clause of the September Convention, Fleury was to declare unequivocally that the Emperor could not abandon the Holy Father and that if there were revolution in Rome he would not hesitate to return the troops he was evacuating from the Eternal City. [107]

By early December, 1866, the debt question had been settled, and before the year was out all the French occupation forces had left Rome. The Italian government exiled Garibaldi to Caprera, supposedly out of harm's way, and Franco-Italian relations assumed a formal cordiality. But soon Italian actionism was to break out again, with serious consequences for all concerned. It would take a further study to demonstrate the relation of Garibaldi's second attack on Rome (and the return of French troops in force to defend the Holy City) to the previous entanglements over Venetia. But even a brief survey of the French documents shows that when Napoleon III sent his troops to stop Garibaldi at Mentana on November 3, 1867, he knew that he was encountering forces that had the encouragement and assistance of the Italian government. [108] This was the first armed conflict between France and the Kingdom of Italy and was doubtless the eruption of pressures built up since July, 1866.

[106] Quoted in Grabinski, *Un ami de Napoléon III*, 231–32.
[107] Comte Emile Félix Fleury, *Souvenirs*, II, 307, 312–14; Marraro, "American Documents on Italy's Annexation of Venetia (1866)," 365.
[108] Villestruex to Moustier, Oct. 21 and 22, 1867, *OD*, XIX, 53f, 60.

Conclusions

NAPOLEON III's decisions and actions were now bold and adventuresome, now shifting and vacillating as he pursued his Venetian prize before, during, and after the Austro-Prussian War. We have attempted to describe his actions and policies as they bore upon Franco-Italian relations, but in doing so we have also tried to illuminate the role of Napoleon in the German conflict itself and bring out of obscurity the mode and manner by which Venetia was finally annexed to Italy.

The conclusions herewith presented have been supported in varying degree. No further analysis is needed to state that desires to obtain Venetia, for whatever reason, were a major preoccupation of French diplomacy between 1864 and 1866. Certainly Venetia was in the background of the September Convention. Whether or not Italy and France made a formal agreement on Venetia while settling the Roman question in September, 1864, is still open to question, but Napoleon III and General La Marmora did have talks about Venetia, and it is probable that the French Emperor made a personal commitment. Venetia was prominent enough to be called the determining element in the policy of Napoleon III with respect to the German conflict. Also, redeeming Venetia amid the complications and tensions of this war made the Emperor's behavior little short of compulsive, affording Italy sufficiently serious embarrassment to destroy hopes of a profitable friendship with that country. Paradoxically, the Venetian venture prepared the way for ultimate failure of French policy in Italy. The following remarks in refocusing the study bear on the latter proposition.

The coming of the German crisis shortly after the September Convention provided an opportunity, enthusiastically received within Italy, to win Venetia in a war on Prussia's side against Austria. Only the president of the cabinet, General La Marmora, held out against this tide of feeling, awaiting some diplomatic magic from the Tuileries, or elsewhere, to obtain Venetia without becoming involved with Prussia. When, however, La Marmora was virtually forced into accepting Bismarck's overtures and looked to Napoleon III for help and guidance, the Emperor faced the first great dilemma in his Venetian policy. He was not yet ready to define his own role in the German crisis because of the pacifistic temper in France and lack of suitable arrangements with Bismarck; neither was he willing to expose Italy to a war against Austria without being at her side.

Through a combination of the Emperor's indecision and the machinations of Constantino Nigra, the Italian ambassador to France, General La Marmora was given to believe in late March, 1866, that Napoleon III gave his approval to an alliance with Prussia. The Emperor did indeed approve a noncommittal pact of friendship with Prussia, but when in the course of the negotiations this pact developed into a defensive and offensive alliance he withdrew all effective support. He gave his unofficial blessing to an alliance he could not now prevent and then attempted to call a general congress either as a needed moratorium or as a genuine effort to prevent an immediate outbreak of war. The congress never met, bringing the Emperor face to face with what he thought to be the strong possibility of an Austrian victory and the exposure of the Italian peninsula to the return in full force of the Hapsburgs. He therefore returned to negotiating with Austria and succeeded in driving a hard bargain with Francis Joseph. The Austrian Emperor guaranteed him Venetia (for retrocession to Italy) and a voice in any further postwar changes in Italy as the price of French neutrality whatever the outcome of the impending war. The secret of this convention was not well kept, and it was only a matter of days before the swift march of Prussian arms made obvious the miscalculations of almost every chancellery in Europe.

The Battle of Sadowa frightened Napoleon III and Francis Joseph into a premature execution of their agreement, and Austria ceded Venetia to France before the war had ended. Austria then withdrew her forces from Venetia to assist in the defense of Vienna. Ignoring the transfer of Venetia to France, the Italian forces proceeded to invade and occupy most of Venetia including the Trentino region. Napoleon III, reluctant to exert force in any sector, turned his attention toward stopping the war and met with surprising success, first in Germany and ultimately in Italy. He secured a cease fire in Germany but was at first stymied in Italy by the occupation of the Trentino. The latter problem was solved to the great embarrassment of the Italian government, for the Austrians, having signed with Bismarck at Nicholsburg, wheeled about to confront the outnumbered Italian contingent in the Trentino. Italy signed the armistice, in the words of Baron Ricasoli, "a miserable peace," and for the moment gave up claims to the Trentino but ever maintained that she had won Venetia by her own force of arms.

The affair over the Trentino was the dénouement of Franco-Italian relations in the 1860's. It revealed to the Italians that in the Emperor's policy Venetia transcended the general objectives of what they thought to be his Italian policy. It reflected on the situation of July 4, when he sacrificed the integrity of Italy by accepting Venetia as a way of checking the Prussian advance on the heart of the Austrian Empire. Subsequent French mediation, which allowed the Italian military forces to be outflanked and outnumbered, was dictated by the need to end the war at any cost. By this series of events Italian leadership was compromised beyond recovery. It not only embittered the liberal forces but also discredited the conservatives, including La Marmora, who having lost his position as president of the cabinet was subsequently replaced as military chief of staff. Those controlling French foreign policy could not afford to appreciate the feelings of the Italian government and people, for settling the peace at Nicholsburg was now too important. As a final humiliation Italy was deprived of her position of independent participant because Austria refused to negotiate a tripartite treaty at Prague, necessitating a separate and unique type of treaty through French mediation.

The settlement between Italy and Austria had to be concluded in the atmosphere of tension set up by the Trentino affair. Two delicate questions had to be settled: the apportionment of the public debt of Venetia to the Kingdom of Italy and the devising and execution of formalities by which Venetia would pass into Italian hands. The first of these was settled ably by the acting minister of foreign affairs, La Valette, who supported the Italian side of the controversy and brought both sides together in acceptable compromise. The second was in effect left to be settled between Italy and France, for Austria refused to acknowledge any direct transfer to Italy. On August 24 she had confirmed the July 4 cession of Venetia to France and did not care what was done with Venetia thereafter.

In this final stage, the transfer of Venetia from France to Italy, further alienation between the two countries was inevitable. Italian forces had overrun seven-eighths of Venetia except for the redoubt of the Quadrilateral, and by virtue of this the Italian government claimed the territory by conquest. They tried to reinforce this argument by claiming the "italianità" of Venetia. Denying French sovereignty over anything but the area of the fortresses, they wanted to circumvent as much as possible the procedures Napoleon III had set up for the transfer. These called for a commission of Venetian citizens to be constituted as the legal recipient of the rights that passed from the Emperor's hands. Thus Venetia would be "rendered up unto itself" and then would express by plebiscite its will to join the Kingdom of Italy. Ricasoli, continually urging that such procedures including the plebiscite violated the sovereignty of Italy, first wanted the plebiscite to be confined to the Quadrilateral area. When this was not found acceptable, the Italian government announced that they themselves were convoking the Venetian communes for a plebiscite, and shortly thereafter Italian troops demanded entrance to the fortresses. Napoleon III, trying to recover his energies at Biarritz, despaired of dealing with these complexities and finally ordered his special representative, General Le Boeuf, to cease his protest against the plebiscite and admit the Italian troops into the fortresses. The grandiose scheme of freeing Italy "from the Alps to the Adriatic" was concluded quietly, obscurely in a Venetian hotel room where General Le Boeuf declared Venetia "remitted to itself." What the Italian populace observed was the virtually unanimous "yes" of the subsequent plebiscite and the solemn triumphal tour of Victor Emmanuel II in garlanded gondola down the Grand Canal.

The mode of annexation of Venetia was almost entirely obscured because of the conflicting contentions of title. Despite his deference to the "principle of nationalities," what Napoleon III ultimately relied upon was the right of one Imperial house to bestow a possession upon another whether the recipient be another Imperial house or a suppliant people seeking independence. Thus older imperial conceptions of sovereignty held sway over the rights of nationalities. On the other hand, the right of conquest by itself did not justify Italian sovereignty, for the failure to overcome the Quadrilateral fortresses left the conquest incomplete, and besides, the territory occupied was technically

French. Ultimately, possession became the law, for without force Napoleon III could not have carried out his proposed formalities.

The whole episode involving the annexation of Venetia spelled doom for the September Convention. It threw the balance of power within Italy to the liberal side and gave Ricasoli's faction a convenient way of reopening the road to Rome by seeming unable to contain the radical elements. Observing this caused Napoleon III to stiffen his resolve on the September Convention, producing an impasse that would lead almost exactly a year later to the battle of Mentana on November 3, 1867. The *ultima ratio regum* was thus invoked by Napoleon III against France's newest antagonist.

It is tempting to construct a relationship between these events of the summer of 1866 and the repeated expressions of the Emperor's willingness, under certain conditions, to see the present state of the Kingdom of Italy undone and replaced by a confederative system. It would seem that, though Napoleon's expressions in this vein were usually made in the presence of Austrian officials, his references to a confederation must have represented policies he was prepared to implement if the price were right.

When the German crisis intervened and an Austrian victory was anticipated, Napoleon III had to consider some adjustment in Italy if Venetia were to be added to the Kingdom of Italy. It is evident throughout his Italian policy that what he desired primarily was the independence of Italy from Austrian control but that he had misgivings about the consolidation of the whole peninsula into one state. As an alternative, he probably envisioned a northern Italian kingdom forming a kind of territorial arch from the French border to the Adriatic buttressed by Genoa and the Romagna. This would at once exclude Austria, guarantee the temporal sovereignty of the Pope, and allow for the heterogeneity and semiautonomous development of the peoples to the south. This territorial arch, as it were, could be a free, loyal Kingdom of Italy, politically, culturally, and economically harmonious with France and setting the symmetry of the whole peninsula. He would not have gone to war for this vision, but it may have been one way to utilize an Austrian victory. This vision can be read into the secret convention with Austria of June 12, 1866; it may even explain Villafranca. It is consistent with the sentiments of an ancient *carbonaro* and worthy of the Bonapartist heritage. The vision was exploded on the field of Sadowa and the rest was improvisation, carried out with skill and courage, but without enough flexibility or finesse to retain Italy as an ally. His desire even after the peace was signed to put Venetia in its proper place with his own hands may have been the fragment of a dream that had vanished.

Finally, the effects of Napoleon III's Venetian policy on the origin, course, and settlement of the famous Austro-Prussian War itself cannot be overlooked. His unwitting delivery of La Marmora into Bismarck's hands in the treaty of April, 1866, doubtless gave the Prussian Minister the one advantage he needed in fomenting a crisis with Austria. The French Emperor's Venetian policy, on the other hand, was partly responsible for the shortness of the war. By entrusting Venetia to Louis Napoleon, Austria was able to deploy forces from Italy to Germany and prevent any real offensive by Prussia. Napoleon III's mediation achieved the cease fire in Germany on June 20 and, in effect, brought about the armistice in Italy on August 11. He continued in the role of mediator until the peace between Italy and Austria was signed on October 3, 1866, and contributed significantly to the success of that settlement. His effect on the war naturally would have been greater had he not been forced to work within the narrow framework of neutrality imposed upon him by French public opinion and by financial and business interests. The June 12 convention with Austria was a brilliant stroke, but it could never have been effective unless the Emperor had been free to intervene when necessary. Sadowa was disastrous only because France did not intervene against Prussia—a failure patriotic Frenchmen regret as they do the failure of 1936.

APPENDIXES

Appendix A

SECRET CONVENTION BETWEEN FRANCE AND AUSTRIA *

Article I: If war breaks out in Germany, the French government undertakes with regard to the Austrian government to keep absolute neutrality and to make every effort to obtain the same attitude on the part of Italy.

Article II: If the outcome of war favors Austria in Germany, she undertakes to cede Venetia to the French government at the time of concluding the peace. If the outcome of war favors her in Italy, she undertakes not to change in this kingdom the status quo ante bellum, unless by agreement with France.

Article III: If the events of war change the relationships of the German powers among themselves, the Austrian government undertakes to reach agreement with the French government before sanctioning such changes of territory as would be of a nature to disturb the European equilibrium.

Vienna
June 12, 1866

Additional Note to the Secret Convention Between France and Austria

In retroceding Venetia to Italy, the French government shall stipulate the maintenance of the temporal sovereignty of the Pope and the inviolability of the territory at present under his authority, without prejudice to the reserves made in favor of the rights of the Holy See.

The French government shall stipulate likewise the recognition of the inviolability of the new frontiers of Austria on the Italian side.

The French government shall stipulate likewise an indemnity in favor of Austria for the fortresses of Venetia and the expenses which the Austrian government must incur to assure the security of her new frontiers. It is also agreed that the state of which Venetia will become part must also take upon itself a part of the public debt of the Empire of Austria, prorated according to the population of that province.

The French government shall stipulate some restrictive clauses relative to the port of Venice in order that that port not be disposed in such a way as to menace the coast and the navy of Austria.

If in consequence of events of the war or otherwise, spontaneous movements are produced in Italy of such a nature to undo Italian unity, the French government shall not intervene either by force or otherwise to re-establish it, and shall leave the population masters of their movements [*maîtresses de leurs mouvements*]. It is understood that there will be no foreign intervention either.

If the outcome of war favors Austria in Germany, the French government shall

* Translated from the French text, which is to be found in *OD,* X, 258–60.

137

sanction all increase of territory conquered by Austria provided that it not be of such a nature as to trouble the equilibrium of Europe by establishing an Austrian hegemony which will unite Germany under one authority.

In case of changes of territory the Austrian government, reserving the rights of sovereignty of the Princes of the Imperial House who have been dispossessed, shall be able to ask compensations for them anywhere except in Italy.

Explanatory Note

To avoid all misunderstanding and prevent all divergence of opinion on the true sense of Article II of the Secret Convention between France and Austria, signed on the 12th of this month at Vienna, it has been specified that the first paragraph relative to the cession of Venetia should have its full effect even though Austria, favored by the outcome of war in Germany, should also be successful in Italy and that, likewise, the second paragraph relative to the maintenance of the status quo ante bellum in Italy should have its full effect in any case, even if Austria be favored by the outcome of war in Italy.

It has also been specified that the words "at the time of concluding the peace" signifies the peace in Germany and Italy.

Vienna
June 15 [,1866]

Appendix B

EXPLANATORY NOTE ON THE TRENTINO

Only since the Napoleonic wars was the Trentino a part of the area generally called the Tyrol. Prior to that time and back through the Middle Ages it had been an ecclesiastical principality adhering to the Holy Roman Empire. During the wars against the first Napoleon, the Emperor of Austria (and Holy Roman Emperor) holding the title of Count of Tyrol, joined Trentino and Tyrol into one principality in order to form a bulwark against the Corsican invader. After the collapse of the Holy Roman Empire in 1806 this whole unit was transferred to the short-lived kingdom of Italy by Napoleon Bonaparte. It was subsequently, after Napoleon's defeat, conferred in toto upon the Austrian Monarchy.

Geographically the area of Trent is separated from the Tyrol proper by two high spurs which come off the principal chain of the Alps across which the Adige River has outlet. The Tyrol, the Italians claimed, was one of the most ancient principalities of Austria, while the Trentino was the most recent.[*] The people of the Trentino—300,000 strong—were Italian speaking and drew their resources from Italy, being shut off from the north by mountain barriers. The Trentino was of great strategic importance because from it Austria could threaten not only Venetia but Lombardy, and from Lake Garda there is easy access to Milan.[†]

[*] Menabrea to Visconti-Venosta, Vienna, October 2, 1866, *Documenti presentati*, 817–25.

[†] Note verbali, Nigra to Drouyn de Lhuys, July 20, 1866, Archivio Storico, Vol. 838.

Appendix C

TREATY OF CESSION OF VENETIA TO FRANCE *
[Signed at Vienna August 24, 1866]

Their Majesties the Emperor of the French and the Emperor of Austria, King of Hungary and Bohemia, desiring to settle the cession of Venetia previously agreed upon between their Majesties have named as their Plenipotentiaries for this purpose the following:

[There follows the enumeration of the
Plenipotentiaries with their titles.]

The aforesaid, having presented their credentials found in due form and proper order, have agreed to the following articles:

Article I: H. M. the Emperor of Austria cedes the Lombardo-Venetian Kingdom to H. M. the Emperor of the French, who accepts it.

Article II: The debts which will be recognized as assignable to the Lombardo-Venetian Kingdom, conformably to the precedents of the Treaty of Zurich, remain attached to the possession of the ceded territory.

They shall be determined more precisely by a special commission designated for this purpose by H. M., the Emperor of the French and H. M. the Emperor of Austria.

Article III: A special arrangement, whose terms shall be agreed upon between the French and Austrian commissioners, authorized for this purpose, shall determine, conformably to military usage and with due respect to Austria's honor, the mode and conditions of evacuating the Austrian fortresses.

The Austrian garrisons shall be able to take with them all transportable equipment.

A further arrangement shall be concluded by special commissioners relative to nontransportable equipment.

Article IV: The actual delivery of possession of the Lombardo-Venetian Kingdom by the Austrian commissioners to the French commissioners shall take place after the conclusion of the arrangement concerning the evacuation of troops and after the peace will have been signed between their Majesties, the Emperor Francis Joseph and King Victor-Emmanuel.

Article V: The commanding officers of the Austrian troops shall act in concert for the carrying out of these provisions with the military authorities who will be assigned to them by the French commissioners, reserving recourse, in case of dispute, to the aforementioned commissioners of H. M. the Emperor of the French.

Article VI: The present convention shall be ratified and ratifications shall be exchanged at Vienna as soon as possible.

In testimony whereof, etc.

Drawn up in duplicate at Vienna, August 24, 1866.

[Signed:]   GRAMONT
              MENSDORFF-POUILLY

* Translated from the French text which is to be found in *OD*, XII, 398–400.

Appendix D

TREATY OF PEACE BETWEEN AUSTRIA AND ITALY °
[Signed at Vienna, October 3, 1866]

In the name of the most holy and indivisible Trinity!

H. M. the Emperor of Austria and H. M. the King of Italy, having resolved to establish a sincere and lasting peace between their respective states; H. M. the Emperor of Austria having ceded the Lombard-Venetian Kingdom to H. M. the Emperor of the French; H. M. the Emperor of the French, on his part, having declared himself ready to recognize the reunion of said kingdom to the states of H. M. the King of Italy on the condition that its population, having been duly consulted, should consent;

H. M. the Emperor of Austria and H. M. the King of Italy have named as their ministers plenipotentiary the following:

[There follows an enumeration of
the ministers and their titles]

The aforesaid, having exchanged their credentials found in due form and proper order, have agreed to the following articles:

Article I: There shall be, from the date of the exchange of ratifications of the treaty, peace and friendship between H. M. the Emperor of Austria and H. M. the King of Italy, their heirs and successors, and their respective states and subjects, forever.

Article II: Austrian and Italian prisoners of war shall be returned immediately by both sides.

Article III: H. M. the Emperor of Austria consents to the reunion of the Lombardo-Venetian Kingdom with the Kingdom of Italy.

Article IV: The frontier of the territory ceded is determined by the present administrative boundaries of the Lombardo-Venetian Kingdom.

A military commission set up by the two contracting powers shall be charged with the task of surveying the boundary line with the least possible delay.

Article V: Evacuation of the ceded territory whose limits are determined by the preceding article shall begin immediately after the signing of this treaty of peace and shall be completed with the least possible delay, in conformity with the arrangements agreed upon among the special commissioners appointed for this purpose.

Article VI: The Italian government shall take under its charge:

1) The share in the Monte Lombardo-Veneto which has been held by Austria in virtue of the convention concluded in Milan in 1860 for the purpose of carrying out the seventh article of the Treaty of Zurich;

2) The debts and obligations incurred by the Monte Lombardo-Veneto bank from June 4, 1859, to the date of the conclusion of the present treaty;

3) A sum of thirty-five million florins, Austrian exchange, payable in cash, in payment of the remainder of the loan of 1854 allocated to Venetia and in payment for nontransportable war matériel.

The mode of payment of this sum of thirty-five million florins, Austrian exchange,

---

° Translated from the French text which is to be found in *OD*, XII, 400–407.

redeemable in cash, shall be determined in conformity with the precedent of the Treaty of Zurich, in an additional article.

Article VII: A commission composed of delegates from Austria, France and Italy shall proceed to carry out the various settlements enumerated in the first two paragraphs of the preceding article, taking account of amortizations previously affected and of the capital goods, of whatever kind, which constitute the basis of amortization. The commission shall proceed to arrange a definitive settling of accounts between the contracting parties and shall fix both the time and the manner of execution of the liquidation of the Monte Lombardo-Veneto.

Article VIII: The government of H. M. the King of Italy shall succeed to the rights and obligations pursuant to contracts duly entered into by the Austrian administration concerning matters of public interest which particularly pertain to the ceded territory.

Article IX: The Austrian government shall retain responsibility for refunding all sums entrusted to the public treasury of Austria by the inhabitants of the ceded territory, by its communes, public establishments and religious corporations under the following headings: securities, deposits, and consignments.

Likewise, the Austrian subjects, communes, public establishments and religious corporations which will have entrusted sums under the headings of securities, deposits and consignments to the treasury of the ceded territory shall be strictly reimbursed by the Italian government.

Article X: The government of H. M. the King of Italy recognizes and confirms the grants of land and other privileges accorded to railways in the ceded territory by the Austrian government in all their stipulations and for the whole of their duration, particularly those concessions granted as a result of contracts entered into on March 14, 1856, April 8, 1857, and September 23, 1858.

Likewise the Italian government recognizes and confirms the stipulations of the convention between the Austrian administration and the Administrative Council of the State Railways Organization of South Lombardy and Central Italy entered into on November 20, 1861, as well as the convention between the Imperial Ministry of Finance and Commerce and the South Austrian Railway Organization entered into on February 27, 1866.

From the date on which formal ratification of the present treaty takes place, the Italian government shall take upon itself all the rights and obligations implied in the previously cited conventions which up to now have belonged to the Austrian government in regard to the railway lines which have been constructed in the ceded territory.

As a consequence, the right of escheat which the Austrian government has over these railways is transferred to the Italian government.

The payments which remain to be made on the sum owed to the state by the grantees in virtue of the contract of March 14, 1856, equal to the construction expenses of the aforementioned railways, shall be paid in full to the Austrian treasury.

The debts owing to construction contractors and purveyors as well as indemnities for land appropriations, going back to the period when the railways in question were administered in the state's account, of which the state shall not yet have acquitted itself shall be paid by the Austrian government and by the grantees in the name of the Austrian government, in as far as they are responsible in virtue of the contract settlement.

Article XI: It is understood that the recovery of credits resulting from paragraphs 12, 13, 14, 15, and 16 of the contract of March 14, 1856, will give

Austria neither right of control nor right of surveillance over the construction and future development of railways in the ceded territory.

The Italian government, on its part, takes it upon itself to make available all information which should be required in this respect by the Austrian government.

Article XII: In order to extend to the Venetian railways the prescriptions of article 15 of the convention of February 27, 1866, the contracting powers take it upon themselves to enter, as soon as is feasible, upon a convention in conjunction with the South Austrian Railway Organization to provide for the administrative and economic separation of the Austrian and Venetian railways.

In virtue of the convention of February 27, 1866, the indemnity which the state must pay the South Austrian Railway Organization shall be calculated on the basis of the gross revenue of all the Austrian and Venetian lines taken together which constitute the system of South Austrian railways actually ceded to the Organization. It is understood that the Italian government will take upon itself a share of this indemnity proportional to the railway lines of the ceded territory, and it is further understood that the total gross product of the Austrian and Venetian lines handed over to said Organization will continue to be taken as the basis for the evaluation of this indemnity.

Article XIII: The governments of Austria and Italy, desirous of expanding the relationships between their two countries, pledge themselves to facilitate communications and to promote the establishment of new railway lines for the purpose of joining the Austrian and Italian systems.

Furthermore, the government of His Imperial and Apostolic Majesty promises to hasten, as much as possible, the completion of the Brenner Line, destined to unite the Adige valley with the Inn valley.

Article XIV: The inhabitants or natives of the ceded territory shall enjoy for the period of one year, commencing on the date of ratification, the right to export, exempt from customs and duties, their personal property and to take up residence with their families in the dominions of His Imperial and Apostolic Majesty, on the condition that they previously enter a declaration of their status before competent authorities. In this case they shall maintain their status as Austrian subjects. They shall be free to retain possession of their real properties which remain within the boundaries of the ceded territory.

The same right and privilege is accorded reciprocally to persons now residing in the territories of H. M. the Emperor of Austria who are natives of the ceded territory.

Those persons who will take advantage of these privileges shall not be personally molested as a result of their choice. Further, they shall receive protection from any possible damage which might, as a result of their choice, be inflicted on their real properties in the respective states.

The period of one year is extended to a period of two years for those natives of the ceded territory who at the time of the ratification of the present treaty will find themselves outside the territories of the Austrian monarchy.

Their declaration may be entered at the nearest mission of the Austrian government or before the governmental authorities of any province of the monarchy.

Article XV: Subjects of the Lombardo-Venetian Kingdom engaged in the Austrian army shall be immediately discharged from military service and sent home.

It is understood that those in the army who will pronounce a desire to remain in the service of His Imperial and Apostolic Majesty will be free to do so and that these will in no way be troubled because of this fact neither in their person nor in their possessions.

The same guarantees are assured to native civil employees of the Lombardo-Venetian Kingdom who will pronounce their intention of remaining in the service of Austria.

The native civil employees of the Lombardo-Venetian Kingdom shall have a choice either of remaining in the service of Austria or of entering the Italian administration, in which latter case the government of His Majesty the King of Italy shall arrange either to place them in positions analogous to those which they held or to grant them pensions, the sum of which shall be determined in accordance with the laws and regulations presently in force in Austria.

It is understood that the employees referred to in the preceding statement will be subject to the laws and disciplinary regulations of the Italian administration.

Article XVI: The officers of Italian origin who find themselves presently in the service of Austria shall have the choice either of remaining in the service of His Imperial and Apostolic Majesty or of entering the army of H. M. the King of Italy with the same rank that they held in the Austrian army provided that they propose their request in a period of six months following the exchange of ratifications of the present treaty.

Article XVII: Regularly discharged pensions, be they civil or military, which formed part of the payroll of the public treasury of the Lombardo-Venetian Kingdom, shall continue to remain payable to their titularies or, in their place, to their widows and children and shall be remitted, in the future, by the government of H. M. the King of Italy.

This stipulation is extended to the pensionaries, whether they be civil or military, and also to their widows and children without distinction as regards national origin, who will hold residence in the ceded territory, and whose stipends, paid since 1814 by the then existing government of the provinces of Lombardy and Venetia, were subsequently charged to the Austrian treasury.

Article XVIII: The archives of the ceded territories containing the property titles, administrative and judicial documents, and also the political and historical documents of the former Republic of Venice, shall be remitted in their entirety to the commissioners who will be designated for this purpose; and to those commissioners shall be submitted all works of art or of scientific interest which are especially attributed to the ceded territory.

Reciprocally, any property titles, administrative or judicial documents concerning the Austrian territories, which can be found in the archives of the ceded territory, shall be remitted in their entirety to the commissioners of His Imperial and Apostolic Majesty.

The governments of Austria and Italy, at the request of high-ranking administrative authorities, agree to hand over to each other all documents and information relative to whatever affairs concern at the same time the ceded territory and the countries contiguous to it.

They shall also allow authentic copies to be made of political and historical documents which will be of interest to the territories remaining in the possession of the other contracting power and which in the interest of learning cannot be removed from the archives to which they belong.

Article XIX: The high contracting powers agree reciprocally to accord the greatest possible convenience regarding customs procedures to the neighboring inhabitants of the two countries for the cultivation of their lands and the managing of their industries.

Article XX: The treaties and conventions which were confirmed by article 17 of the peace treaty signed at Zurich November 10, 1859, shall remain in force provisionally for a year and shall be extended to all the territories of the Kingdom of Italy.

If these treaties and conventions are not disclaimed by three months before the expiration of a year from the time of the exchange of ratifications, they will remain in force and in this manner continue from year to year.

In any case, the two high contracting parties agree at the end of a year to submit these treaties and conventions to a general revision in order to bring about with common accord the modifications which will be judged in conformity with the interest of the two countries.

Article XXI: The two high contracting powers agree to enter into negotiations as soon as possible in order to conclude a treaty of commerce and navigation on the broadest possible basis to facilitate, reciprocally, transactions between the two countries.

In the meanwhile, for the period determined in the previous article, the treaty of commerce and navigation of October 18, 1851, will remain in force and will apply to all the territory of the Kingdom of Italy.

Article XXII: The princes and princesses of the Austrian royal line, as well as the princesses who have entered the royal family by way of marriage, shall return, retaining claim to their titles, into full and complete possession of their private property, both landed and personal, which they shall be able to use and dispose of without being vexed in any manner in the exercise of their rights.

All the rights of the state are at all times reserved, as well as rights of private persons when asserted by the proper legal means.

Article XXIII: In order to strive with all their efforts towards a pacification of spirits, H. M. the Emperor of Austria and H. M. the King of Italy declare and promise that in their respective countries there shall be a full and complete amnesty for all individuals liable to discredit as a result of political events which have transpired on the peninsula up until this day. Consequently, no individual of whatever class or condition, may be pursued, troubled, or disquieted either in his person, in his possessions, or in the exercise of his rights by reason of his conduct or his political opinions.

Article XXIV: The present treaty shall be ratified and the ratifications shall be exchanged in Vienna in a period of two weeks or sooner if possible.

In testimony whereof, etc.

Drawn up at Vienna, the third of the month of October in the year of grace 1866.

Signed: WIMPFFEN
MENABREA

Additional Article

The government of H. M. the King of Italy pledges itself to the government of His Imperial and Apostolic Majesty to make payment of thirty-five million florins, Austrian exchange, equivalent to eighty-seven million, five hundred thousand francs as stipulated by article VI of the present treaty in the manner and at the times determined as follows:

Seven million florins shall be paid in cash through seven cheques or treasury drafts on demand of the Austrian government, each for one million florins, redeemable at Paris, at one of the leading banking houses or at a reliable credit establishment, without interest, at the expiration of the third month from the date of the signing of the present treaty. These cheques or treasury drafts shall be remitted to the minister plenipotentiary of His Imperial and Apostolic Majesty at the time of the exchange of ratifications.

The payment of the remaining twenty-eight million florins, readily transferable, shall take place at Vienna through ten cheques or treasury drafts payable to the Austrian government, redeemable at Paris, at the rate of two million, eight hundred thousand florins each, Austrian exchange, falling due every second month in succession. These ten cheques or treasury drafts shall likewise be remitted to the minister plenipotentiary of His Imperial and Apostolic Majesty at the time of the exchange of ratifications.

The first of these cheques or treasury drafts shall mature two months after the payment has been made on the cheques or treasury drafts for seven million florins stipulated above.

The interest for that period and for the following periods shall be calculated at 5 percent from the first day of the month following the exchange of ratifications of the present treaty.

The payment of interest shall be made in Paris at the date of maturity of each cheque or treasury draft.

The present additional article shall have the same force and validity as if it had been inserted word for word in today's treaty.

[Signed:]   Wimpffen
Menabrea

Protocols *

Among the debts consolidated under the Monte de Venise [sic] and which H. M. the King of Italy undertakes conformably to the Treaty of October 3, 1866, there is a sum of five million francs (two million florins) representing a title of the French government.

It remains understood that the Italian government will continue to turn over the interest on this sum to the French government following the mode of payment observed hithertofore by the Austrian government.

In testimony whereof, etc.

At the time of the signing the official document of the peace treaty the Plenipotentiaries have agreed that the question relative to the administration, liquidation and inscription of the former Lombardo-Venetian debt, which were the object of the declaration annexed to the convention signed at Milan September 9, 1860, will remain reserved and will be regulated in every respect with full consideration to those whose claims are involved.

In testimony whereof, etc.

[Signed:]   Wimpffen
Menabrea

The Two Protocols Appended to the Treaty
of Vienna, October 3, 1866 †

Parmi les dettes inscrites au Monte de Venise et que le Gouvernement de Sa Majesté le Roi d'Italie prend à sa charge conformément à l'article VI du traité du 3 octobre 1866 se trouve une somme de cinq millions de francs (2 millions de florins) représentant une créance du Gouvernement français.

Il demeure entendu que le Gouvernement italien continuera à verser les intérêts de cette somme entre les mains du Gouvernement français, suivant le mode de paiement observé jusqu'ici par le Gouvernement autrichien.

* Translated from copies contained in FAE, Autriche, Vol. 493, p. 189. These protocols are not contained in OD. As far as I know the protocols have not heretofore been published. Consequently, there follows the original French version.

† FAE, Autriche, Vol. 493, p. 189.

En foi de quoi les Plénipotentiares ont signé le présent Protocole et y ont opposé le sceau de leurs armes.

Au moment de signer l'instrument du traité de paix les Plénipotentiares sont convenus que les questions relatives à l'administration, la liquidation et l'inscription de l'ancienne dette Lombardo-Venitienne qui on été l'objet de la déclaration annexée à la convention signée a Milan le 9 septembre 1860, resteront réservées et seront reglées sous tous les rapports entre qui le droit.

En foi de quoi...

Bibliography

MANUSCRIPT COLLECTIONS

France

Archives du ministère de la guerre, Vincennes.

Archives Historiques: Italie, 1862–67, Mission du Colonel Schmitz; Autriche, 1866–67, Mission du Colonel Merlin.

Archives du ministère de la Marine, Paris.

Archives centrales de la Marine. Mouvements de la flotte, 1866.

Archives du ministère des affaires étrangères, Quai d'Orsay, Paris.

Correspondance politique: reports from and instructions to French Ambassadors. Pieces are numbered within each volume. Consulted were Italie, 1863–66, Vols. 6–16; Autriche, 1865–66, Vols. 487–93; Prusse, 1866, Vol. 355.

Correspondance consulaire: reports from and instructions to French Consuls, classified according to country and consular post. Consulted were Italie, Milan, 1865, Vol. 4; Autriche, Venise, 1864–66, Vols. 25–27.

Mémoires et documents: special collections of correspondence in which pertinent material is found under Italie, No. 37, and Autriche, No. 67.

Papiers de Rouher: special collection of the correspondence and private papers of Eugène Rouher, Minister of State. Material on Venetia is found in Section I, Allemagne (1862–68), and Section II, Italie (1830–67).

Archives nationales, Paris.

Correspondance privée: especially the private papers of the duc de Gramont, French Ambassador in Vienna, preserved on microfilm; pertinent sections are Bobines, 52, 53, 67–70.

Papiers des Tuileries: letters between Napoleon III and Prince Jerome Napoleon, carton 174.

Austria

Haus Hof und Staatsarchiv, Vienna.

Politisches Archiv: reports from and instructions to Austrian ambassadors. Pieces are numbered and classified in "Kartons" according to country, and within the "Karton" according to Berichte, Weisungen, und Varia. Consulted were P.A. IX, Frankreich, Kartons 78–85; P.A. IX, Italien, Kartons 207–208, both covering the years 1864–66. Under separate classifications are Protokolle, No. 11, 1864–66; Parlaments-papiere, 1855–92; Friedensverhandel, 1864–66.

Italy

Archivio del ministero degli affari esteri, Piazza dei Crociferi, Rome.

Archivio Storico: reports from and instructions to Italian ambassadors. Consulted were Rapporti della legazione a Parigi, 1864–66, Vols. 833–38; Istruzione alla legazione a Parigi, 1865–66, Vols. 452–53. Although above volume numbers were used in references in this work, reader is cautioned that the numbering system is being changed.

Great Britain

British Public Record Office, London.

Foreign Office: reports from British ambassadors and consuls. Consulted were Domestic and Various from Italy, July–December, 1864, FO 45, Vol. 67; from Rome, July–December, 1864, FO 43, Vol. 91B; from Turin, September–November, 1864, FO 45, Vol. 59; from France, August–November, 1864, FO 27, Vols. 1533–35; special collection of reports of the ambassador to Vienna entitled "Bloomfield Papers," FO 356, 1864–65, Vols. 20–21.

BIBLIOGRAPHIES

Droz, Jacques, Genêt, Lucien, and Vidalenc, Jean. *"Clio": Introduction aux études historiques,* Vol. I. *L'époque contemporaine, Part I, 1815–1871.* Paris: Presses Universitaires de France, 1953.

France, Centre d'information de la recherche d'histoire de France. *Bulletin* (1953—— by year).

France, Centre nationale de la recherche scientifique. *Bibliographie annuelle de l'histoire de France, du 5 siècle à 1939.* Paris: Editions du C.N.R.S., 1955—— by year.

Rota, Ettore. *Questioni di storia del Risorgimento e dell' Unità d'Italia.* Milan: Carlo Marzorati, 1951.

Schnerb, Robert. "Napoleon III and the Second Empire," *Journal of Modern History,* Vol. VIII (1936), 338–55.

Société d'histoire moderne, Paris. *Répertoire méthodique de l'histoire moderne et contemporaine de la France.* Paris: G. Bellais, 1898–1913.

Société française de bibliographie. *Répertoire bibliographique de l'histoire de France.* Paris: A. Picard, 1923—— by year.

PUBLISHED SOURCE MATERIAL

Bloomfield, Georgiana. *Reminiscences of Court and Diplomatic Life.* 2 vols. London: K. Paul, 1883.

Bortolotti, Sandro. *La guerra del 1866.* Milan: Istituto per gli studi di politica internazionale, 1941.

Castellani, Carlo. *La Marmora e Ricasoli nel 1866 con documenti.* Rome: G. Bertero e.c., 1903.

Chiala, Luigi. *Ancora un po' più di luce sugli eventi politici e militari dell'* *anno 1866.* Florence: G. Barbèra, 1902.

Cochin, Augustin. "Lettres à ses amis 1866–68," *Revue Hebdomadaire,* Vol. IV (1926), 472–88.

Drouyn de Lhuys, Edouard. *Documents pour l'histoire contemporaine.* Paris: M. P. Pradier, 1871.

Fleury, Emile Felix. *Souvenirs.* 2 vols. Paris: Plon, 1897–98.

France, Archives diplomatiques. *Recueil de diplomatie et d'histoire.* Paris: Amyot (by year).

France, Ministère des affaires étrangères. *Origines diplomatiques de la* *guerre, 1870–1871.* 20 vols. Paris: Imprimerie Nationale, 1910–32.

Germany, Historische Reichskommission. *Die auswärtige Politik Preussens,* *1855–1870.* 10 vols. Oldenburg: G. Stalling, 1932–39.

Govone, Giuseppe. *Mémoires.* Edited by U. Govone. Paris: A. Fontemoine, 1905.

Govone, Uberto. *Il Generale Giuseppe Govone, frammenti di memorie.* Turin: F. Casanova, 1902.

Hauterive, Ernest d'. *Napoléon III et le prince Napoléon; correspondance* *inédite.* Paris: Calmann-Levy, 1925.

Italy, Ministero degli affari esteri. *Documenti diplomatici e negoziati com-* *merciali, 1866. Documenti diplomatici presentati al Parlamento, dal* *Ministero degli affari esteri il 21 dicembre 1866.* Libri verdi italiani No. 9. (Documents on the Venetian Question from Jan. 11, 1866, to Oct. 1866). Florence: Eridi Botta, 1866.

Loftus, Augustus. *The Diplomatic Reminiscences of Lord Augustus Loftus* *1862–79.* 2 vols. London: Cassell, 1894.

La Marmora, Alfonso. *Les secrets d'état dans le gouvernement constitu-* *tionnel.* Translated from Italian by M. M. Marcel. Paris: J. Dumaine, 1877.

————. *Un peu plus de lumière sur les événements politiques et militaires* *de 1866.* Translated from the Italian by Niox et Descoubes. 4th ed. Paris: J. Dumaine, 1874.

Marraro, Howard R. "American Documents on Italy's Annexation of Venetia (1866)," *Journal of Central European Affairs,* Vol. VI (January, 1946), 354–77.

————. "Unpublished American Documents on the Naval Battle of Lissa (1866)," *Journal of Modern History,* Vol. XIV (September, 1942), 342–56.

Merimée, P. *Lettres à M. Panizzi.* 2 vols. Paris: Levy, 1881.

Metternich, Pauline Clémentine. *Eclairs du passé 1859–1870.* Paris: Plon, 1935.

Minghetti, Marco. *Carteggio tra Marco Minghetti e Giuseppe Pasolini.* 4 vols. Turin: Fratelli Bocca, 1924.

Oncken, Herman. *Die Rheinpolitik Kaiser Napoleons III von 1863 bis 1870* *und der Ursprung des Krieges von 1870–71.* 3 vols. Stuttgart: Deutsche Verlagsanhalt, 1926.

Passamonti, E. "Constantino Nigra ed Alfonso La Marmora dal 1862–1866," *Risorgimento italiano,* Vol. XXII (1929), 323–469.

Ricasoli, Bettino. *Lettere e documenti.* Edited by Tabarrini and Gotti. 9 vols. Florence: Successori le Monier, 1893.

Srbik, Heinrich von. *Quellen zur deutschen Politik Oesterreichs von 1859 bis 1871.* 5 vols. Oldenburg: G. Stalling, 1934–38.

Steefel, Lawrence D. "A Letter of Francis Joseph" (to Beust July 9, 1866, on the urgent necessity of French intervention), *Journal of Modern History,* Vol. II (1930), 70–71.

Revel, Genova Thaon di. *La cessione del Veneto. Ricordi di un commissario regio militare.* Milan: Fratelli Dumolard, 1890.

Victor Emmanuel II. *Vénétie.* Paris: no publisher, 1866.

Wellesley, Henry R. C. (Lord Cowley). *The Paris Embassy During the Second Empire: Selections from the Papers of Lord Cowley, 1852– 1867.* Edited by F. A. Wellesley. London: Butterworth, 1928.

BOOKS

Barbier, Jean Baptiste. *Outrances sur le Second Empire.* Paris: Librairie Française, 1956.

Bardoux, Jacques. *Quand Bismarck dominait l'Europe (1863–1892).* Paris: Hachette, 1953.

Beyens, Napoléon. *Le Second Empire vu par un diplomate belge.* 2 vols. Bruges: Desclée, de Brouwer et cie., 1924–26.

Bonghi, Ruggiero. *L'alleanza prussiana e l'acquisto della Venezia.* Florence: Le Monnier, 1870.

———. "La Marmora," *Nuova Antologia,* Vol. XXIV (1873); Vol. XXV (1874).

Cameron, Rondo E. *France and the Economic Development of Europe, 1800–1914.* Princeton: Princeton University Press, 1961.

Case, Lynn M. *Franco-Italian Relations, 1860–1865.* Philadelphia: University of Pennsylvania Press, 1932.

———. *French Opinion on War and Diplomacy During the Second Empire.* Philadelphia: University of Pennsylvania Press, 1954.

Cataluccio, Francesco. *La politica estera di E. Visconti-Venosta.* Florence: Marzocco, 1940.

Charles-Roux, François. *Alexandre II, Gortchakoff et Napoléon III.* Paris: Plon, 1913.

Chiala, Luigi. *Le général La Marmora et l'alliance prussienne.* Paris: Dumaine, 1868.

Clark, Chester W. *Franz-Joseph and Bismarck: The Diplomacy of Austria Before the War of 1866.* Cambridge: Harvard University Press, 1934.

Corti, Egon C. *The Reign of the House of Rothschild.* Translated from German by Brian and Beatrix Lunn. New York: Cosmopolitan Book Co., 1928.

Craig, Gordon. *The Battle of Königgrätz, 1866.* Philadelphia: Lippincott, 1964.

Diamilla-Müller, Demetrio E. (ed.). *Politica segreta italiana, 1863–1870.* Rome: E. Loescher e.co., 1897.

Farat, Honoré. *Persigny, un Ministre de Napoléon III, 1808–1872.* Paris: Hachette, 1957.

Fletcher, Willard A. *The Mission of Vincent Benedetti to Berlin, 1864–1870* (The Hague: Martinue Nijhoff, 1965).

Friedjung, Heinrich. *Der Kampf um die Vorherrschaft im Deutschland, 1859 bis 1866.* 2 vols. Stuttgart: Cotta, 1898.

————. *The Struggle for Supremacy in Germany, 1859–1866.* Translated by A. J. P. Taylor and W. L. McElwee. London: Macmillan, 1935.

Grabinski, Joseph. *Un ami de Napoléon III, le comte Arese et la politique italienne sous le Second Empire.* Paris: Bahl, 1897.

Gramont, Antoine A. duc de. *L'Allemagne nouvelle, 1863–67.* Paris: E. Dentu, 1878.

Grunwald, C. de. *Le duc de Gramont, gentilhomme et diplomate.* Paris: Hachette, 1950.

Hallberg, Charles W. *Franz-Josef and Napoleon III, 1852–1864.* New York: Bookman Associates, 1955.

Halperin, S. William. *Diplomat Under Stress: Visconti-Venosta and the Crisis of July 1870.* Chicago: University of Chicago Press, 1963.

Hansen, Jules. *À travers la diplomatie, 1864–1867.* Paris: E. Dentu, 1875.

Harcourt, Bernard d'. *Les quatre ministères de M. Drouyn de Lhuys.* Paris: Plon, 1882.

King, Bolton. *History of Italian Unity 1814–1871.* 2 vols. London: Nesbet and Co., 1912.

Kulessa, Adolf. *Die Kongressidee Napoleons III im mai 1866.* Giessen: University of Giessen Press, 1927.

Lavisse, Ernest. *Histoire de France contemporaine (depuis la Révolution jusqu'à la paix de 1918).* Vol. VII. Paris: Hachette, 1921.

Lemoyne, Jules V. *Campagne de 1866 en Italie. La bataille de Custozza.* Paris: Berger-Levrault, 1875.

Mack Smith, Denis. *Italy, A Modern History.* Ann Arbor: University of Michigan Press, 1959.

Massari, Giuseppe. *Il Generale Alfonso La Marmora.* Florence: Barbèra, 1880.

Maurain, Jean. *La politique ecclésiastique du second empire de 1852–1869.* Paris: Felix Alcan, 1930.

Mori, Renato. *La questione romana, 1861–1865.* Florence: le Monnier, 1963.

Mosse, Werner E. *The European Powers and the German Question, 1848–1871.* Cambridge: Cambridge University Press, 1958.

Ollivier, Emile. *L'empire libéral.* 18 vols. Paris: Garnier Frères, 1903.

Osti, Anselmo. *Rapporti fra Vittorio Emmanuele II e Giuseppe Mazzini.* ("Circolo di Cultura et di Educazione," No. 3) Rome: Arti Grafici S. Barbara, 1950.

Pottinger, E. Ann. *Napoleon III and the German Crisis, 1865–1866.* Cambridge: Harvard University Press, 1966.

Ramsay, Anna Augusta. *Idealism and Foreign Policy.* London: John Murray, 1925.

Riker, Thaddeus W. *The Making of Roumania: A Study of an International Problem, 1856–1866.* London: Oxford University Press, 1931.

Rothan, Gustave. *La politique française en 1866.* Paris: Levy, 1879.

———. *Souvenirs diplomatiques. L'affaire du Luxembourg, le prélude de la guerre de 1870.* Paris: Levy, 1884.

Salmon, Henry. *L'ambassade de Richard de Metternich à Paris.* Paris: Firmier, Didot et cie., 1931.

Silva, Pietro. *Italia e la guerra del 1866.* 2nd ed. Milano: Rana and Co., 1915.

Schnerb, Robert. *Rouher et le Second Empire.* Paris: Colin, 1949.

Steefel, Lawrence D. *The Schleswig-Holstein Question.* Cambridge: Harvard University Press, 1932.

Taylor, A. J. P. *The Struggle for Mastery in Europe, 1848–1918.* Oxford: Oxford University Press, 1954.

Vecchiato, Lanfranco, *Constantino Nigra, diplomatico, erudito, poeta.* Verona: Nova Historia, 1959.

ARTICLES

Barker, Nancy Nichols. "Austria, France, and the Venetian Question, 1861–1866," *Journal of Modern History,* Vol. XXXVI, No. 2 (June, 1964), 145–55.

———. "France, Austria, and the Mexican Venture, 1861–1864," *French Historical Studies,* Vol. III, No. 2 (Fall, 1963), 224–45.

Bernstein, Paul. "The Economic Aspects of Napoleon III's Rhine Policy," *French Historical Studies,* Vol. I, No. 3 (Spring, 1960), 335–48.

Bossy, Raoul. "Napoléon III et l'Autriche de Villafranca à Sadowa 1859–1866," *Revue d'histoire diplomatique,* Vol. LXXIII (July–September, 1959), 220–30.

Cameron, Rondo E. "Economic Growth and Stagnation in France, 1815–1914," *Journal of Modern History,* Vol. XXX (March, 1958), 1–3.

———. "French Finance and Italian Unity: The Cavourian Decade," *American Historical Review,* Vol. LXII (April, 1957), 552–69.

———. "Papal Finance and the Temporal Power, 1815–1871," *Church History,* Vol. XXVI (June, 1957), 132–42.

Carpi, Luigi. "Biografie di M. Pepoli," *Risorgimento italiano, Biografie,* Vol. III (1885), 370–426.

Case, Lynn M. "French Opinion and Napoleon III's Decisions After Sadowa," *Public Opinion Quarterly,* Vol. XIII, No. 3 (Fall, 1949), 441–61.

Cochut, André. "La situation financière en Italie," *Revue des deux mondes,* Period 2, Vol. 63 (May, 1866), 221–51.

Corti, Egon C. "Napoléon III après Sadowa d'après les rapports du Prince Richard Metternich," *Revue des études napoléoniennes,* Vol. XIX (1922), 229–35.

Diamilla-Müller, Demetrio E. "Il riscatto della Venezia. Prologo, Preparazione, Epilogo. Ricordi di un testimone oculare," *Gazetta di Venezia* (July 19–20, July 29–30, July 31–August 1, August 9–10, 1890).

Fester, Richard. "Biarritz, eine Bismarck-Studie," *Deutsche Rundschau*, Vol. CXIII (November, 1902), 212–36.

Frahm, Friedrich. "Biarritz, " *Historische Vierteljahrschrift*, Vol. XV (1912), 337–61.

Gallavresi, Giuseppe. "Le Marquis Visconti-Venosta," *Revue des deux mondes*, Period 6, Vol. XXV (January, 1915), 64–73.

Hauterive, Ernest d'. "La mission du Prince Napoléon en Italie, 1866," *Revue des deux mondes*, Period 8, Vol. XXVIII (June, 1925), 83–120.

Hoffmann, Georg. "Die venezianische Frage Zwischen den Feldzügen von 1859–1866," *Schweizer Studien Zur Geschichtswissenchaft*, Vol. XX (1941), 363–442.

Klaczko, Julian K. "Les préliminaires de Sadowa," *Revue des deux mondes*, Period 2, Vol. 507 (September, 1868), 365–90; (October, 1868), 513–56.

Long, Dwight C. "The Austro-French Commercial Treaty of 1866," *American Historical Review*, XLI (April, 1936), 474–91.

Luzio, Alessandro. "La Missione Malaguzzi a Vienna nel 1865–66 per la cessione del Veneto," *Risorgimento italiano*, Vol. XV (1922), 125–200, 414–48; Vol. XVI (1923), 213–60.

Miko, Norbert. "Zur Geschichte der Konvention vom 15 September 1864 Zwischen Frankreich und Italien," *Römische Historische Mitteilungen*, Vol. II (1957–58).

Nola, Carlo di. "La Venezia nella Politica Europea dalla Pace di Zurigo (November, 1859) alla Pace di Vienna (October, 1866), *Nuova Rivista Storica*, Vol. XLV (January–April, 1961), 109–39; (May–August, 1961), 230–79.

Ollivier, Emile. "L'entrevue de Biarritz, 1865," *Revue des deux mondes*, Period 5, Vol. IX (June, 1902), 481–518.

―――. "Un cas de conscience diplomatique," *Revue des deux mondes*, Period 5, Vol. XV (March, 1903), 5–40, 312–48.

Orsi, Defino. "Il mistero dei 'ricordi diplomatici' di Constantino Nigra," *La Nuova Antologia* (November, 1928), 10–154.

Rain, Pierre. "Sadowa," *Revue des deux mondes*, No. 14 (July 15, 1966), 190–98.

Rothan, Gustave. "La France et l'Italie, 1866–1870," *Revue des deux mondes*, Period 3, Vol. 66 (November–December, 1884), 298–321, 503–45.

Salomon, Henry. "Napoléon III à la veille et au lendemain de Sadowa," *Monde slave*, Vol. IV (April, 1925).

―――. "Le Prince Richard de Metternich et sa correspondance pendant son ambassade à Paris 1859–1871," *Revue de Paris*, 31st Year, Vol. I (January–February, 1924), 507–41, 762–804.

Srbik, Heinrich von. "La convenzione segreta tra Austria e la Francia del 12 giugno, 1866," *Revista storica italiana,* Series V, Fasc. 12 (December, 1937).

————. "Der Geheimvertrag Oesterreichs und Frankreichs vom 12 juni 1866," *Historisches Jahrbuch,* Vol. LVII (1937), 454–507.

Vidal, César. "La question vénitienne et la diplomatie française en 1866," *Revue d'histoire diplomatique,* Vol. LIII (October–December, 1939), 328–52.

UNPUBLISHED MATERIAL

Armengaud, André. "Opinion française au moment de Sadowa et la crise nationale allemande." Unpublished Ph.D. dissertation, Faculté des belles lettres, Sorbonne, 1955.

Bernstein, Paul. "The Rhine Problem During the Second Empire." Unpublished Ph.D dissertation, Department of History, University of Pennsylvania, 1955.

Cameron, Rondo E. "French Foreign Investment, 1850–1880." Unpublished Ph.D. dissertation, Department of Economics, University of Chicago, 1953.

Miko, Norbert, "Verbale della deliberazione del Concilio degli Ministri, I, 12 Junio 1861–30 Maggio 1867, Session of July 26, 1866, p. 130." Manuscript notes taken verbatim from Archivio Centrale Roma, Archivio di stato, by Norbert Miko.

Renouvin, Pierre. "La politique extérieure du Second Empire." Paris: Tournier et Constans, 1940. (mimeographed.)

Spenser, Warren F. "Edouard Drouyn de Lhuys and the Foreign Policy of the Second Empire." Unpublished Ph.D dissertation, Department of History, University of Pennsylvania, 1955.

Index